Schopenhauer's Fourfc

This volume collects 12 essays by various contributors on the subject of the importance and influence of Schopenhauer's doctoral dissertation (*On the Fourfold Root of the Principle of Sufficient Reason*) for both Schopenhauer's more well-known philosophy and the ongoing discussion of the subject of the principle of sufficient reason. The contributions deal with the historical context of Schopenhauer's reflections, their relationship to (transcendental) idealism, the insights they hold for Schopenhauer's views of consciousness and sensation, and how they illuminate Schopenhauer's theory of action. This is the first full-length, English volume on Schopenhauer's Fourfold Root and its relevance for Schopenhauer's philosophy. The thought-provoking essays collected in this volume will undoubtedly enrich the burgeoning field of Schopenhauer studies.

Jonathan Head is a Teaching Fellow at Keele University, UK. He has recently published papers on Kant's philosophy of religion and various aspects of Schopenhauer's philosophy.

Dennis Vanden Auweele is a postdoctoral researcher at the Faculty of Philosophy, KU Leuven (University of Leuven), and assistant professor in philosophy of religion at the Faculty of Theology, RUG (University of Groningen). His publications deal mostly with Kant's philosophy of religion, Schopenhauer's philosophy, and contemporary philosophy of religion.

Routledge Studies in Nineteenth-Century Philosophy

For a full list of titles in this series, please visit www.routledge.com

Schopenhauer's Fourfold Root

Edited by Jonathan Head
and Dennis Vanden Auweele

Routledge
Taylor & Francis Group

LONDON AND NEW YORK

First published 2017 by Routledge

2 Park Square, Milton Park, Abingdon, Oxfordshire OX14 4RN

52 Vanderbilt Avenue, New York, NY 10017

*Routledge is an imprint of the Taylor & Francis Group,
an informa business*

First issued in paperback 2019

Library of Congress Cataloging in Publication Data
Names: Head, Jonathan, editor.
Title: Schopenhauer's fourfold root / edited by Jonathan Head and
    Dennis Vanden Auweele.
Description: 1 [edition]. | New York : Routledge, 2016. | Series:
    Routledge studies in nineteenth-century philsophy ; 12 | Includes
    bibliographical references and index.
Identifiers: LCCN 2016038390 | ISBN 9781138195042
    (hardback : alk. paper)
Subjects: LCSH: Schopenhauer, Arthur, 1788–1860. èUber die
    vierfache Wurzel des Satzes von zureichenden Grunde. | Sufficient
    reason. | Will. | Schopenhauer, Arthur, 1788–1860.
Classification: LCC B3124 .S36 2016 | DDC 193—dc23
LC record available at https://lccn.loc.gov/2016038390

ISBN: 978-1-138-19504-2 (hbk)
ISBN: 978-0-367-87689-0 (pbk)

Typeset in Sabon
by Apex CoVantage, LLC

Contents

Preface

At the time the plan was conceived to cooperate on an edited volume on Schopenhauer's doctoral dissertation, we were very much involved with our own dissertations—Jonathan Head was still in the midst of writing his, and Dennis Vanden Auweele had defended his only one month prior. Needless to say, this project proved to be a daunting challenge to two junior scholars in philosophy. We are as a result immensely grateful for all the guidance and support we received during the time—a little bit less than two years—working on this volume. First of all, we would like to thank the editors at Routledge, first Margo Irvin and for the majority of this process Andrew Weckenmann, who have been particularly helpful and professional—as well as flexible when change was needed—throughout the entirety of this process. Next, we express our gratitude to our contributors. While this volume was conceived in the aftermath of a specialized conference, not all contributors participated at this conference. Numerous of these papers were commissioned specifically for this volume. The level of diligence in conceiving and actualizing their contributions was more than we could have hoped for. Work on this volume was greatly assisted by financial support of Keele University, the APRA Foundation Berlin, the Research Foundation Flandres (FWO), the Academische Stichting Leuven (ASL), and the Research Fund of the KU Leuven.

When young Arthur proudly presented his dissertation to his mother, she derisively described the book as intended for pharmacists (the German *Wurzel* has the same connotation as the English 'root'). Dismayed, Schopenhauer would respond that she would only later be known as the 'mother of Schopenhauer' and that scarcely a copy of her writing would be available. To this, Johanna Schopenhauer replied that the entire printing of Schopenhauer's dissertation could easily be found. They would still be in the shops since they were never sold (a remark eerily true for a long time). The editors would like to dedicate this volume to their mothers, in which respect they feel much more fortunate than Schopenhauer.

Note on Abbreviations and Referencing

References to the works of Schopenhauer are to the pagination of Hübscher's edition: Schopenhauer, A. *Sämtliche Werke in 7 Bänden*. Edited by A. Hübscher, Leipzig: F.A. Brockhaus, 1937. The translation is based on the *Cambridge Edition of the Works of Arthur Schopenhauer* (when available): Schopenhauer, A. *On the Fourfold Root of the Principle of Sufficient Reason and Other Writings,* translated and edited by David Cartwright, Edward Erdmann and Christopher Janaway, Cambridge: Cambridge University Press, 2012; Schopenhauer, A. *The World as Will and Representation: Volume 1,* translated and edited by Judith Norman, Alistair Welchman and Christopher Janaway, Cambridge: Cambridge University Press, 2010; Schopenhauer, A. *The Two Fundamental Problems of Ethics,* translated and edited by Christopher Janaway, Cambridge: Cambridge University Press, 2009; Schopenhauer, A. *The World as Will and Representation. Volume Two,* translated by E.F.J. Payne, New York: Dover, 1969; Schopenhauer, A. *Parerga and Paralipomena. Volume 1,* translated and edited by Christopher Janaway and Sabine Roehr, Cambridge: Cambridge University Press, 2014; Schopenhauer, A. *Parerga and Paralipomena. Volume 2,* translated and edited by Adrian Del Caro and Christopher Janaway, Cambridge: Cambridge University Press, 2015; Schopenhauer, A. *Manuscript Remains in Four Volumes,* edited by Arthur Hübscher and translated by E.F.J. Payne, Oxford: Berg, 1988.

Individual works are referenced using the following sigla: FR: *Fourfold Root*; EF: *First edition of Fourfold Root* (pages refer to the book pages of the *Cambridge Edition*); VC: *On Vision and Colours*; WWR1/2: *The World I/II*; WN: *Will in Nature*; FW: *Prize-essay on Freedom*; BM: *Prize-essay on Morals*; PP1/2: *Parerga I/II*; MR: *Manuscript Remains*.

Texts from *Immanuel Kant* are referenced through the *Akademie Ausgabe*: Immanuel Kant, *Gesammelte Schriften*. Edited by Bd. 1–22 Preussische Akademie der Wissenschaften, Bd. 23 Deutsche Akademie der Wissenschaften zu Berlin, ab Bd. 24 Akademie der Wissenschaften zu Göttingen (Berlin: Verlag Walter de Gruyter, 1900 ff). Translation from the work of Kant are taken from the *Cambridge Edition of the Works of Immanuel Kant*: Immanuel Kant, *The Critique of Pure Reason. Cambridge Edition of the Works of Immanuel Kant*. Edited by Paul Guyer and Allen Wood (Cambridge: Cambridge University Press, 1999).

Authors

Marco Casucci, *University of Perugia*

Sebastian Gardner, *University College London*

Jonathan Head, *Keele University*

Christine Lopes

Eric v.d. Luft, *SUNY Upstate Medical University*

Graham McAleer, *Loyola University Maryland*

Sandra Shapshay, *Indiana University—Bloomington*

Luis de Sousa, *Nova Institute of Philosophy/New University of Lisbon*

Gudrun von Tevenar, *Birkbeck College*

Dennis Vanden Auweele, *KU Leuven/University of Groningen*

Bart Vandenabeele, *Ghent University*

Robert Wicks, *University of Auckland*

Günter Zöller, *Ludwig-Maximilians-Universität München*

Introduction

Jonathan Head and Dennis Vanden Auweele

When Schopenhauer began, in 1813, to write his doctoral dissertation, *On the Fourfold Root of the Principle of Sufficient Reason (Ueber die vierfache Wurzel des Satzes vom zureichenden Grunde)*, he was twenty-five years old. Though first a student of medicine at Göttingen, he changed his field of study to philosophy and moved to Berlin to attend the lectures of Schleiermacher and Fichte. Little time had passed before he became deeply disappointed with the lack of existential engagement these thinkers displayed with regard to their respective philosophical projects. Abandoning the idealism of the day, Schopenhauer chose to focus on what he came to consider the greatest event in the history of philosophy, namely Kant's transcendental idealism. Desiring then to escape the threat of potential military service in the face of Napoleon's advances—Hegel's world-spirit made flesh—Schopenhauer had left Berlin to live with his mother and sister in Weimar. Once there, however, with ongoing familial tensions coming to the fore, he was unable to find the peace he desired and thereafter ensconced himself in a small inn in the town of Rudolstadt to write *Fourfold Root*.

The solitude of his situation must have been very helpful to him, as the doctorate was completed in the space of a few months over the summer of that year under conditions that many a graduate student would nowadays envy: no pesky undergraduates to educate or supervise, no professors who offer their constructive criticisms, and no pressure to publish articles or procure research grants. The topic of this dissertation was one of the key principles of 18th century German philosophy—the principle of sufficient reason, advanced most prominently by Leibniz, Wolff, and Baumgarten. This is the idea that everything ought to have a reason: *nihil est sine ratione*. In late September, the manuscript was submitted to the University of Jena (with an accompanying letter that was uncharacteristically obsequious in tone[1]), and word would spread quickly across Jena that the son of the famous *Autorin*, Johanna Schopenhauer, had submitted his doctoral thesis for their scrutiny. Perhaps then with the benefit of his mother's notoriety and her friendly relations with Goethe (who had strong links with Jena), Schopenhauer was quickly granted his doctorate in absentia *magna cum laude*. Following this success, he paid to have five hundred copies of his dissertation printed, but as with his other early works, it remained in obscurity until nearly the end of Schopenhauer's life.

Unlike many scholars who may be tempted to later write off their doctoral dissertation as mere juvenilia, Schopenhauer continued to view *Fourfold Root* as an intrinsic part of his philosophy. Indeed, he did not mince words when he wrote in the First Preface to *The World as Will and Representation*: "It is absolutely impossible to truly understand [*The World as Will and Representation*] unless the reader is familiar with [*Fourfold Root*], and the contents of that essay are presupposed here as much as if they had been included in the book" (WWR1 x); and in the second preface to *Fourfold Root*, he even calls this work "the underpinning of [his] whole system" (FR v). Very few scholars, however, have taken these assertions seriously, and most have treated *Fourfold Root* as a work of relatively minor importance, often even reading it as Schopenhauer paying his dues to academic philosophy. Admittedly this work does seem a bit out of place in Schopenhauer's oeuvre since his more well-known work, such as the two volumes of *The World as Will and Representation*, the two prize-essays and the two volumes of his *Parerga and Paralipomena,* deal mostly with matters of metaphysics, ethics, aesthetics, and anthropology rather than epistemology. Perhaps it is because of Schopenhauer's aversion to be repetitive that he refused to revisit the subject of his doctoral dissertation? Schopenhauer has such "strong aversion to copying [himself]" (WWR1 x)—and in fact reminds his readers repeatedly of this aversion—that he likely considered the subject matter settled once and for all.

One of the few scholars in the English-speaking world who has taken *Fourfold Root* seriously was Frank C. White,[2] who summarized the threefold purpose of this work as: "To establish the world as representational, to establish that the principles of reasoning governing that world license no inference to a reality beyond it, and to refute the many claims of those who hold otherwise."[3] Despite the fact that Schopenhauer made impressive changes in the different published editions of this work (respectively in 1813 and 1847), the general aims of the work remain the same, namely to show how the proper conclusion from Kantian philosophy ought to be that the principle of sufficient reason is only valid for representational reality and cannot either be used 'as a window' into the in-itself or to positively determine noumenal reality. As such, there arises a radical, perhaps unbridgeable, dualism between the phenomenal reality, which is structured in accordance with the principle of thought and explanation, and noumenal reality, which foregoes from all thought and explanation.

Schopenhauer became displeased with the first edition of *Fourfold Root* early on. Already in the preface to the first volume of *The World as Will and Representation*, he would inform his readers that

I could now present the material in that essay [*Fourfold Root*] rather better, particularly by cleansing it of many concepts that stem from my (then excessive) entanglement with the Kantian philosophy . . . Yet those concepts are there only because I have never really engaged with them on a very profound level, and thus only as side issues that do not touch on the main subject. This is why the reader who is familiar with the present work will automatically correct those passages in the essay.

(WWR x)

In this way, Schopenhauer signals that he has somewhat distanced himself from the Kantianism of *Fourfold Root* in a manner that could be discerned through a careful reading of *The World as Will and Representation*, which in turn should have an impact upon the way we read *Fourfold Root* itself. Schopenhauer would continue to reflect at great length upon his doctoral dissertation. It is noteworthy that often when scholars talk about a text called *Fourfold Root*, they do not mean the text that was originally published in 1813. Rather, they are referring to a somewhat different work, namely, an extensive reworking of the dissertation published in 1847 in Frankfurt as a second edition of *Fourfold Root*. The question of the relationship between the two editions of *Fourfold Root* is an important one and will be touched upon at points in this volume. The Cambridge translation of *Fourfold Root* brings out the stark contrast between the two editions, with 44 pages noting the ways in which the two editions depart from each other.

One of the intentions of this collection is to mark, somewhat belatedly, the 200th anniversary of the first appearance of *Fourfold Root*. The anniversary itself, of course, passed in 2013. After a German-language conference in Naumburg to mark the occasion in that year, an English-language conference followed at Keele University in November 2014. At that latter event, it became clear to the editors that there is still much exciting research being undertaken on *Fourfold Root*. Further, it was refreshing to hear papers that treated the text the way in which Schopenhauer wished it to be treated, namely, as a significant part of Schopenhauer's corpus, and not just as a minor work of 'juvenilia'. At the obligatory after-conference alcohol-induced collegial network-building in the local pub, the conference organizer and a cohort realized the outstanding level of the conference presentations and the dire need of the broader Schopenhauer scholarly community for an urgent revisit of Schopenhauer's doctoral dissertation. They then took the decision to bring together selected papers from the conference in a single volume, alongside new contributions from senior scholars. This collection of essays is a first humble move in the direction of inspiring young and old Schopenhauer scholars, but also scholars of German Idealism, intellectual history, and the history of epistemology, to revisit this necessary preamble to Schopenhauer's philosophy. We hope that this collection will demonstrate that *Fourfold Root* is worthy of in-depth study, and thus inspire further research not only on Schopenhauer's first major work but also his philosophy generally.

The papers collected in this volume were conceived separately from one another, and while attempts were made to streamline the content, many of the authors subscribe to different points of views. Rather than looking for superficial agreement, the editors decided to let the controversy stand. The volume begins with papers that place *Fourfold Root* in its historical context. Sebastian Gardner had published earlier a highly influential paper in which he shows how Schopenhauer's philosophy departs from German idealism by taking a standpoint beyond representation, without first querying whether such a standpoint is in fact possible. Such a new perspective on things allows for Schopenhauer's philosophy to follow from Kant's transcendental idealism.[4] In his present contribution, Gardner continues this train of thought and further vindicates Schopenhauer's alternative to German Idealism from the viewpoint of *Fourfold Root*. For more of a future-oriented and critical perspective, Eric v.d. Luft argues that there are two ways to interpret the principle of sufficient reason, analytic and speculative. He argues that Schopenhauer follows the former approach, which tends to restrict consideration of the PSR to epistemological matters, and fails to recognize that the principle of sufficient reason should have a ground outside of itself. He then continues to argue that Heidegger's approach to the principle of sufficient reason, which sees PSR as the ultimate ground of being, supersedes Schopenhauer's approach.

The next group of contributions focuses on the relationship of *Fourfold Root* to (transcendental) idealism. Jonathan Head engages the two different editions of *Fourfold Root* intimately and argues that changes between the editions reveal a growing sympathy for a Berkeleyan form of idealism. The paper also reviews further evidence for reading Schopenhauer as a subjective idealist, including the possible influence of Indian thought. Schopenhauer's relationship to idealistic philosophy is still very much unclear, and Head's contribution not only sheds some light on Schopenhauer's own evolution on this subject but also shows Schopenhauer's sustained sympathy for Berkeleyan idealism. Günter Zöller re-contextualizes Schopenhauer within the era of early 19th-century German Idealism by showing how Schopenhauer's philosophy is a parody (in a technical sense) of the systems of the idealists. Schopenhauer's stance toward freedom is usually characterized as a hard form of determinism: everything that occurs does so by means of a sufficient cause. Sandra Shapshay revisits this presupposition by showing how the 'ghost of Kantian freedom' remains explicit in Schopenhauer's philosophy. Going back to the earliest edition of *Fourfold Root*, Shapshay shows how Schopenhauer initially endorsed Kant's compatibilism of freedom and determinism and that this view is kept in the later works, though with some development. By taking this as a vantage point, some of Schopenhauer's more troubling assertions on freedom and responsibility in the *Prize-Essay on Freedom* are clarified. Shapshay argues that though some mystery regarding freedom will inevitably remain, nevertheless it is revealed to some extent through the experiences engendered through engagement with art-works and ascetic practices, as well as through the feeling of responsibility that we have for our own character. Finally, Schopenhauer's metaphysics has often been found to be inconsistent with Kant's transcendental idealism. Dennis Vanden Auweele revisits this debate and develops a new reading of Schopenhauer's metaphysics from the latter's objection to the ontological argument. Much like Schopenhauer objected to the ontological argument—which in his view confused the ground of something with its cause—Schopenhauer similarly objects to Kant's way of introducing the thing in itself as the cause of phenomenal reality, not merely as its ground. As such, Schopenhauer argues that the will is the ground of phenomenal reality without being its cause. By then correcting even Kant's own mistakes with regard to transcendental idealism, Schopenhauer is enabled to circumscribe a metaphysics fully consonant with the principles of transcendental idealism.

The next group of contributions discusses the notions of consciousness and sensation in Schopenhauer's early writings. Graham McAleer discusses the issue of 'angelism' in Schopenhauer and Reid, which is the view that human essence is best considered spiritual, rather than material. Schopenhauer famously reintroduced a level of materiality, as body, as central to properly understanding reality, and thus avoiding a slide into Berkeley's ontology of minds and mental events. Nevertheless, McAleer argues, it is Reid's response to angelism that has the upper hand. Marco Casucci more explicitly delves into the early manuscripts to understand Schopenhauer's evolution from the philosophy of better consciousness to his new understanding of consciousness and reflection in *Fourfold Root*. His focus is specifically on the relationship between idea (*Idee*) and concept (*Begriff*) in these early manuscripts, as well as the important early notion of the 'better consciousness', which is potentially key to a new way of approaching Schopenhauer's system as a philosophy of levels of consciousness, rather than as a metaphysics of will. Luis de Sousa continues this discussion by looking into Schopenhauer's theory of subjective consciousness. Schopenhauer famously departs from the Cartesian tradition in this respect by blurring the distinction between human and animal consciousness. However, de Sousa argues that there is still an important distinction between human and animal consciousness with regard to the reflexivity of consciousness in relation to the Kantian notion of transcendental apperception. Complete subjectivity is still only possible with the uniquely human capacities for reason, conceptual reflection, and the use of language. Last, Bart Vandenabeele takes up the issue of aesthetical perception in Schopenhauer's philosophy. His argument is that Schopenhauer's theory of aesthetical perception is not, as critics such as Friedrich Nietzsche argued it to be, life-denying. Instead, Schopenhauer's aesthetics is remarkably life-affirming if this is interpreted from the appropriate phenomenological point of view. Rather than interpreting Schopenhauer as viewing aesthetic consciousness as passive and disengaged, Vandenabeele argues that Schopenhauer rightly sees the aesthetic beholder as 'energetically active', but unjustly downplays the significance of personal interests, emotions, and desires.

The final group of contributions deals with an issue that goes to the heart of Schopenhauer's more well-known philosophy, namely ethics, motivation, and action. These authors claim that important insight for Schopenhauer's views can already be found in *Fourfold Root*. Gudrun von Tevenar and Christine Lopes recognize that the fourth root of the principle of sufficient reason—the one dealing with motivation and morality—is slightly different from the first three roots. Nevertheless, Schopenhauer consistently and adamantly emphasizes that the same strict sense of causal determination applies to human agency as to physical causes and organic stimuli. Lopes and von Tevenar investigate this claim further and show that Schopenhauer only successfully justifies this claim in his *Essay on the Freedom of the Will*, not yet in *Fourfold Root*. The final contribution by Robert Wicks investigates in what sense Schopenhauer's metaphysics of will is impacted by Kant's theory of freedom. Schopenhauer claims that Kant's antinomy of speculative reason is what directly leads toward his philosophy. Wicks takes this claim particularly seriously, and even develops this all the way toward Schopenhauer's endeavor toward a 'philosophy of tranquility'. In particular, Wicks argues for the potential importance of the notion of the 'acquired character', attained by an individual after self-reflection upon patterns of behavior. In order to make sense of the tranquility found through pursuit of ascetic practices, we can understand the will as itself coming to an acquired character, ultimately turning away from itself in horror.

Other efforts have recently been made to pull Schopenhauer's views of epistemology and metaphysics from the obscurities of merely historical research.[5] Taking these efforts together with the present volume, Schopenhauer's philosophy proves not altogether outdated. At one point, Schopenhauer himself expressed the fear that any philosophical author of truth would only enjoy renown for a short time (after being ridiculed extensively) but would then disappear as superfluous: "[Truth is] granted only a short victory celebration between the two long periods of time when it is condemned as paradoxical or disparaged as trivial. The author of truth usually meets with the first fate as well" (WWR1 xv). This volume is then a humble attempt to keep the exciting innovations of Schopenhauer's philosophy fresh in mind.

Notes

1 In this letter, Schopenhauer requested the dean of the philosophy faculty to advise him "if they found anything unclear, rambling, untrue or even offensive" and he even believed it unwise to "rely on one's own judgment" when it comes to matters of philosophy (David Cartwright and Edward Erdmann, 'Introduction'. In: *On the Fourfold Root of the Principle of Sufficient Reason and Other Writings.* Edited by David Cartwright, Edward Erdmann and Christopher Janaway (Cambridge: Cambridge University Press, 2012), p. xiii).

2 See: Frank C. White, *On Schopenhauer's Fourfold Root of the Principle of Sufficient Reason* (Leiden: Brill Publishing, 1992).

3 Frank C. White, 'The Fourfold Root' in: *The Cambridge Companion to Schopenhauer*. Edited by Christopher Janaway (Cambridge: Cambridge University Press, 1999), p. 64.

4 Gardner, S. 'Schopenhauer's Contraction of Reason: Clarifying Kant and Undoing German Idealism', *The Kantian Review* 17, 2012: 375–401.

5 *Schopenhauers Wissenschaftstheorie: Der "Satz vom Grund". Beiträge zur Philosophie Schopenhauers, Bd. 16.* Edited by D. Birnbacher, Würzburg: Verlag Königshausen & Neumann, 2015.

Part I

The Historical Context of *Fourfold Root*

1 Schopenhauer's Metaphilosophy

How to Think a World without Reason

Sebastian Gardner

I suggested in a previous paper that Schopenhauer's decision to focus his doctoral dissertation on the principle of sufficient reason owes a great deal to his opposition to Fichte, Schelling, and Hegel.[1] The thesis concerning the limits of thought advanced in *Fourfold Root*, though effective in undermining the speculative idealism of his post-Kantian contemporaries, is however both problematic on its own account and directly responsible for well-known difficulties facing Schopenhauer's metaphysics of will. The relation of *Fourfold Root* to *The World as Will and Representation* is thus ambiguous, for while it prepares the way for Schopenhauer's reinstatement of Kant's transcendental idealism as he understands it, it at the same time obstructs a literal metaphysical reading of his identification of world with *Wille*. In response I offer, first, an account of the historical context that helps to make sense of Schopenhauer's metaphilosophical decisions, and second, a construal of Schopenhauer's metaphilosophy designed to protect his claim to offer a coherent alternative to rationalist forms of post-Kantian idealism (though not his claim to have undermined or surpassed them).

I

When we look back at *Fourfold Root* from the standpoint of *The World as Will and Representation*, as Schopenhauer tells us to do in the latter's preface (WWR1 ix–x), the claims of the earlier work are readily intelligible: *Fourfold Root* spells out a number of key theses, elaborated at length in WWR, concerning the structure and limits of human knowledge and the different types of objects and relations corresponding to its different ordering principles. Whether it also offers support for those theses in addition to what is argued in WWR, as Schopenhauer leads us to expect,[2] is more doubtful, but Schopenhauer clearly has good reason to describe *Fourfold Root* as an effective introduction to WWR.

Considered in isolation from the later work, what is most striking about *Fourfold Root*—and what, from the evidence of reviews, puzzled its readers in 1813[3]—is that Schopenhauer appears to resurrect a principle with a long and distinguished history in early modern rationalism which he at the same time regards Kant as having disposed of. If Kant has stripped the PSR of its former authority as an epistemological principle and tool of metaphysical enquiry, what then is the point of revalidating it? Why not instead offer the principle as a revised version of Kant's principles of the understanding? Given that the new principle is so unlike the old—the mere husk of it, in effect[4]—there seems little point in reemploying the old title. One of the chief implications of Schopenhauer's critical discussion of the use made of the PSR by pre-Kantian philosophers is that a good number of central arguments in the rationalist tradition can be charged with confusing different senses of ground or reason,[5] but this hardly required a new theory of the PSR, and in any case, all of the relevant work in support of this verdict was done already by Kant.[6] In fact not even the critical philosophy was required for this: Kant's very early *New Elucidation* (1755), following Crusius, had already sharply discriminated logical from real grounds, and Euler had made the key anti-Wolffian point that the substantial issue is not the PSR itself but whether or not we have the capacity to use it to generate explanations and render things like corporeality intelligible. Leibnizians, according to Euler, have confused the truth of the principle with our capacity to employ it to positive ends.[7]

It is true that Schopenhauer's claims concerning the structure of human cognition in *Fourfold Root* do not merely repeat Kant but include vital disagreements with him and that postulation of the PSR as a single principle at work across the board in human cognition is of assistance to Schopenhauer, insofar as it makes it easier for him to set causality on a par with space and time, and to assimilate practical reason to a sub-form of theoretical reason, thereby dismantling key pieces of Kant's architecture. But these purposes would have been served just as well if not better by advertising his work as an innovative reformulation of transcendental idealism and the Kantian system as a whole—which is how he, in effect, presents his position in Book 1 and the Appendix of WWR respectively. The puzzle, in short, is why Schopenhauer should offer what is actually a study in the history of metaphysics as seen through the lens of the Critical Philosophy, followed by a set of revisions to Kant, as the correct account of a principle still associated firmly, in 1813, with the Wolffian philosophy that Kant had, in Schopenhauer's own view, rendered metaphysically impotent.

The answer to this puzzle lies, I suggest, in Schopenhauer's antagonism toward the German Idealists,[8] whom he perceives as the modern incarnation of the malign optimistic tendency in Western thought, and that his aim in *Fourfold Root* is to reinstate in clarified and purged form Kant's original insights, as he understands them. The main points in this account of Schopenhauer's reasons for focussing on the PSR can be summarized under three interconnected headings: Schopenhauer's distinctive metaphilosophical position; his absorption of one key idea that he takes from the German Idealists, concerning the proper way to develop Kant's philosophy; and his intention of undercutting at its root the Fichte-Schelling-Hegel development.[9]

1   *Minimalist metaphilosophy in* Fourfold Root. I raised the question of whether Schopenhauer is justified in regarding *Fourfold Root* as providing support for the relevant key theses of WWR1. Whether it does so depends, of course on what counts as support, and if our expectation is of finding in *Fourfold Root* transcendental arguments of a Kantian or Fichtean sort, or even just a *Prolegomena*-style regressive argument, then we will be disappointed: in §14 Schopenhauer explicitly rejects as fruitless, circular, and absurd all attempts to prove PSR. His alternative to Kant's proof of the causal principle, for example, is mere asseveration of 'the unshakeable certainty' of our convictions concerning the future course of experience.

(FR 89)

What needs to be taken on board—in order for Schopenhauer's position in WWR not to seem unaccountably dogmatic or peculiarly naive—is Schopenhauer's *ab initio* commitment to an ultra-minimal account of synthetic *a priori* knowledge.[10] I will come back to this shortly, but the point to emphasize for now is that by redescribing principles that Kant would have regarded as in need of and as capable of being provided with deductions, as forms of the PSR, Schopenhauer signals his view that it is a mistake to even contemplate equipping them with any sort of justification: just as the PSR in the eyes of the rationalists is epistemically final—justified by its being simply constitutive of ideation and knowledge—so too, Schopenhauer is indicating, are his four principles. The absence of justification is no deficiency because to refuse to acknowledge their validity is, for Schopenhauer, a bootless attempt to blind oneself to what is immediately subjectively certain, and to require more, in Schopenhauer's view, is to demand the transcendent perspective on our cognition that Kant rightly denies us. Kant's use of the table of judgements to give a higher, non-contingent status to the categories is in this light incoherent: by his own account, Kant is missing the necessary external authorization.[11]

2   *Reduction of reason to the transcendental.* The idea which Schopenhauer takes from Fichte and the early Schelling is that the limits of reason or the thinkable, and the limits of cognition or knowable truth, should be understood to coincide, *contra* Kant.

Kant draws a clear distinction between (on the one hand) the 'land of truth' defined by the *transcendental* principles of the *understanding*, which employ schematized categories and possess rational necessity on account of the cognitions which they enable; and (on the other hand) the broader sphere opened up by the faculty of *reason*, which employs unschematized categories in its attempt to determine noumenal objects and whose Ideas remain merely problematic, or serve only for regulative employment (or for pure practical reason). The shortfall of Kant's transcendentally grounded cognition in relation to the PSR is expressed in the concept of the unconditioned. The various transcendental necessities that condition human cognition—space and time, the 'I think', the principles of the understanding—are *empirically* unconditioned but not *self*-grounding, and hence not *absolutely* necessary or necessary *in themselves*. We have no knowledge of their individual or collective grounds: we cannot understand why our intuition should be spatial and temporal, and we cannot grasp the ground of the I or the common root of sensibility and understanding, any more than we can grasp the ground of the manifold of sensation; indeed we cannot even form a determinate concept of the totality which our cognitive powers jointly form. The transcendental frame of human cognition holds itself together *from the inside* but as far as we are concerned—from our confined perspective—must be regarded as floating unanchored in the unconditioned, which we can think, but not know, as containing the sufficient reason for our mode of cognition.

Now from this point there are two directions in which one may proceed in order to get understanding and reason to coincide. *Either* the limits of the transcendental can be pushed back, *or* the scope of reason can be contracted. The German Idealists do the former; Schopenhauer does the latter. Both allow it to be said that the PSR is the highest principle of transcendental philosophy and *vice versa*, but the direction taken is crucial for where we end up: if we enlarge the sphere of the transcendental, then we are affirming that reason plays as much of a transcendental role as the understanding, and that the unconditioned can be determined conceptually; while if we contract reason, we reduce the unconditioned to the principles of the understanding and rule out any other conception of a thinkable object or cognitive power. Schopenhauer's conviction that reason needs to be contracted derives from his belief that, if Kant's position is left as it is, it will inevitably (under pressure from skeptics such as Schulze) end up being converted into German Idealism.[12] This is the lesson Schopenhauer had learned from his years of exposure to Schelling and Fichte.

3   *Undermining German Idealism*. Schopenhauer is correct in his perception of the German Idealists as implicitly endorsing and in effect reactivating the PSR. Within each of their systems, the PSR emerges in new dress and does essential work. Fichte (in the later Jena *Wissenschaftslehre*) affirms it in the form of what he calls the 'principle of reciprocal determination' (*Wechselbestimmung*). Hegel validates it in his Doctrine of Essence in *The Science of Logic*. These are, however, only its explicit manifestations. At a more fundamental level, the German Idealists' commitment to the PSR is expressed in their demand for full systematicity, which they hold to be a condition of *Wissenschaft* and invoke as a reason for judging Kant's Critical philosophy inadequate: if it were not for the pressure exerted by the PSR, there would be nothing objectionable *per se* in Kant's dualism and the German Idealists would have no compelling ground for going beyond Kant in his own name by expanding

the transcendental to take in reason and the unconditioned—demands which are explicit in Schelling's earliest publication.[13]

Schopenhauer's strategy is therefore well conceived: if the PSR *could not* amount to more than the four sub-principles, then all of German Idealism's inflationary metaphysics fall to the ground, clearing the way for the path that Schopenhauer wants to build from Kant to an anti-optimistic axiological vision, or in the more positive terms characteristic of his earliest reflections, for the vindication of his 'better consciousness'.

II

One question which now arises, of a systematic rather than historical nature, concerns the effectiveness of *Fourfold Root* as a criticism of German Idealism. The immediate difficulty is of course that Schopenhauer's deflation of the PSR does not, as noted, rest on any kind of proof: its argument appears to consist simply in Schopenhauer's reiteration of Kantian doctrines concerning the *a priori* conditions of cognition, and this suffices only to *separate* the transcendental from the merely rational, not to *reduce* reason to the transcendental.

There is an obvious danger that the basic assumptions of both parties are so flatly contradictory that no critical exchange between them is possible, but what mitigates the difficulty, and gains for Schopenhauer a momentary advantage, is an issue which neither can shirk and on which Schopenhauer puts a great deal of weight, namely the requirement that metaphysical discourse be demonstrably meaningful. Schopenhauer's vocal complaints of the unintelligibility and emptiness of German Idealist philosophy suggest at times a bare refusal on his part to attempt to understand Fichte, Schelling, and Hegel, but they also contain a serious philosophical point, one that Fichte and Hegel (if not Schelling) themselves acknowledge: if philosophy is to complete its task, then it needs to explain and justify, in the eyes of *ordinary* understanding, its ascent to a putatively higher (transcendental for Fichte, and speculative for Hegel) standpoint and to demonstrate that its concepts are not cognitively defective in the manner of, according to the first *Critique*, transcendent metaphysics.

The philosophical discourse of German Idealism is built up by way of metaphilosophical reflection on Kant and other earlier philosophy, which is why so much of the systematic reconstruction of German Idealism consists characteristically in attempting to trace its basic notions back to Kant. Even if we find convincing the German Idealists' attempts to justify their speculative discourses, Schopenhauer is right to point out the greater proximity of his own metaphysical discourse to ordinary thought, and to claim that it gives his own system all of the advantages of immanence over the dubious quasi-transcendence of the German Idealists. Even transcendental idealism in Schopenhauer's hands becomes, like Berkeley's idealism, less a solution to technical problems concerning the justification of knowledge claims and more of a would-be immediately ascertainable truth of ordinary consciousness. And as Schopenhauer argues repeatedly and in detail, ordinary human life abounds with cues and intimations, provocations and invitations, to rise to the standpoint of 'better consciousness'. Aside from Fichte's intermittent appeals to Kant's moral Fact of Reason—the authenticity of which as a component of ordinary consciousness is in any case disputed—this groundedness in how-things-are-actually-given has no real parallel in Fichte, Schelling, and Hegel, who segregate philosophical reflection sharply from the natural attitude, which they treat as an *explanandum*, and not as a resource for philosophical *explanantia*.

However, it is precisely here, in connection with the question of the conditions of meaning of philosophical discourse, that we also encounter a deep and all-too-familiar problem in Schopenhauer's philosophy, which bears on the basic structure of his system and very plausibly, cannot be resolved by any fine-tuning of his claims about representation and will.

If Schopenhauer is right that the limits of thought are determined by the content of intuitive representations and our power of abstraction from these,[14] then thought cannot determine any object, and so cannot have any content that does not contain reference to, and is not derivable in some way from, the intuitive representations of the subject.[15] The implications of such concept empiricism, as just stated, are not completely clear, since everything depends on what counts as abstraction or derivation. And here the claims of *Fourfold Root* are decisive: no legitimate abstraction or derivation can go further than spelling out the presence of the four forms of the PSR in the objects and relations given in intuitive representation.

This restrictive condition on conceptual meaning allows Schopenhauer to immediately close down speculation concerning an 'absolute ground of reason' or a 'ground in general', but it creates a problem with regard to Schopenhauer's own aim to describe in concepts the excess of reality over representation, which now seems by his own lights not merely unwarranted but strictly nonsensical. The problem shows up at many points—most obviously and prominently in WWR1, in the idea that will is the ground of the world as representation, but also to a lesser extent in the theory of Ideas, which involves application of the category of quantity ('degrees' of objectification) and individuation beyond the sphere of representation (the difference of one Idea from another).[16]

In *Fourfold Root*, this problem does not show up *as such*, because there Schopenhauer does not say anything about what lies outside the world as representation. There is, however, another problem in the early text suggesting a breach of immanence. This lies in the ambiguity surrounding the either-unitary-or-aggregative character of the PSR, and the assumed-but-ungrounded harmony of its various sub-forms. Is the PSR one principle, differentiated into four forms, or is it a mere conjunction of discrete principles? Schopenhauer equivocates throughout—in fact the equivocation is expressed in the title of the work—but the question is crucial, and both options create difficulties, which explains why his answer should appear so undecided.

If the former—if the PSR is a genuine unity—then there *is* an essence of reason, which may be expressed necessarily in each of the four sub-forms but cannot be regarded as expressed *fully* in any of them individually. The concept of this essence could not have arisen through mere abstraction. The question also then arises—since it is hard to see why, if no individual sub-form exhausts reason, the conjunction of the four sub-forms should do so—what prevents us from constructing new sub-forms of the principle: for example and in particular, a principle governing the relation of the realm of representation as a whole to its ground.

If on the other hand the PSR is a mere aggregate—if there are four principles each with their own root, and 'reason' is a disjunct which *means* 'one or other of the four underived basic structuring principles'—then Schopenhauer is missing an explanation for why the sub-forms of the PSR do not part company with one another. What ensures the coordination of the various domains of objects attached to each sub-principle? What, for instance, ensures that the portions of matter-filled space and time that we individuate in accordance with the third sub-form are related coherently to the causal sequences determined by the first sub-form? What stops *this* portion of matter-in-space, this table, being directly plugged in causally to some other portion on the other side of the planet? Again, what ensures that the order of truth and inference tracks the causal order? Why should the order of my judgements, the beliefs that I have reason to form, follow the order of the empirical content of my experience?

These are not ('mere') skeptical problems, which might be dismissed as expressing only hyperbolical doubt: they are properly *transcendental* questions, closely related to those that define the tasks of Kant's Transcendental Deduction (why should appearances not "be so constituted that the understanding [does] not find them in accord with the conditions of its unity?" [A90/B123]) and Second Analogy ('How am I to understand *the fact that, because something is, something else is?*'[17]).

Kant has the basis for an answer to such questions—if the various principles of the understanding did not harmonize with one another, and with the forms of intuition, then no unity of consciousness would be possible—which is not available to Schopenhauer, given his abnegation of transcendental proof. And if Schopenhauer does not recognize the questions as meriting attention, then that is because (so it may be argued) he has surreptitiously assumed a fifth, superordinate form of the PSR, which keeps the four subordinate principles aligned, operating, so to speak, behind the back of representation—that is, playing the role of Kant's transcendental unity of apperception.

If correct, this immediately reverses the balance of argument between Schopenhauer and the German Idealists. Their success in securing the meaningfulness of speculative philosophical discourse—by appeal to 'intellectual intuition', the method of *Konstruktion*, the experience of pure thinking, and so on—may be *doubtful*, but their efforts do not result in inconsistency. Schopenhauer's claims, by contrast, seem to generate exactly that: a strict contradiction between his restrictions on conceptuality on the one hand, and his metaphysics of the world as will and need for a unitary ground of the world as representation on the other.

III

The problem of how to give systematic form to the limitations of systematicity is of Kantian provenance and Schopenhauer's aggravated version of it has a long and well-explored after-history. As commentators have suggested, its effects can be felt in the skepticism of Nietzsche's early 'On Truth and Lies' essay, in Hartmann's suggestion that Schopenhauer's system needs to be fused with Hegel's in order to supply the ideational components missing from his metaphysics of will, and in the *Tractatus*' distinction of what can be said from what can only be shown.

That Schopenhauer should put himself in the situation of advocating such a metaphilosophically convoluted form of post-Kantianism deserves as much explanation as can be provided. I have already suggested what provides his motive—his wish to force philosophical reflection to a conclusion which is alien to its inherently rationalistic nature. The question which needs to be addressed is how and why—by what logical path—this essentially axiological conviction gets translated itself into the doctrines expounded in *Fourfold Root* and WWR.

We find a great deal in Schopenhauer's immediate philosophical environment that can be taken to point in the direction he takes. Haym puts it well when he describes the history of the genesis of Schopenhauer's philosophy as 'the solution to the riddle of how so many incongruent features can nonetheless give the impression of a single, attractive and distinctive physiognomy'.[18] There is much to be said on this topic, but I will confine myself to three points.[19]

1   *Kant*. Schopenhauer thinks of himself as retrieving Kant's true insight and stripping away the retrograde features with which Kant had unfortunately bound it up, due to his immersion in Wolffian philosophical culture. When we see how much of Kant's system Schopenhauer wants to jettison, we may wonder what exactly his professed Kantian allegiance amounts to, but Schopenhauer is surely right to emphasize his incorporation of the Aesthetic's doctrine of transcendental idealism and Kant's theory of intelligible character as testifying to his genuine continuity with Kant. Less obvious but also of huge importance, I suggest, is his appropriation of what might be called Kant's affirmatively aporetic metaphilosophical stance, by which I mean the following.

There is, as noted, a close relation between the problem of bounding cognition that faces Schopenhauer, and the familiar high-level problem encountered by transcendental idealism. In effect the error that Schopenhauer appears to make at the level of meaning is the one that Kant is standardly charged with making at the level of epistemology: allegedly, Schopenhauer should not, but does, think that a ground of the world as representation can be conceived, and Kant should not, but does, think that we can know that things in themselves are the grounds of appearances. And the closely allied charge levelled by Hegel, that Kant must overstep the limits of knowledge in order to draw them, appears to have straightforward application to Schopenhauer too.

This familiar line of objection to Kant's transcendental idealism has been restated very clearly, and endorsed, by Adrian Moore in his recent history of metaphysics.[20] Moore describes the task of metaphysics as that of making sense of things in the most general terms, which involves making sense of its own making sense of things. And the problem with transcendental idealism, according to Moore, is that it fails to do this, for it is embroiled, if not in contradiction then at least in self-stultification: "At a more general level, we cannot represent limits to what we can represent. For if we cannot represent anything beyond those limits, then we cannot represent our not being able to represent anything beyond those limits."[21] Therefore, Moore concludes, transcendental idealism is incoherent.

This is not the place for detailed discussion,[22] but my view is that, while Moore is quite right to highlight the sense in which transcendental idealism fails to account for itself, it does not result in contradiction or self-stultification, for the reason that the Kantian transcendental idealist disavows any intention to make sense of sense-making in the way that Moore requires—that is, in a way that is symmetrical or continuous with our making sense of objects—and also *justifies* this disavowal: it is a *positive claim* of transcendental idealism that we have no insight into the real ground of our sense-making capacities. Kant's transcendental epistemology offers itself as a means for avoiding the skepticism that might seem to follow from this admission of our cognitive limitation: it shows that and how we give justified application to, and claim necessity for, principles whose ultimate real grounds are indiscernible to us. Transcendental idealism, rather than stultifying itself, registers the *actual* stultification of the task of human cognition, with respect to the ultimate ends of theoretical reason, in the account that it gives of our-situation-in-relation-to-reality.

My suggestion is that the affirmatively aporetic feature of Kant's system is consciously carried over into Schopenhauer, who raises it to a higher power by extending to our conceptual capacities the bare contingency and surd quality exhibited on Kant's account by space and time; hence the denial in *Fourfold Root* that there can be a derivation of the PSR or any account of its source.

2   *Maimon.* Salomon Maimon—who is referenced in the first edition of *Fourfold Root* (FR 22)—is of particular interest in the narrative of Schopenhauer's development in so far as he was the key progenitor of the systems of German Idealism, ultimately more important than Reinhold, and also, non-coincidentally, the only important early post-Kantian to lay stress on the relevance of the PSR in the critical estimate of Kant's philosophy. We find rehearsed in Maimon a line of thought that Schopenhauer could have taken to further support his conviction (as I have attributed it to him) that aporeticity is unavoidable and which also shows him, indirectly, a way to depart from the path which leads to German Idealism.

Stated very briefly, and in the sketchiest terms, Maimon's contribution to the post-Kantian development consists in his claim to demonstrate that Kant fails to satisfy the demands of the PSR, which he cannot escape, for the decisive reason that he fails in his endeavour to provide an epistemologically satisfactory alternative: even when the conditions on knowledge are scaled down and made immanent to subjectivity in the way transcendental idealism proposes, our knowledge claims are, Maimon argues, insufficiently grounded. This failure, according to Maimon, stems from Kant's thesis of the aboriginal independence and heterogeneity of sensibility and understanding, which makes it impossible to give grounds for thinking that what we *take* to be the objective application of the categories is really any such thing (i.e., that the categories of substance and cause are genuinely *constitutive* of any object given in experience). In other words, Kant's Analytic leaves Humean skepticism unscathed, and this is ultimately because Kant denies all intrinsic conceptual character to the data of sense.

The moral drawn by Maimon is that, since the demands of the PSR cannot be met through Kant's transcendental logic, and since failure to meet them entails radical skepticism, the PSR needs to be reinstated as a supreme principle of philosophical reflection (in the novel form of what he calls the *Satz der Bestimmtbarkeit*, the Principle of Determinability). Maimon's further argument is that this principle requires us to revert to Leibniz's intellectualist conception of the data of sensibility and forms of intuition, and moreover, to treat finite minds as moments of an infinite intellect.

If Maimon is right that Kant's transcendental deduction of the categories fails because of his dualism of sensibility and understanding, then German Idealism, insofar as it seeks to overcome this dualism, is well motivated. However, the *other* way in which one could respond to Maimon's discovery—instead of following him in his attempting to upgrade the transcendental in the direction of Leibniz,[23] a move which demands epistemic transcendence (the positing of the infinite intellect)—is to downgrade the PSR in the direction of Hume: that is, to declare that *there can be nothing more to reason* than the forms of representation that we, as a matter of fact, find ourselves with, and that there can be *nothing more to objectivity* than the *de facto* internal structure of representation. Such a move obviates the need for transcendental logic, by disposing of the idea that there could be anything constitutive of objects beyond the reach of proof.[24] This is what Schopenhauer does in *Fourfold Root*. In this way his strategy can be seen to emerge from the very same source as German Idealism, even as it heads in the opposite direction.

3   *Schelling.* I have described Schopenhauer as presenting a critique of German Idealism from a putatively Kantian standpoint and as offering a systematic alternative, but he was not the first to do so. Fries had done the same in his *New Critique of Reason* (1807), as Schopenhauer knew (MR2 417–425), and so too, in a quite different way and with much greater importance for Schopenhauer, had Schelling in his writings following his exposition of the Identity Philosophy (1801–04). Schopenhauer's Berlin manuscripts contain notes on Schelling's *Philosophie und Religion* (1804) and later writings including the *Freiheitsschrift* (1809—see MR2 353–355, 371–378, 389–391) in which Schelling does exactly what Schopenhauer will later do in WWR: he draws a limit to the space of reasons and characterizes what lies outside it as *Wille*. He does so moreover in the name of acknowledging the reality of evil: the *Freiheitsschrift* argues that human freedom has reality only if evil has reality, and that evil is possible only if the absolute has a certain structure, whereby 'blind longing' precedes the genesis of reason and functions thereafter as its continuing, indispensable source.[25]

This is but one of the numerous points of contact with Schelling—others include the double aspect structure of the system of philosophy, the elevation of art to parity with philosophy, and the general notion that the task of philosophy is born from our "egress from the absolute".[26] What matters presently, however, is not Schopenhauer's reproduction of Schelling's teachings but his creatively destructive relation to Schelling's later philosophy, in which the PSR has been demoted but is never abandoned. Schelling's high wire act, seeking to balance the claims of reason with the insight into a volitional reality which transcends it, continues into the 1840s, and in Schopenhauerian perspective seems a forlorn attempt to reconcile the irreconcilable. Schopenhauer might, therefore, have described WWR (Hartmann for one suggests) as a radical revision to Schelling's later metaphysics, doing with Schelling in Book 2 of WWR1 what he describes himself as doing in Book 1 with Kant, and *Fourfold Root* as the only tenable account of the PSR once the inadequacy of reason to the traditional task of metaphysics has been grasped.

IV

Having argued that *Fourfold Root* fails to supply Schopenhauer with the metaphilosophy that he needs in WWR, I now want to consider the possibilities for his defence. What other metaphilosophy might serve Schopenhauer's purposes in WWR?

We may begin with a brief comparison of Schopenhauer's metaphysics of will with Kant's theory of reason. In the Transcendental Dialectic, Kant explains away reason's Ideas of unconditioned objects in terms of, on the one hand, the conditions and objects of the understanding, and on the other, the specific need of reason, which Kant suggests can be identified with the purely formal function of achieving absolute unity and totality. Such transcendental reflection resolves the Ideas of reason back into the elements from which they were formed, whereby they lose their power to project objects (this is so for philosophical reason if not for natural reason). Once all this has been done, however, Kant has the Ideas return in the contexts of reason's regulative employment and the postulates of pure practical reason, which require that their object-projecting power be restored to them. Kant's solution to the problem which he at this point faces—how can we legitimately attempt to think the supersensible determinately, for example, think of God as endowed with infinite power and wisdom, and do so without reanimating a transcendental illusion?—is to say that judgement here proceeds by analogy, that is, by treating supersensible objects as analogical with sensible objects.[27]

Why cannot Schopenhauer say the same, that is, describe his use of concepts in order to think the relation of the world-as-will to the world-as-representation as a case of analogical thinking?[28] The reason is simply that analogical cognition—moving predicates across the sensible/supersensible divide—can get going only once the two domains have already been established. If I am to think A on the analogy with B, then A must already be posited, hence must be *thinkable*. Now Kant is entitled to presuppose the supersensible domain, because he has affirmed that thought *per se* has an *a priori* foundation which does not tie conceptual significance exclusively to sensible representation, and because he has also shown that the sensible domain fails to account sufficiently for itself. In other words, the unconditioned is securely in place for Kant *before* we undertake to determine it by an analogical use of concepts. Schopenhauer by contrast has scotched the very possibility of another 'domain' capable of bearing analogical relation to the world-as-representation: if we try to talk of a 'determinable domain analogous to the domain governed by the PSR', then we are either, Schopenhauer must say, talking about the world as representation once again, a mere duplicate thereof, or we are saying nothing at all.

What makes Schopenhauer think otherwise, in WWR, is that he believes himself to have discovered in the experience of willing a *rift* in the fabric of the world as representation, an item *within* experience which testifies to the existence of an extra-representational domain or other 'aspect' of the domain of representation. Now the problem concerns the nature of this alleged fact of consciousness. It cannot (by Schopenhauer's rules) be inherently conceptualized in the same manner as perception, for if it were then it would represent an *object*, in accordance with the PSR.[29] So its conceptual articulation—our thinking of this putative fact in a way that permits our extraction of meaning from it—must, it seems, involve our bringing concepts to it. But what concepts? Certainly we can think that this experience—of volition or hedonic affect—is something which has *nothing in common* with representations structured by the PSR, but what we cannot do, with the conceptual resources Schopenhauer allows us, is move from this wholly negative characterization to any positive determination (we can think, as it were, 'this doesn't fit', but cannot say what 'this' *is*, nor what about it makes it incongruent with representation).

It seems that only one alternative remains. If we cannot get the experiential datum to speak by bringing concepts *to* it, then it must speak for *itself*. That is, in order to extract anything positive from volitional experience, Schopenhauer must affirm that the experience contains, or makes provision for, its own conceptualization—it *tells us* what its nature is. The suggestion is of course not supported by the letter of Schopenhauer's texts, but it has (just) enough coherence to do the work needed.

One worry here is that, if Schopenhauer posits an intuition which is independent of the PSR yet for all that *not blind*, then he seems to have allowed himself, in effect, the intellectual intuition that he derides in Fichte and Schelling.[30] Putting the point in the terms of *Fourfold Root*, it may seem that he has allowed a further form of reason additional to those that structure the world as representation, and thus has done exactly what he objects to in German Idealism. Some commentators have indeed suggested that Schopenhauer here shows himself to be a Fichtean or Schellingian. Arguably this is too quick. While it is true that Schopenhauer has expanded his epistemology and come close to admitting a 'higher faculty of knowledge', he has certainly not licensed the project of speculative philosophy. What Schopenhauer needs to maintain, regarding the experience of will, is only that (i) it *manifests* its own incongruity with the world as representation, displaying itself as independent from and foreign to the PSR, as being of a nature that repugns our *a priori* concepts; and (ii) it presents itself as *more primitive* than representation. These relational properties must be held to flow directly from the non-relational essence of will as it is disclosed to us, the intrinsic self-intimating quality of the experience of volition. But Schopenhauer is not obliged to agree that, having registered the meaning of the experience of volition, there is anything more that we can do with it, epistemologically. On the contrary, his position can be that, precisely because what is revealed is *without thinkable internal structure*, it does not put us in possession of a conceptual form that could be redeployed in metaphysical reflection. Unlike the intellectual intuition of Fichte and Schelling, therefore, it does not supply a metaphysical template, a clue to the hidden *reason* of things. It marks an end point for philosophical reflection, not a launching pad. And yet it qualifies as insight.

A question nonetheless remains. Even granting that volitional experience can contain this metaphysical information, which we grasp in the mode of feeling, still we need to be able to take it up in reflection and extract from it the philosophical concept of will *as* a domain or world-aspect, distinct from that of representation. So what in our conceptual repertoire enables us to do this? It seems that we are back with the question we started with.

What Schopenhauer must say, under such intense pressure and for want of any alternative, is that the use made of concepts in thinking the relation of the world-as-will to the world-as-representation as a relation of grounding, is, as several commentators have proposed, a species of *metaphorical* usage.[31] In a way this is to go back to the analogical predication idea. But the new formula avoids the earlier difficulties. If the case is one of metaphor, then we do not commit ourselves to specifying the likeness that underpins it, but only to *exhibiting* the route by which we *arrive* at it—this is the only sense in which we are bound to justify discursively the metaphorical transference of intra-representational grounding to extra-representational relations. This surrender of discursive responsibility is what makes it a case of metaphor, not one of analogy. Nonetheless, we can affirm its rightness, metaphorical aptness, in light of the experience of willing.

If this means, and perhaps it does, that when we think of the world-as-will as ground of the world-as-representation, we are not strictly thinking that *anything is the case*, then Schopenhauer must accept the implication and agree that to think the world as will is not, formally speaking, to *judge* any state of affairs. But this does not leave him empty-handed. The species of thought (or 'quasi'-thought) that the world-as-will admits of, Schopenhauer may say, is instead *expressive*. Leaning on the etymology of expression, the 'object' or 'content' of thought—here, *Wille*—may be regarded as pressing itself out into thought, and so perhaps as being also, in some admittedly strange sense, the *subject* that does the thinking. What matters at any rate is that the world's 'being in essence will' is a thought that *comes to us*, rather than a conclusion that *we come to* through the spontaneity of our thinking. This passive, receptive mode of philosophical cognition would therefore contrast, in an appropriate way, with the way in which we come to know the apodictic truths of the PSR: truths concerning the world-as-will would semi-literally force themselves upon us—they 'strike' us, as one says[32]—rather than being simply and banally self-evident in the manner of the principle of causality.

This would mean that Schopenhauer's system is not really, appearances to the contrary, a rival standing on the same plane as the systems of the German Idealists. When Schopenhauer declares that the world in itself is unindividuated *Wille*, this thesis is not of the same order as Hegel's claim that it is the movement of the Concept or Fichte's claim that it is the activity of the pure I. Schopenhauer's disagreement with Fichte and Hegel would then consist, not in his offering a *competing* conceptual determination of the essence of reality, but in a *denial* that any such characterization is possible.

To be sure, it must seem initially that Schopenhauer loses something in his argument with German Idealism by relinquishing claims for the literal truth of his metaphysics of will, but if so, he gains on the other side by relocating his disagreement at an even more fundamental level. And again, if the result is to make Schopenhauer's metaphysics akin to an aesthetic construction, this is not necessarily to their disadvantage: if their truth is a matter of their *aesthetic force*, and if aesthetic force is understood in the (semi-realist) way described above, and if this is the *only* kind of truth (correctness, warrant) available and appropriate to talk of the ground of the world of representation, and if *no other* theory has comparable aesthetic force, then Schopenhauer's aesthetically validated metaphysics has a full complement of epistemic virtues (and is not aesthetic in any sense which contrasts with the serious business of thinking). It lacks, of course, the pure rational foundation which the German Idealists regard as the sole virtue worth having, but it is Schopenhauer's claim, which his system in a certain sense explains, that that demand is in error. If Schopenhauer is right, there is a good sense in which we do *not* know what we are doing when we engage in metaphysical reflection—this is a direct implication of *Fourfold Root*, which tells us that the transcendent perspective required to conceive reason as grasping reality in itself is an absurdity. What sustains our commitment to the warrantedness of his metaphysics, Schopenhauer may insist, is the absence of any alternative: face-to-face with the world as we find it, there are certain things that, we find, we *have to* think.

It must be asked of course to what extent this extreme construal of Schopenhauer's metaphilosophy matches his own understanding. While we do not find anywhere an outright affirmation of this view as just formulated, it certainly coheres with passages, particularly in the early *Nachlaß*, in which Schopenhauer classifies philosophy alongside *Kunst* in opposition to *Wissenschaft*, and describes the philosopher as possessing genius and engaged in *painting in concepts*, deploying reflection in order to *refract* the content of intuition but not in the service of *explanation*. Philosophy is, or should be, Schopenhauer says, "a reflected image [reflektirtes Abbild] in permanent concepts" of the inner nature of the world (WWR1 453). Also relevant are Schopenhauer's statement in the Appendix of WWR1 that Kant sought a "science *from* [or *of: aus*] concepts", whereas his own philosophy is a "science *in* concepts" (WWR1 537), and the continuity of art with philosophy implied by his description of it, in the conclusion of Book 3, as providing clarification, *Verdeutlichung*, of the visibility of the world (WWR1 315).[33]

V

I have claimed that the minimalist metaphilosophy of *Fourfold Root*, even if it were adequate in its own terms, could not serve the purposes of WWR. Even if *Fourfold Root* is justified in supposing that the PSR hangs in the void, neither grounded nor self-grounding, an ultimate bare *factum*, more is needed metaphilosophically when Schopenhauer steps out of its sphere, specifically, an account of the source of the significance of the claims which compose his metaphysics of will. Whether or not the aesthetic construal is satisfactory, it is highly unlikely that a straightforward, logical solution to the difficulties indicated above can be found: even if Schopenhauer's metaphysics of will could be formally reconciled with his thesis of the limitation of thought, so much twisting and turning will be required that it will be doubtful that we remain in the spirit of Schopenhauer's thought. Here is an alternative perspective on the problem, which supplements the aesthetic construal.

That Schopenhauer was fully aware of the peculiarity of his position seems not open to doubt. His allusion to a 'miracle' at the core of his system (WWR1, 126 [121], and FR, 136 [143]) acknowledges that it is not a theory of the standard type familiar from German Idealism, and the inconsistencies it exhibits are not buried but at the surface: they were rapidly identified and spelled out comprehensively in the earliest 19th-century commentaries on Schopenhauer.[34]

My suggestion is that Schopenhauer is willing to tolerate formal inconsistences in his system because he believes them to be justified in an oblique fashion by what it brings to light. Schopenhauer's standpoint may be reconstructed as follows. Systematicity is inescapable for philosophical reflection insofar as it expresses an aspiration to totality and all-comprehension. However, it cannot properly be determined in advance what direction our reflection will take and what different forms of consciousness will weigh with us, and nor, therefore, can it be determined what will result from the combination of our findings and what shape the system will finally have. In order for philosophical reflection to be genuinely open and *unbefangen*, a wholly indeterminate conception of the system of philosophy as simply whatever we find ourselves once all things have been run through is required—*contra* Kant, Fichte, Schelling, and Hegel, who all maintain that the very concept of a system is given in advance and properly *constrains* the path of philosophical reflection. If it seems otherwise—if it seems to us that achieving systematicity is necessarily equivalent to making the All transparent to Reason and explaining Reality all the way down—then that is because we are victims of the prejudice (rooted in the will to life) that *Fourfold Root* attacked, of supposing the PSR to be not a mere form of cognition but the very substance of the Real. If the failure of Schopenhauer's system to 'add up' is attributable to its object (viz., reality-and-our-situation-within-it), then its inconsistencies can be condoned, and to deploy them as criticisms is merely to wish that things were not as they are and that our situation were not as it is. In sum, if we want to see reality rendered comprehensively (and philosophy can have no other mission), then we commit ourselves to accepting the final product of our endeavour, whatever its logical character. The systematic endeavour is not abortive, since Schopenhauer's system does not return us to where we started from; rather, it takes us to a point where the questions with which we were originally confronted have been dissolved away.

To return to the aesthetic analogy: though we may begin philosophy with the expectation that the system of philosophy will have the form of a piece of classical architecture, the lesson of reflection, if it remains faithful to actual experience, is that the true system has a much stranger shape and incorporates all of the juxtapositions and dissonances of artistic modernism.

To thus urge comparison with appropriate works of art is not to say that Schopenhauer ought really to have employed an artistic medium for articulating his vision, or that his worth lies merely in his having paved the way for *The Man Without Qualities*. It is quite true, as the spectacular history of his influence on artists and writers attests, that internalization of Schopenhauer's thought conduces naturally to non-philosophical forms of expression, but the essential point, not to be lost sight of, is that his system *validates the transition* to these other modes of sense-making: in providing this bridge, the system does not discharge itself or make itself redundant, for we do not and could not find Schopenhauer's system reexpressed in any work of art. It retains its position, as an arrow pointing the way. Systematic philosophy and fine art thus form a unity, not in the way described in Book 3 of WWR1 but at the level of Schopenhauer's metaphilosophy.

Notes

1 See Gardner (2012).
2 The firm implication of the Preface to WWR is that the earlier work is *logically* presupposed, not merely an aid to understanding.
3 The review by Georg Klein, a Schellingian, in the *Jenaischen Allgemeinen Litera-tur-Zeitung*, July 1814, nos. 123–124, imputes confusion: Schopenhauer's PSR is neither the traditional principle nor properly Kantian. Schopenhauer sent *Four-fold Root* to Schulze, Reinhold, Schleiermacher, and August Wolff, but (to my knowledge) received no responses, aside from Schulze's unenthusiastic review in the *Göttingischen Gelehrten Anzeigen*, Stück 70, 30 April 1814, 701–703, which complains that Schopenhauer over-extends the PSR.
4 Or even its antithesis: Wolff (1738, 16–17, 74–76 [§30 and §143]) describes the PSR as sufficient for the distinction of empirical reality from dream, whereas Schopenhauer's PSR entails that empirical reality can only be a certain kind of dream.
5 Another, stronger, and more general implication is that being or existence in general is not something for which there *could* be a reason. Schopenhauer also attacks the assumption in Wolff that essence or determinacy (being thus and not otherwise) is something for which there must be a reason (FR 18–19).
6 Thus in his crucial argument with Wolff in FR, §10, everything turns on Schopenhauer's invocation of Kant's restrictive account of the concept of possibility.

That Schopenhauer's PSR is, at least as regards its content, reducible to (and a mere restatement of) two principles that Kant had already established, is pointed out by Friedrich Ueberweg (1909, 260n).

7 In his *Letters to a German Princess* (1768), Letters XIII–XIV, in Watkins, 2009, 224–228.

8 I use the term 'German Idealism' here, obviously, in a narrow sense.

9 What follows is argued in more detail in my 'Schopenhauer's Contraction of Reason: Clarifying Kant and Undoing German Idealism' (2012, 375–401).

10 Schopenhauer complains of both the fogginess of Kant's conception of method and its intellectualism (see WWR1 537–539). His criticism of Kant for elevating the merely abstract understanding recalls Hegel, but in its place Schopenhauer recommends immediacy, not further mediation. If Schopenhauer is right, the very method of Kantian transcendental proof is ill-conceived.

11 See WWR1 536–559 on the categories. Schopenhauer allows that the Table of Judgements can be accepted, but says that the forms of judgement can all be derived from perception, the content of which they re-express in reflection: they are in fact one and all elaborations of the causality sub-form of the PSR. This coheres with Schopenhauer's criticism of Kant regarding the absurdity of supposing a causality of things in themselves. Thus, just as Kant's Transcendental Deduction is reversed by Schopenhauer—for whom we go *from* the understanding's perception *to* the categories—so too is Kant's Metaphysical Deduction: we go *from* the categories *to* the forms of judgement.

12 See the reconstruction of Paul Franks (2005).

13 See *On the Possibility of a Form of All Philosophy* (1794), in Marti, 1980, esp. 49–51 and *Of the I as Principle of Philosophy* (1795), in Marti, 1980, 120. Schelling asserts the autonomy of the PSR, its superordinate position in relation to Kant's principles of knowledge, and Kant's reliance on it.

14 A position not short of antecedents, one of the most interesting being Herder: see the semantic skepticism of *Fragments on German Literature* (1767–68), in Forster, 2002, 33–64.

15 See, e.g., FR, 97–99; WWR1 47–50; MR2 298–299, 468 and 471.

16 The theory of Ideas either presupposes the independence of the form 'subject-object' from the form determined by the PSR, or it introduces an entirely new sense of 'objectification', which Schopenhauer leaves unexplained. The whole issue comes to a head in the 'Epiphilosophy' conclusion of WWR2 640–643.

17 As Kant first posed it in *Attempt to Introduce the Concept of Negative Magnitudes into Philosophy* (1763), in Walford, p. 239 [2: 202]. Kant supposes there to be a problem, because what allows such a relation to be understood in the case of concepts—containment and the law of identity—makes it puzzling that we can understand it in the case of objects. *FR* implies that there is no puzzle.

18 Haym (1864, 84). Haym affirms, however, that what ultimately fuses these features together is something deeper.

19 On the background to Schopenhauer's development, see Weiß (1907), Hübscher (1989) and Cartwright (2010). A narrower focus is offered in Schröder (1911). Schröder sets against Schopenhauer's own claim that his philosophy sprang whole from his head like Minerva, the charge made by several critics that it is almost entirely 'borrowed': Volkelt and von Hartmann point to sources in the Vedanta, Eleatics, Scotus, Bruno, Spinoza, and Schelling; Seydel describes Schopenhauer's philosophy as corresponding to one stage of Fichteanism and the doctrine of objectification of the will as Hegelian; Windelband considers that Schopenhauer merely rearranges pieces from Kant, Fichte, and Schelling. Schröder's own thesis is that Schopenhauer takes his Kant critique and subject-object correlationism (without acknowledgement) from Schulze, Bouterwek and Jacobi, in opposition to the intellectualist post-Kantian trajectory represented by

Maimon and Beck which leads to Fichte. My highlighting of Maimon below, as a resource for Schopenhauer's abreaction to intellectualism, is of course consistent with this.

20 Moore (2012).

21 Moore (1997 119–120; see also 112–113, 125–126).

22 See Gardner (2015).

23 We find a clear illustration in Maimon (1794, 134): given two drops of water indistinguishable by their concepts and distinguished only by their external relations, it is to be inferred by the PSR that their concepts are inadequate.

24 The task of transcendental logic for Maimon is to demonstrate the existence of 'reale Denken', as he believes Kant fails to do. Schopenhauer disposes of it by reducing transcendental knowledge to immediate awareness of the given fact of certain *a priori* necessities. Other important elements in Schopenhauer's philosophy can be related back to Maimon. Maimon assimilates space and time to the categories—they become *Verstandesbegriffe*—thereby removing the gap between intuition and conceptuality; they are, for Maimon, *Fiktionen*, in parallel with the essentially illusory spatio-temporal world in Schopenhauer. Second, Maimon's rejection of Kant's Antinomies of Pure Reason, on the grounds that their theses are meaningless, is replicated in Schopenhauer. Third, Maimon reduces general logic to transcendental logic (this is central to both of the Maimon texts that Schopenhauer is known to have read), which for Schopenhauer eliminates a further ground for thinking that there is such thing as reason outside the world as representation or as distinct from the PSR: see the section on metalogical truth, *FR*, §33, where Schopenhauer tells us that the non-transcendental laws of thought, inclusive of the Principles of Non-Contradiction and the Excluded Middle, share the epistemology of the PRS, namely immediate experience of repugnance of their contradictories, and have the same root. With regard to their attitudes toward the PSR, we find the following neat inversion: in Maimon's combination of rationalism and skepticism, a rational Real stands opposed to an irrational Given; in Schopenhauer's anti-rationalist and non-skeptical system, a rational Given is opposed to an irrational Real.

25 Schelling (2006, 40). Schopenhauer's deep but disavowed debt to Schelling was remarked upon long ago: see Haym (1864, 83–84) and Liebmann (1865, 187–189).

26 *Philosophical Letters on Dogmatism and Criticism* (1795), in *The Unconditional in Human Knowledge: Four Early Essays 1794–1796*, in Marti, 1980, 163.

27 E.g., *What Real Progress has Metaphysics Made in Germany Since the Time of Leibniz and Wolff?* (1793), in Allison, 370 [20: 280].

28 Schopenhauer makes use of this notion in his treatment of music (WWR1 §52), but notes its limitations (WWR1 303).

29 Liebmann notes the problem (1865, 200).

30 Schopenhauer was aware of the issue: see, e.g., MR1 373.

31 The option is explored and defended by G. Stephen Neeley (1997, 47–67), taking off from remarks in F.C. White (1992, 58–59). Aestheticist construals of Schopenhauer's metaphilosophy are developed in Sandra Shapshay (2008, 211–229) and Sophia Vasalou (2013).

32 In this phenomenological respect (though of course in no other) they bear comparison with Kant's Fact of Reason.

33 To describe Schopenhauer's conception of the aim of philosophy as therapeutic, though tempting, would give a misleading suggestion of instrumentality: Schopenhauer considers that philosophy serves its true purpose when it cancels the putative purposiveness of empirical consciousness, which it can do only if the vision or 'image' it sets before us is intuited in the same way we apprehend a

work of art, as simply 'there for its own sake' (hence the scope, exploited by Hartmann, for representing philosophical insight as achieved on behalf of the world). The aim of philosophical reflection is therefore to reach a point which cannot properly be brought under either explanatory or instrumental categories, and once the system of philosophy achieves total completeness, it melts back into the 'single thought' from which, Schopenhauer tells us, his system was born (WWR1 vii–viii). In MR2 412, Fichte is criticized for regarding philosophy as 'the art of explaining the world, like any instrument', and in the 1820 lectures we find: 'Die ganze Aufgabe der Philosophie wird erst deutlich, durch ihre Auflösung selbst' (in Spierling, 1986, 572).

34 See Zeller (1873, 702–719) and Fischer (1897, Ch. 21). A sizeable list can be gleaned from Ueberweg's *History of Philosophy*. More recently, see Neeley (2012, 105–119).

Bibliography

Cartwright, D. *Schopenhauer: A Biography*. Cambridge: Cambridge University Press, 2010.

Euler, L. *Letters to a German Princess* (1768), extracts in Eric Watkins (ed.), *Kant's Critique of Pure Reason: Background Source Materials*, trans. Eric Watkins. Cambridge: Cambridge University Press, 2009.

Fischer, K. *Geschichte der neuern Philosophie, Vol. 9: Schopenhauers Leben, Werke und Lehre*. Heidelberg: Winter, 1897.

Franks, P. *All or Nothing: Systematicity, Transcendental Arguments, and Skepticism in German Idealism*. Cambridge, MA: Harvard University Press, 2005.

Gardner, S. 'Schopenhauer's Contraction of Reason: Clarifying Kant and Undoing German Idealism', *The Kantian Review* 17, 2012: 375–401.

Gardner, S. 'Transcendental Idealism at the Limit: On A. W. Moore's Criticism of Kant', *Philosophical Topics*, 43, 2015.

Haym, R. *Arthur Schopenhauer*. Berlin: Reimer, 1864.

Herder, J.G. 'Fragments on German Literature (1767–68)', in Michael Forster (ed.), *Philosophical Writings*. Cambridge: Cambridge University Press, 2002, 33–64.

Hübscher, A. *The Philosophy of Schopenhauer in Its Intellectual Context: Thinker against the Tide*. Lewiston, NY: Mellon, 1989.

Kant, I. 'Attempt to Introduce the Concept of Negative Magnitudes into Philosophy (1763)', in David Walford and Ralf Meerbote (trans. and ed.), *Theoretical Philosophy, 1755–1770*. Cambridge: Cambridge University Press, 1992, 203–242.

Kant, I. *Critique of Pure Reason*, trans. and ed. Paul Guyer and Allen Wood. Cambridge: Cambridge University Press, 1998.

Kant, I. 'What Real Progress has Metaphysics Made in Germany since the Time of Leibniz and Wolff? (1793)', in Henry Allison and Peter Heath (eds.) and Gary Hatfield, Michael Friedman, Henry Allison and Peter Heath (trans.), *Theoretical Writings after 1781*. Cambridge: Cambridge University Press, 2002, 337–424.

Liebmann, O. *Kant und die Epigonen. Eine kritische Abhandlung*. Stuttgart: Schober, 1865.

Maimon, S. *Versuch einer neuen Logik oder Theorie des Denkens, nebst angehängten Briefen des Philaleles an Aenesidemus*. Berlin: Felisch, 1794.

Moore, A.W. *Points of View*. Oxford: Oxford University Press, 1997.

Moore, A.W. *The Evolution of Modern Metaphysics: Making Sense of Things*. Cambridge: Cambridge University Press, 2012.

Neeley, G.S. 'Schopenhauer and the Limits of Language', *Idealistic Studies* 27, 1997: 47–67.

Neeley, G.S. 'The Consistency of Schopenhauer's Metaphysics', in Bart Vandenabeele (ed.), *A Companion to Schopenhauer*. Oxford: Blackwell, 2012, 105–119.

Schelling, F.W.J. 'On the Possibility of a Form of All Philosophy (1794)', in Fritz Marti (ed. and trans.), *The Unconditional in Human Knowledge: Four Early Essays 1794–1796*. Lewisburg: Bucknell University Press, 1980(a), 38–58.

Schelling, F.W.J. 'Of the I as Principle of Philosophy (1795)', in Fritz Marti (ed. and trans.), *The Unconditional in Human Knowledge: Four Early Essays 1794–1796*. Lewisburg: Bucknell University Press, 1980(b), 63–128.

Schelling, F.W.J. 'Philosophical Letters on Dogmatism and Criticism (1795)', in Fritz Marti (ed. and trans.), *The Unconditional in Human Knowledge: Four Early Essays 1794–1796*. Lewisburg: Bucknell University Press, 1980(c), 156–196.

Schelling, F.W.J. *Philosophical Investigations into the Essence of Human Freedom and Matters Connected Therewith* (1809), trans. Jeff Love and Johannes Schmidt. Albany, NY: State University of New York Press, 2006.

Schopenhauer, A. 'Vorlesung über die gesammte Philosophie d.i. Die Lehre vom Wesen der Welt und von dem menschlichen Geiste. In vier Theilen. Erster Theil: Theorie des gesammten Vorstellen, Denkens und Erkennens (1820)', in Volker Spierling (ed.), *Theorie des gesammten Vorstellens, Denkens und Erkennens. Aus dem handschriftlichen Nachlaß*. München: Piper, 1986, 85–572.

Schröder, W. *Beiträge zur Entwicklungsgeschichte der Philosophie Schopenhauers. Mit besonderer Berücksichtigung einiger wichtiger frühnachkantischer Philosophen (Maimon, Beck, G. E. Schulze, Bouterwek und Jacobi)*. Rostock: Bold, 1911.

Shapshay, S. 'Poetic Intuition and the Bounds of Sense: Metaphor and Metonymy in Schopenhauer's Philosophy', *European Journal of Philosophy* 16(2), 2008: 211–229.

Ueberweg, F. *History of Philosophy, Vol. 2: History of Modern Philosophy*, trans. George Morris. New York: Scribner, 1909.

Vasalou, S. *Schopenhauer and the Aesthetic Standpoint: Philosophy as a Practice of the Sublime*. Cambridge: Cambridge University Press, 2013.

Weiß, O. *Zur Genesis der Schopenhauerschen Metaphysik*. Leipzig: Thomas, 1907.

White, F.C. *On Schopenhauer's "Fourfold Root of the Principle of Sufficient Reason"*. New York: Brill, 1992.

Wolff, C. *Vernunfftige Gedancken von Gott, der Welt, und der Seele der Menschen, auch allen Dingen überhaupt*, 7th edn. Frankfurt and Leipzig, 1738.

Zeller, E. *Geschichte der deutschen Philosophie seit Leibniz*, 2nd edn. München: Oldenbourg, 1873.

2 The Fivefold Root of the Principle of Sufficient Reason

Eric v.d. Luft

The main question before us is how atheism can be compatible or consistent with accepting any form of the principle of sufficient reason (PSR). This issue concerns Schopenhauer because he is a historical example of an atheist who accepted PSR, and even wrote a treatise in defence of his interpretation of PSR.[1] Questions can be raised whether Schopenhauer correctly understood PSR. Schopenhauer's interpretation will be confronted with Heidegger's interpretation of PSR, and the argument will be made that Heidegger's interpretation is superior. PSR is usually and disproportionately associated with Leibniz (even though it was first clearly formulated by his disciple Wolff), but it can be traced much further back: it occurs embryonically in Plato's *Timaeus* 28a and *Phaedo* 99b, but more substantially and coherently in Aristotle's *Posterior Analytics* 71b8–12 and following Aristotle, in Aquinas's *Summa Contra Gentiles* 15.[2]

The Principle of Sufficient Reason

Principle of sufficient reason is the English translation of the German 'Satz vom Zurreichende Grunde' or the Latin 'principium sufficientis rationes'. Basically, this principle suggests that nothing is without reason (*nihil est sine ratione*). The translation is troublesome, however. The Latin 'ratio' and the English 'reason' can each be translated into either the German *Grund* or the German *Vernunft*. 'Ratio', as Aquinas uses it, and as Leibniz and Wolff use it whenever they refer to *principium rationis sufficientis*, would properly translate the Greek *logos*, not *arche* or *aition*. The meaning of *logos* is *Grund* as reason in the sense of foundation, basis, cause, or ground, not *Vernunft*, which is reason in the sense of intellect, intelligence, or judgment. As will be discussed in more detail below, for Heidegger PSR says nothing about reason but has 'beings' (*Seiende*) and their ground as subject matter. For Heidegger, PSR then says something about the ontology of their 'ontic-ness'. The word 'reason' suggests design or intention; the word 'ground' is neutral on this point. Accordingly, in English, it may be more precise to speak of 'The Principle of Sufficient Ground'—but tradition is against us. In Latin, *ratio* is ambiguous; in German, *Grund* is not. It may help, whenever one sees the abbreviation 'PSR', to think of *principium sufficientis rationis* rather than principle of sufficient reason.

PSR has been under critical scrutiny from two main camps, which I shall name the analytic and the speculative.[3] Respective paradigms of the two camps are Schopenhauer and Heidegger. The former camp sees the topic of PSR as causality, generation, or the metalogic of propositions, and is likely to bracket, ignore, or discount the problem of infinite regress;[4] while the latter sees the topic of PSR as the ultimate ground of being (*Seinsgrund*), and thus should reject the possibility of infinite regress.[5] Analytic versions of PSR are generally conceived in response to problems raised by the First and Second Ways of Thomas Aquinas, while speculative versions are consistent with, and perhaps even sometimes equivalent to, the Third Way.

Schopenhauer, although the fountainhead of the analytic side of the PSR debate, was not an analytic philosopher himself, any more than Kant was, *avant la lettre*. Unlike subsequent analytic philosophers, Schopenhauer (FR 18–20, 23–24) avows that PSR is *a priori* and criticizes Wolff in §§ 10–11, 14 for trying to prove it. He begins *Fourfold Root* by praising Plato for being a lumper and Kant for being a splitter (§ 1). It is not much of an oversimplification to claim that lumping is the essence of speculative philosophy and that splitting is the essence of analytic philosophy. Schopenhauer's decision in § 2 to favor Kant in this regard reveals Schopenhauer as a proto-analytic philosopher rather than a member in good standing of the speculative tradition. He approaches PSR much as subsequent analytic philosophers do, namely as seeing it only in terms of finite relationships, such as those of causality and generation, rather than as an expression of the eternal ontological relationship between the finite things that we see and the infinite absolute that we do not see.

Schopenhauer's Analytic Approach

In *Critique of Pure Reason* (A201-A204 / B246-B249), Kant attempts to prove PSR by reading it as the ground of either possible experience or objective knowledge of phenomena in sequential temporal order. He sees PSR as relevant only to issues of causal succession, or specifically in reaction to Hume's criticisms of causality, and thus considers PSR as either more basic than or equivalent to the principle of causal relation. Schopenhauer follows and amplifies Kant, thus establishing himself as foremost in the analytic school of interpreting PSR. From this perspective, no proof of PSR is likely to be forthcoming, not because PSR is false or problematic, but because it is axiomatic and self-evident. PSR is not inferential. It is not a sequential argument. Rather, it is 'analytic' in the sense that to understand it requires only to 'unpack', as it were, the concepts which are already contained within it as soon as it is stated.

Those on the speculative side tend to see PSR as self-evident, *a priori*, or axiomatic, and those on the analytic side tend to see it as *a posteriori* and thus try either to prove or disprove it. The question of whether PSR is self-evident and incontrovertible or subject to proof remains widely discussed. Even though Schopenhauer differs from analytic philosophy in calling PSR *a priori*, he nevertheless agrees with it in restricting PSR to epistemology and denying its application to ontology, especially to cosmology (FR 24). His interpretation of the principle of sufficient 'reason' (Latin: *ratio*; German: *Grund*) does not deal with either *ratio* or *Grund*, but with 'cause' (*Ursache*). According to the well-established distinction in pre-Schopenhauerian philosophy between reason and ground on the one hand and cause on the other, Schopenhauer, in order to reflect accurately his own interpretation of PSR and the actual content of his book, should have entitled it *Über die vierfache Wurzel des Satzes von der zureichenden Ursache* (i.e., *On the Fourfold Root of the Principle of Sufficient Cause*).[6]

In limiting PSR to causality, Schopenhauer never strays far from efficient or 'billiard ball' causality, the immediate relationship between particular cause and particular effect. Because he claims it does not apply to the world as a whole, but only to its parts, Schopenhauer's PSR refers only to a nexus of interconnected causes, grounds, and reasons—all *Vorstellungen*—but to no first cause, ultimate ground, or primal reason. His assertion, then, in § 5, "Nothing is without a [ground or] reason why it is" (FR 5) should be supported in § 52 when he says, "Always and everywhere each thing is only *by means of another thing*" (FR 158; Schopenhauer's emphasis); but he seems to contradict it in WWR2, § 4, by saying, "the mere *existence* of a thing does not entitle us to conclude that it has a cause" (WWR2 49; Schopenhauer's emphasis). He appears either not to understand or implicitly not to accept the difference between a 'thing' or a 'state' as cause, on the one hand, and a pre-causal 'ground' of causality, on the other. Granted, as long as we regard the *causa mundi* as either a 'thing' or a 'state', then common sense demands that we reject Wolff's *principium essendi* (FR 18–19), the application of PSR to the question of existence in general, just as Schopenhauer has done—but there seems to be no call to assume that a ground of existence would be either a 'thing' or a 'state'.

To regard causality as Schopenhauer does, only in terms of changing states and not in terms of ultimate ground, would entail the eternity of matter, therefore the necessity of matter; and this, for Schopenhauer, is exactly what it does entail (FR 43). Let us grant this point (i.e., that matter neither comes to be nor passes away but only changes form). His argument for this is intuitively cogent and accords with physics, even post-Einsteinian physics, where matter may take on the form of sheer energy. Schopenhauer then appears to reject the cosmological claims of the Leibniz-Wolff version of PSR because they presume to provide a ground to explain how matter and the world came into being out of non-being, and because such a concept, for him, is absurd. But Schopenhauer is not necessarily called upon to provide a ground for how the world *came into being*—that was indeed Leibniz's and Wolff's mistake. Rather, he is called upon by the full and consistent extension of all aspects of PSR to provide a ground for why the world exists *now* (i.e., a ground for why matter is in fact *eternal*). Aristotle provided such a ground of the world's eternity with his prime mover. We may well jettison the idea of a creative ground, an ultimate originative ground, or God as creator, for we may legitimately doubt whether the world was created out of nothing; but we cannot jettison the idea of a sustaining ground, or God as sustainer, for we cannot possibly doubt that the world actually exists *now*. The world exists. Therefore it must have a ground of existence; otherwise it would not exist.

Schopenhauer believed that he could both be an atheist and accept PSR at the same time. Yet he recognized that since proof of the reality of God follows trivially via an implicit cosmological argument from the full-fledged Leibniz-Wolff version of PSR (i.e., the universal application to of PSR), he had to limit PSR to the extent that such a logical consequence could be avoided. His limiting of PSR could be seen as an overly closecut with Ockham's razor. As an atheist, he could not tolerate the free exercise of reason leading him to such a position. So he checked the free exercise of reason. That is, he just asserted, with minimal argument, that PSR applied only to the physical or phenomenal world and its causality and not to any first cause outside this world. If he ever offered any such argument, it was circular, as follows:

> the general sense of the principle of sufficient reason may be reduced to the fact that always and everywhere each thing is only *by means of another thing*, Now, however, the principle of reason is *a priori* in all its forms, thus rooted in our intellect; therefore, this principle cannot be applied to the totality of all existing things—the world—including this intellect in which the world resides. For such a world, presenting itself by means of *a priori* forms, is for just this reason mere appearance; therefore, what applies to this world as a consequence of just these forms can have no application to the world itself; i.e. to the thing in itself presenting itself in the world. Therefore, one cannot say 'the world and all things in it exist by means of something else'—which proposition is simply the cosmological proof.
>
> (FR 158; Schopenhauer's emphasis)

In the above passage, note especially the following two arguments: Argument one. (1) PSR is *a priori*; (2) therefore, PSR is rooted in the human intellect; (3) therefore, PSR cannot apply to the totality of existing things, to the world, or to the intellect itself. Argument two: (2) PSR is *a priori*; (2) a world presented through *a priori* forms is merely phenomenal; (3) what holds true of a phenomenon does not necessarily hold true for the thing-in-itself; (4) therefore, PSR applies to appearances in the world and not to the world itself.

The first is a fallacious argument in that it excludes any class of things from being subject to PSR. How Schopenhauer moves from the *a priori* character of PSR to these exclusions seems arbitrary and mysterious. The move from the second to third premise is an example of *ignoratio elenchi*. It may also involve an instance of the *ad hominem* (circumstantial) fallacy (i.e., Schopenhauer may be poisoning the well by suggesting that if the universal application of PSR is what Leibnizian theists believe, then such universal application cannot be the case). The move from the first to the second premise is even more problematic. Interpretations of it would naturally divide into Platonic/Cartesian 'innate ideas' and Lockean *tabula rasa* camps.

The second argument is stronger but still not strong enough to make his point. He claims that not everything is subject to PSR. He seeks to limit the use of PSR to explanations of the physical or phenomenal world alone. Many commentators have remarked upon this oddity in Schopenhauer's thought,[7] yet they seem not to have penetrated deep enough to mention how illogical this notion is. Bryan Magee comes close to embarking upon a challenge to Schopenhauer's constriction of PSR, but stops short of a real attack.[8]

A Limited Understanding of PSR?

To say that things in the world are subject to PSR but that the world itself is not subject to it is to set up a double standard. The world is, after all, just another 'thing' writ large. Since he does not allow PSR to be applied universally (i.e., to every possible question, including the ontological ground of the world's existence), he seems confused about the difference between ground (*Grund*) and cause (*Ursache*)—in spite of his discussion of Aristotle in § 6. Above all, he seems not to recognize that the very concept of 'groundlessness' does not make sense, and consequently, that either the will, his ultimate principle, is the ground of the world or has a ground of its own. Or rather, he seems to recognize the difference between ground and cause (FR 7–8) but then ignores it.

How could anything be 'groundless' for anyone who accepts PSR? Why must PSR be restricted to *individual* phenomena? If we look at the passages in *Fourfold Root* where Schopenhauer claims that PSR cannot be applied to the question of the world's existence, we see that he does not offer much of an argument for truncating PSR in this way. In § 10 he dismisses Wolff's *principium essendi* in cavalier fashion; in § 49, 'Necessity,' he lists all good reasons for adopting such a Wolffian principle, but then again just dismisses it out of hand without saying why; and in § 52 he asserts that because PSR is rooted in our intellect and is always *a priori*, it thus cannot be applied to the whole world. These unsatisfying passages are supplemented to a meager extent by Schopenhauer's discussion of the cosmological argument in WWR2, § 4; but in FR, even though we are given a more lengthy treatment of these issues, what we are really given is equivocation and contradiction with other assertions elsewhere in the corpus.

His reliance on causality leads him to some bizarre or paradoxical positions. For example, he at once recognizes and does not recognize the reality of the universal ground, which for him is the will or, as he calls it here, the force:

> The force itself lies entirely outside the chain of causes and effects that presupposes time . . . the force lies outside time as well. . . . Because, however many times it may occur, a case derives its efficacy from a force of nature which is groundless as such, i.e. lies completely outside the chain of causes and the province of the principle of sufficient reason in general.
>
> (WWR1 155)

It would be intelligible and coherent to say that there is a ground of existence, a *causa mundi*, or the-cause-without-which-the-things-or-states-which-act-as-causes-would-not-be-able-to-act-as-causes. We need not also be able thereafter to say anything intelligible or coherent about the nature of that ground. We would not be committed to a full-fledged Thomistic or even Aristotelian *Weltanschauung* by claiming such a ground of existence. In other words, we could easily say, in accord with the full extension of PSR, *that* such a ground is, but we could never say *what* such a ground is. We could not even call it the 'first cause'. We could point toward it, but we would not be competent to name it. To assume that it must be like a thing, a state, or even a cause, is simply stifling. But Schopenhauer refuses even to say *that* it is, and this refusal lands him in a sea of contradictions and incompletenesses. He is thereby led to truncate his PSR, but he seems unable or unwilling to say why. He thus eviscerates PSR, claiming that it "cannot be applied to the totality of all existing things—the world—including this intellect in which the world resides" (FR 158). He makes a straw man argument out of PSR and moreover, seems to do so arbitrarily. Analogously, and just as absurdly, he might as well say that the law of gravity cannot be applied to all existing things, but only to heavy things, and only when they are actually in the process of falling.

Fourfold Root is the *locus classicus* of most of Schopenhauer's systematic premises. There, in § 5, he takes over Wolff's *nihil est sine ratione cur potius sit quam non sit* (Wolff, 1736, 28)—"Nothing is without a [ground or] reason why it is"—*Nichts ist ohne Grund warum es sei* (FR 5) as his preliminary working definition of PSR. But by this formula he does not mean what Wolff, Leibniz, or their predecessors mean at all. They do not limit PSR. They literally mean what they say (i.e., that *nothing*, even the world or the universe itself, is without a ground, reason, or cause why it is rather than is not). This is Wolff's *principium essendi*, which Schopenhauer does not refute but just boldly rejects (FR 18–19). Schopenhauer (§ 10) notices in Wolff's formulation that *ratio* may refer either to (1) the cause of an effect, (2) the ultimate ground of the existence of entities, or (3) the reason why a proposition is true. Schopenhauer rejects the second outright, calls the first ontological and the third logical. That he wants to reduce the second to causality shows that he does not understand what Wolff is talking about (Wolff, 1736, 386–389) (i.e., the ground of essence, or the reason why things are what they are and are as they are). Wolff reveals in § 908 (396) that his topic, and the actual focus of PSR, is *causa sui*. That Schopenhauer, in discussing Spinoza, identifies *causa sui* with Baron Münchhausen (§ 8) is clear evidence that he does not understand PSR in general.

Even though he admits that PSR is *a priori*, he nevertheless wants to name what he regards as its four separate 'roots'. His argument for this decision is sound. Just because something is *a priori* does not mean it also has to be atomic. He claims that PSR is actually a compound of four simpler *a priori* principles (§ 5), which he chooses to call its 'roots', but which he could just as well have called its 'parts', 'factors', or 'aspects'. Indeed, they are not really 'roots', but classes of existential instantiations of 'the real root without which the other roots would not be roots'—that is, (1) physical, (2) logical, (3) mathematical, and (4) moral principles (FR 7), comparable and perhaps respectively analogous to Aristotle's four types of causality: efficient, formal, material, and final (*Physics*, 194b-195a, 198a-b). Schopenhauer's principle of physical necessity, becoming, or change (FR 93–95) corresponds to Aristotle's determining factor of efficient causality or propelling cause; Schopenhauer's principle of logical necessity, knowing, or judgment (FR 105) to Aristotle's determining factor of formal causality or definition; Schopenhauer's principle of mathematical necessity, being, or relation (FR 131–132) to Aristotle's determining factor of material causality or existence; and Schopenhauer's principle of moral necessity, willing, or motivation (FR 145–146) to Aristotle's determining factor of final or telic causality, the goal or *telos*.

Taken together, these four principles pretty much define the analytic approach to PSR. But this four-root analysis commits a category mistake. Here are Sills Hall, Hyde Hall, Coles Tower, and Pickard Theater, but where is Bowdoin College? Here are the physical root, the logical root, the mathematical root, and the moral root, but where is PSR?[9] Statements such as *Nichts ist ohne Grund warum es sei* (FR 5) suggest that the actual 'root' of PSR would be *fivefold*, not fourfold as Schopenhauer claims. There should also be a fifth, an *existential* principle (i.e., an ultimate ontological principle of existential instantiation, not only of individuals or particulars, but of anything at all). But Schopenhauer misses this fifth root (i.e., Tillich's 'ground of being', or what Heidegger sees on the other side of the ontological difference, i.e., that without which nothing would exist to be either a cause or an effect). The fifth 'root' of Schopenhauer's four-headed propositional version of PSR is PSR itself—in its axiomatic Aristotelian-Thomistic-Leibnizian version. This fifth root is what defines the speculative.

The Speculative Approach as an Alternative

In what remains, some notes will be made on a different approach to PSR that might address the difficulties expressed with regard to the analytic approach. Somewhat surprisingly, given the long history of PSR, the first philosopher to recognize the ultimate or absolute ontological significance of PSR was Heidegger, although inklings of this speculative interpretation exist in Aristotle, Aquinas, Leibniz, and Hegel. Not even Wolff or Leibniz's other main disciple, Baumgarten, managed to move beyond the merely analytic view of PSR. Analytic thought about PSR occurs only in what Heidegger would call the ontic realm, never touching the truly ontological ground of whatever exists.

The early and the later Heidegger, each, wrote a small book about PSR: *Vom Wesen des Grundes* (*On the Essence of Ground*) in 1929 and *Der Satz vom Grund* (*The Principle of Ground*) in 1957, the latter a critique of the former. One purpose of the former is to define the ontological difference (ER/VWG 2–3; OEG 97), and one purpose of the latter is to refine this definition. First, Heidegger investigates whether *das Problem des Grundes* is even raised by PSR at all (ER/VWG 6–9; OEG 100–107). For Heidegger, PSR points toward bridging the gap between beings and being by understanding the ontological difference. To understand PSR we must understand and accept the ontological difference. The last few paragraphs of Lecture 12 in the later work, on calculative vs. meditative thinking (*rechnendes* vs. *besinnliches Denken*) (PR 100–101), imply that calculative thinking is inevitably ontic but that meditative thinking may eventually become ontological, and thus may lead us to recognize the other side explicitly. The other side of the ontological divide from us does not include the efficient, material, formal, or even final cause of any particular entities. Rather, there is only their ground. The ground of being is being (i.e., being is its own ground). It is *causa sui* (cause of itself)—or better said—*ratio sui* (ground of itself), *der selbstgegründete Grund* (self-grounded ground), or *der sich gründende Grund* (self-grounding ground).

Just as, for Leibniz, the reality of God follows trivially from PSR, so for Heidegger, the reality of *Sein* behind *Seiende* follows trivially from it. That is, the speculatively interpreted PSR immediately answers Heidegger's question, "Why is there something rather than nothing?"[10] There is something rather than nothing because the ontological must become ontic in order to be known as ontological. Speculatively understood, PSR is a version of the Aquinas' Third Way. Moreover, PSR is necessarily involved in all arguments for the reality of God, both cosmological and ontological. Recognizing the interrelatedness and even complementarity of particular arguments for the reality of God can strengthen each separate argument involved in the relation. The ontological and cosmological arguments are complementary insofar as to understand the nature of being and existence to the extent that therefrom one may infer the reality of God (as in the ontological argument) is essentially the same as to understand the nature of necessity and contingency to the extent of the same inference (as in the Third Way).[11] Any claims that the Third Way does not depend upon PSR would hold that PSR emphasizes causality as the ultimate ground of cosmological arguments. But the speculative PSR does not depend on causality, especially efficient causality, nor formal, material, or even final causality, but rather on the nature of ontology itself. All we have to do is unpack the meaning of ontology—as Heidegger did—to discover the meaning and importance of PSR. Paradoxically (or ironically), the speculative PSR is 'analytic' in that sense. Its meaning lies within itself, not in pointing toward anything else.

Sein is the reason that there are *Seiende* rather than nothing. It is the answer to the central question of Heidegger's *Introduction to Metaphysics* (IM 1–7; EM 1–7). In other words, *Sein* is the ultimate focus of what in English is PSR but in German is more accurately denoted as *der Satz vom Grund*, the principle of ground. *Sein* is the ground of both being and beings (i.e., the ground of itself as well as of all specific entities). It is uncaused, *sui generis, causa sui*, and purely self-reflexive. Heidegger (PR 75; SG 129) is clear that PSR refers to *Sein* as the ultimate ground, even as the ground of itself, or as identical with itself *qua* ground.

Heidegger regards Schopenhauer's analysis of PSR as superficial and misbegotten (MFL 112–115). He does not shirk from discussing Leibniz, Aristotle, and Goethe in connection with PSR, but scarcely gives a second thought to Schopenhauer after mentioning FR merely bibliographically (ER/VWG 6–9; OEG 99). We can easily imagine Heidegger's contempt for the author of the lines: "the principle of sufficient reason . . . cannot be applied to the totality of all existing things—the world—including this intellect in which the world resides" (FR 158). Heidegger's appropriation of PSR is more or less traditional (i.e., close to the Aristotelian-Thomistic-Leibnizian interpretation of PSR as a self-evident axiom). Heidegger claims, however, against Leibniz, that PSR is more fundamental than the principle of non-contradiction (MFL 52–53), but in so doing he still allies himself with Leibniz *et al.* against Schopenhauer.

"Nothing is without a reason why it is" or "Nothing is without a ground of its being" means not only that everything is an effect and therefore has a cause, but also that every cause, in order to be a cause at all, must have an effect, else it would just be inert.[12] Every 'thing' (*Seiendes*) is a predicate (SG 23) (i.e., an effect, contingent upon something else). The *Grund* in PSR may refer either to (1) the cause of an effect, (2) the reason why a proposition is true, or (3) the ultimate ground of the existence of entities. In the third case the *Grund* is the *Seinsgrund* and is ontologically different from any other kind of *Grund*. In the first two cases the *Grund* is ontologically of the same type as the effect or the proposition (i.e., it is, like them, a finite entity with properties). Analytic philosophy would typically regard the third case as nonsense. But for Heidegger, ground equals being (i.e., the ultimate cause of beings is being itself). We experience *Sein* as *Grund* (SG 210; PR 129). With just a slight change of terminology, not of content, the following passage would make Heidegger sound almost theistic:

> Because beings (*jedes Seiende*) are brought into being by being *qua* ground/reason (*Grund*), every being inevitably is alloted a ground/reason. For otherwise it would not be (*seiend*). Understood as the fundamental principle of rendering sufficient reason (*Grundsatz vom zuzustellenden zureichenden Grund*), the principle of reason (*Satz vom Grund*) is thereby true only because a word of being (*Wort vom Sein*) speaks in it that says being and ground/reason: the same (*Sein und Grund: das Selbe*).
>
> (PR 125; SG 205)

Because a cause would not be a cause unless it had an effect; hence the effect is, in effect, the cause of the cause being a cause. PSR transcends the ontological difference and provides a genuine ontological reason for the existence and succession of ontic beings, not just a series of ontic reasons for this existence and succession. Without Heideggerian being (*Sein*) qua *causa sui*, nothing would be. That is, unless there were being in general, there would be no particular beings; no entities would exist. In other words, for Heidegger, PSR points directly beyond the ontic and toward the ontological, whereas for other philosophers (such as Schopenhauer and Russell), it points only toward other aspects of the ontic.

PSR and Ockham's razor could be seen in relation to each other as not exactly complements, but as opposite versions of a single implicit admonition to try to achieve an Aristotelian mean of explanations. That is, the one urges us not to posit too few explanatory factors, while the other urges us not to posit too many. By the speculative PSR we can say *that* there is a ground, reason, or cause for the being of the entire world or universe, but we cannot say *what* that ground, reason, or cause is. This is the standard theological problem of knowing *that* God is (*quod sit*), but not knowing *what* God is (*quid sit*). Ockham's razor can never be at odds with the *quod sit*, but must always be at odds with the *quid sit*. If a simple and a complicated explanation, each *fully* adequate to fit the facts of some case, compete with each other for acceptance in that case, the simple is always to be preferred because we ought not to posit the existence or reality of anything unless we must. This winnowing process would exclude from the sphere of *knowledge* most of the dogmas of most of the particular religions of the world and relegate such dogmas to the sphere of *faith*. For example, the reality of God *per se* (*quod sit*) is a matter of knowledge (through the proofs and through PSR), but the reality of Jesus Christ, Krishna, or Glooskap (each an example of *quid sit*) are, partially because of Ockham's razor, matters of faith alone, since there can be no *knowledge* of Jesus Christ, Krishna, or Glooskap, but only stories and *beliefs* about them.[13]

The proofs—ontological, cosmological, teleological, moral—only demonstrate the reality or necessity of some presence which must be completely different from the world. They do not provide any specific information about any nameable deity. Rather, they only show *that* there must be (*quod sit*) what Aristotle calls *energeia*; Aquinas (following Aristotle) calls *actus purus*; Hinduism calls Brahman Nirguna; Pseudo-Dionysius calls the 'superessential'; Plotinus calls to 'en; Eckhart calls the Godhead; Otto calls the 'numinous', the *mysterium tremendum et fascinans*, or (following Schleiermacher) *das ganz Andere*; or perhaps most to the point, what Tillich calls the 'ground of being'. Neither PSR nor any theistic proofs say anything about the attributes or character of this presence. This is because it is ontological and infinite, not ontic or finite, which is why Heidegger calls it *Sein*. To personify, anthropomorphize, worship, pray to, or otherwise pretend that we can have any certain knowledge of, justifiable beliefs about, or personal contact with *Sein*, this essentially Aristotelian God, is impossible. Through the speculative PSR we can be certain *that* God is real (*haecceitas*), but cannot be justified in believing anything about *what* God is (*quidditas*). There can be no human knowledge of divine attributes or character; that is, any judgments about *what* such a presence actually is (*quid sit*) must remain matters of faith and imagination.[14]

Notes

1 See also: Griffiths (1976) and Hamlyn (1980b, 78–94).
2 In an extended version of this paper, these earlier versions of PSR were treated in more detail. Because of constraints of space, these sections were cut out.
3 Jacek Wojtysiak (2007, 112) designates as PSR-O (i.e., the ontological PSR) approximately what I call the speculative PSR. Within what I call the analytic PSR, he distinguishes PSR-E and PSR-M (i.e., the epistemological and methodological PSR). George N. Schlesinger (1995) discusses something akin to Wojtysiak's PSR-M. Also on the analytic side, Lois Frankel (1986, 324) distinguishes between PSR_g = "Every true proposition has a proof" and PSR_c = "Every event or state of affairs has cause."
4 Wilbur Marshall Urban (1898, 82–83) claims that Schopenhauer reduces ground, even the ground of the will, to "mechanical causation."
5 Cf. Luft (2004, 15–16, 37).
6 Some commentators—for example, Hamlyn (1980a, 12–14)—protest the word *Wurzel* as well, claiming that Schopenhauer's topic is not really four 'roots' of PSR, but four forms or aspects of it, since there is but a single root of PSR, namely, for Schopenhauer, our consciousness and its process of knowing via the subject/object relation (cf. FR, § 16).
7 For example: John Atwell (1988, 18; 1995, 64–65, 106, 116, 127–128, 133, 135–136, 141–142, 160). Surprisingly uncritical of Schopenhauer on this and most other points is F.C. White, who scarcely even mentions the oddity, except for a brief allusion (White, 1992, 9). White seems as little bothered by

Schopenhauer's refusal to grant universal application to PSR as does Schopenhauer himself—this has been asserted by at least one reviewer (Lance Richey, 1995)

 8 Magee (1983, 28–48).
 9 Cf. Gilbert Ryle (1949, 16–17).
10 Cf. Hermanni (2011).
11 Cf. Luft (2010).
12 Cf. "Nichts ist ohne Grund" vs. "Jegliches/Jedes Seiende hat einen Grund" (SG 16–17).
13 Cf. Luft (2008).
14 Conversations with Dennis Vanden Auweele, David E. Cartwright, Marco Casucci, G. Scott Davis, Sebastian Gardner, Tom Rockmore, Ivan Soll, David Woods, the late John Atwell, the late George L. Kline, and the late C. Douglas McGee, as well as notes taken by my wife, Diane, at conferences and in several courses on religion and philosophy which I taught at the Humanistic Studies Center of Syracuse University, were all of great help to me in writing this paper. I thank these people very much.

Bibliography

Atwell, J. 'Doers and Their Deeds: Schopenhauer on Human Agency', in E. Luft (ed.), *Schopenhauer: New Essays in Honor of His 200th Birthday*. Lewiston: Edwin Mellen Press, 1988, 1–23.

Atwell, J. *Schopenhauer on the Character of the World: The Metaphysics of Will*. Berkeley: University of California Press, 1995.

Frankel, L. 'From a Metaphysical Point of View: Leibniz and the Principle of Sufficient Reason', *Southern Journal of Philosophy* 24, 1986: 321–334.

Griffiths, A.P. 'Wittgenstein and the Fourfold Root of the Principle of Sufficient Reason', *Proceedings of the Aristotelian Society* 50, 1976: 1–20.

Hamlyn, D.W. *Schopenhauer*. London: Routledge & Kegan Paul, 1980(a).

Hamlyn, D.W. 'Schopenhauer on the Principle of Sufficient Reason', in M. Fox (ed.), *Schopenhauer: His Philosophical Achievement*. Totowa, NJ: Barnes & Noble, 1980(b), 78–94.

Heidegger, M. *An Introduction to Metaphysics*, trans. Ralph Manheim. Garden City, NY: Anchor Doubleday, 1961; cited as IM.

Heidegger, M. *Kant and the Problem of Metaphysics*, trans. James S. Churchill. Bloomington: Indiana University Press, 1962; cited as KPM.

Heidegger, M. *Einführung in die Metaphysik*. Tübingen: Niemeyer, 1966.

Heidegger, M. *The Essence of Reasons: A Bilingual Edition, Incorporating the German Text of Vom Wesen des Grundes [1929]*, trans. Terrence Malick. Evanston: Northwestern University Press, 1969; cited as ER/VWG.

Heidegger, M. *Sein und Zeit*. Tübingen: Niemeyer, 1972.

Heidegger, M. *The Principle of Reason*, trans. Reginald Lilly. Bloomington: Indiana University Press, 1991; cited as PR.

Heidegger, M. *The Metaphysical Foundations of Logic*, trans. Michael Heim. Bloomington: Indiana University Press, 1992; cited as MFL.

Heidegger, M. *Being and Time*. trans. Joan Stambaugh. Albany: SUNY, 1996; cited as BT.

Heidegger, M. *Der Satz vom Grund [1957]*, 8th edn. Stuttgart: Neske, 1997; cited as SG.

Heidegger, M. 'On the Essence of Ground' [1929], in William McNeill (trans.), *Pathmarks*. Cambridge: Cambridge University Press, 1998, 97–135; cited as OEG.

Heidegger, M. *Geschichte der Philosophie von Thomas von Aquin bis Kant: Marburger Vorlesung Wintersemester 1926/27*. Frankfurt am Main: Klostermann, 2006.

Hermanni, F. 'Warum ist überhaupt etwas? Überlegungen zum kosmologischen und ontologischen Argument', *Zeitschrift für philosophische Forschung* 65, 2011: 28–47.

Luft, E.v.d. 'The Empirical Version of the Ontological Argument and the A Priori Version of the Cosmological Argument', in J. Jacobson and R. Mitchell (eds.), *Existence of God: Essays from the Basic Issues Forum*. Lewiston, New York: Edwin Mellen Press, 1988, 149–161.

Luft, E.v.d. *God, Evil, and Ethics: A Primer in the Philosophy of Religion*. North Syracuse, NY: Gegensatz Press, 2004.

Luft, E.v.d. 'Ockham's Razor', in B. Lerner and K. Lerner (eds.), *Scientific Thought in Context*. Farmington Hills, MI: Gale Cengage Learning, 2008, 950–954.

Luft, E.v.d. *Ruminations: Selected Philosophical, Historical, and Ideological Papers, Volume 1*. North Syracuse, NY: Gegensatz Press, 2010.

Magee, B. *The Philosophy of Schopenhauer*. Oxford: Clarendon, 1983.

Richey, L.B. 'Book Review of F.C. White: On Schopenhauer's "Fourfold Root of the Principle of Sufficient Reason"', *Journal of Speculative Philosophy* 9, 1995: 241–245.

Ryle, G. *The Concept of Mind*. New York: Barnes & Noble, 1949.

Schlesinger, G. 'A Pragmatic Version of the Principle of Sufficient Reason', *Philosophical Quarterly* 45, 1995: 439–459.

Urban, W.M. *The History of the Principle of Sufficient Reason: Its Metaphysical and Logical Formulations*. Princeton: Princeton University Press, 1898.

White, F. *On Schopenhauer's "Fourfold Root of the Principle of Sufficient Reason"*. Leiden: Brill, 1992.

Wojtysiak, J. 'On the Principle of Sufficient Reason', *Polish Journal of Philosophy* 1, 2007: 111–135.

Wolff, C. *Philosophia prima sive ontologia methodo scientifica pertractata*, 3rd edn. Veronae: Typis Dionysii Ramanzini Bibliopolae apud S. Thomam, 1736.

Part II

(Transcendental) Idealism in and beyond the Fourfold Root

3   Idealism in *Fourfold Root*

Jonathan Head

The place of Schopenhauer within the philosophical realm of idealism is still up for debate.[1] Of course, we can follow the usual interpretive line and straightforwardly designate him as a transcendental idealist.[2] However, taking into account Schopenhauer's numerous objections to aspects of Kant's Critical system, the ways in which he modifies aspects of Kant's epistemology and other areas, as well as the presumably idiosyncratic manner in which Schopenhauer would understand what it would be to be a Kantian philosopher, we would perhaps do well to take another look. In this paper, I will argue that Schopenhauer's sympathies lie closer to a Berkeleyan subjective idealism than is usually supposed. This paper can only present the very beginnings of such an argument, but at the very least, it is hoped that the question of the precise nature of Schopenhauer's idealism will be shown to be worthy of further consideration.

After considering various types of idealism that might conceivably have acted as an influence upon Schopenhauer in the construction of his philosophy (section 2), I will compare the first and second editions of *Fourfold Root* with an eye on the differing approaches to idealism found in these works (section 3). I will argue that a close reading of relevant sections reveals a softening of attitude toward subjective idealism between the writing of Schopenhauer's doctoral dissertation and the publication of the second edition of *Fourfold Root* in 1847. I will consider further evidence from *WWR* for my view. I will then consider aspects of Berkeley's philosophy that may appear Schopenhauerian in tenor, the possible idealistic influence of Indian philosophy, and some of the difficulties that might seem to be insuperable barriers to interpreting Schopenhauer as a subjective idealist (section 4). I argue that such barriers can be overcome.

Varieties of Idealism

In order to orient our reflections, I will give a brief characterisation of three different types of idealism that were prevalent in the 18th and 19th centuries, and thus conceivably could have influenced Schopenhauer in some way. First, we can consider subjective idealism, a position whose perhaps most famous proponent is George Berkeley. According to this view, material objects are construed as collections of ideas in a given mind. All that exists are minds and their ideas. In the *Principles of Human Knowledge*, he writes,

> all those bodies which compose the mighty frame of the world, have not any subsistence without a mind . . . [,] their being is to be perceived and known . . . [,] consequently so long as they are not actually perceived by me, or do not exist in my mind, or that of any other created spirit, they must either have no existence at all, or else subsist in the mind of some Eternal Spirit.
>
> (Berkeley, 1901, 260–261)

More specifically, we can boil it down to some key claims regarding objects in the world: 1) There are no material (only mental) substances, 2) material objects consist in their sensible qualities, which are nothing more than ideas (so sensible things are mind-dependent), and 3) all that exists are minds and their sensations.

Second, we can consider transcendental idealism, the position first famously held by Kant, from his *Inaugural Dissertation* of 1770 onward. We can view this position as a weaker form of idealism, in that we find the rejection of ontological idealism as a corollary of the postulation of a thing-in-itself underlying the world of experience in some way, a 'something' that does not depend for its existence upon being thought. Instead of focusing on the mind as providing the very matter for sensation, the mind is investigated as to the form which it imposes upon our experience, such that we can still claim that the world of our experience is in some non-negligible way mind-dependent. Kant characterises transcendental idealism in *The Critique of Pure Reason*:

> We have sufficiently proved in the Transcendental Aesthetic that everything intuited in space or in time, hence all objects of an experience possible for us, are nothing but appearances, i.e, mere representations, which, as they are represented, as extended beings or series of alterations, have outside our thoughts no existence grounded in itself.
>
> (Kant, 1998, A490/B518f.)

A straightforward reading of Schopenhauer would undoubtedly place him in this category, following Kant as a transcendental idealist, with space, time, and causality being the forms that we impose on our experience, and the Will in place as the 'thing-in-itself' underlying all experience.

The final type of idealism we can look at is absolute idealism, which boasts among its followers Hegel and Bradley.[3] Under this view, all parts of the world have a purpose or function in relation to an Absolute Idea, which can be understood as a final unfolding of all things (see Dunham, 2011, 150). In this discussion, we will be more interested in Schopenhauer's relation to both subjective and transcendental idealism, mostly because Schopenhauer rejects absolute idealism out of hand (for example, he writes in the first edition of *Fourfold Root*, "an intellectual intuition of the absolute identity of [subject and object], which places them under the category of unity, would have the advantage of leaving one unknown quantity instead of two. However, [we lack] such [an] intuition" (EF 184), and in the notebooks, in the context of critiquing the philosophy of Schelling, he writes of "an unspeakable clumsiness to appear after [the Kantian philosophy] with the system of the *absolute identity of the real and the ideal*" (MR3 186)).

Before we move on to consider the text of *Fourfold Root* itself, it is worth noting that in what follows, we will presume that Schopenhauer's philosophy certainly falls under the rubric of idealism, broadly conceived. However, some have even denied this basic claim (see Snow & Snow, 1991). Such a view, I argue, arises from overlooking the potential impact of subjective idealism upon Schopenhauer's philosophy, and instead focusing on transcendental and absolute idealism, on the basis of which his commitment to idealism is questioned. Rather, Schopenhauer's rejection of parts of Kant's transcendental idealism could be seen as a commitment to a more thoroughgoing idealism such that we find in Berkeley, rather than as a rejection of idealism *per se*. Further, I am interested in the development of Schopenhauer's relation toward idealism, whereas Snow and Snow quote interchangeably from earlier and later works, which makes the underlying assumption that one can retrieve one constant Schopenhauerian view with regard to idealism throughout the works, and such an assumption is what I wish to challenge in this paper. For these reasons, I will leave Snow and Snow's paper aside for the rest of this discussion.

Idealism in *Fourfold Root* and beyond

We will now compare the treatments of idealism found, respectively, in the first and second editions of *Fourfold Root*. When reading through *EF*, it seems that Schopenhauer has little time for subjective idealism. To begin with, he accuses subjective idealists of extending the law of causality beyond the limits of its validity, from objects to the knowing self. He writes, "According to [subjective idealism], the representation arises through the causality of the subject: thus, the subject is actively subject to the law of causality. This forms the basis of *idealism*" (EF 173). As such, Schopenhauer argues that subjective idealism falls foul of his claim that one cannot come to know the knowing subject, as to do so would be to attempt to turn the knowing subject into an object, which is an impossible task. Later on in *EF*, Schopenhauer criticises subjective idealism on a slightly different basis. Having stressed the interconnection between subject and object, he criticises subjective idealism on the basis that it "[imagines] that it can think of a subject without object" (EF 184). This is perhaps just another way of putting the first objection—if we separate subject from object, we still have to posit some form of relation between them, and it makes sense to assume some sort of quasi-causal relation between them, which, as Schopenhauer notes, goes beyond the legitimate validity of the application of the law of causality.

In the first edition of *Fourfold Root*, then, we have two straightforward rejections of subjective idealism, both times on the basis of a misunderstanding of the subject-object relation. However, it is interesting to note that the first objection is removed from the second edition, and that Schopenhauer entirely rewrites the second objection, notably implicating Kant in the dispute between realism and idealism, which is glossed as "the dispute between the old dogmatism and the Kantians" (FR 142). Schopenhauer explicitly admits that he makes substantive changes from the first edition. For example, in the preface he writes, "I have, therefore, as far as it is possible, helped the present youthful work . . . where he advanced something incorrect or superfluous, or even omitted the best part, I have had to cut him off" (FR v-vi). It is admittedly the case that, in a section added to the second edition discussing Hume's treatment of causality, Schopenhauer described Kant as leading us to "an incomparably more profoundly conceived and well-founded idealism that that which had existed earlier, which was principally Berkeley's" (FR 21). However, I do not believe that this is evidence for Schopenhauer rejecting subjective idealism; rather, it is part of his continuing praise of Kant as focusing upon the contribution that the human mind makes to the construction of the world of experience, which allows him to move decisively away from the necessity of the role that God plays in Berkeley's system. As such, Kant is praised by Schopenhauer for this anti-theistic consequence of his system, rather than for displacing subjective idealism altogether.

We see, then, a couple of potentially revealing changes in passages regarding idealism from the first edition of *Fourfold Root* to the second, which invites a question, and the question we are left with is whether this reflects a changing attitude and a growing sympathy toward subjective idealism on the part of Schopenhauer, and perhaps a shift away from Kantian transcendental idealism. Perhaps not if he has just moved his critique of subjective idealism elsewhere, maybe to *WWR*. Where the first objection, on the basis of the misuse of the law of causality, should be in the second edition, we instead find a reference to the fourth chapter of the second volume of *WWR*, originally published three years earlier (FR 93). So we would do well to examine this text, as well as the first chapter of the volume, entitled 'On the Fundamental View of Idealism'.

In this first chapter of *WWR2*, it is striking how much Berkeley is praised, taken as an equal with Kant in the development of 'true idealism', and even seems to be taken as superior to the latter on some points. Berkeley, to begin with, is trumpeted as coming to the "very correct and deep insight" that "the objective, material world in general, exists as such simply and solely in our *representation*, and that it is false and indeed absurd to attribute to it, *as such*, an existence outside all representation and independent of the knowing subject" (WWR2 5). Later on, Schopenhauer distinguishes between

"*Berkeleyan idealism*, which concerns the *object in general*" and "*Kantian* idealism, which concerns the specially given *mode and manner* of objective experience", and affirms the importance of both in establishing that "the whole of the material world . . . has its fundamental presuppositions in our brain-functions, *by means of* which and *in* which along is *such* an objective order of things possible" (WWR2 9–10). Indeed, Schopenhauer's explication of his understanding of the distinction between Berkeleyan and Kantian idealism here may be rather illuminating for our purposes. Berkeley is credited here with the general claim that the subject conditions the material, in that the subject is in some sense responsible for the very existence of phenomena, whilst Kant is credited with explicating the manner in which the subject gives phenomena a certain form (which Schopenhauer simplifies to the forms of space, time, and causality), which is a more specific claim.

Given such an understanding of the distinction between Berkeley and Kant, and the wider context of Schopenhauer's system, a shift away from a straightforward affirmation of transcendental idealism toward a more general Berkeleyan idealism may appear to make more sense. Following *FR* and Book 1 of *WWR*, Schopenhauer will go on to describe further forms of experience for a subject, namely, those connected with aesthetic experience, compassion, and ascetic practices. In these forms of experience, the world of empirical reality, on the one hand, and the individuality of the subject, on the other, will break down. In such circumstances, the object of experience is no longer subject to the normal forms of experience (so space, time, and causality no longer apply).

An even more intriguing passage occurs in a discussion where Schopenhauer rehearses the familiar argument regarding the use of the subjective law of causality to project back from our sensation to a 'really existing object', a process which he calls "the foundation of all sense-perception" (WWR2 13). Schopenhauer praises the 'Kantian conclusion' related to this that states

> the fact, on the occasion of certain sensations occurring in my organs of sense, there arises in my head a *perception* of things . . . by no means justifies me in assuming that such things also exist in themselves . . . that they exist with such properties absolutely belonging to them, independently of my head and outside it.
>
> (WWR2 13)

This key Kantian claim is then connected to the Lockean view that notes that there need be no strict resemblance between things as they appear to us and things as they are in themselves. However, perhaps surprisingly, Schopenhauer then writes, "But to all this we still have to add the result of Berkeley, which has been revised by me, namely that every *object*, whatever its origin, is, *as object*, already conditioned by the subject, and thus is essentially only the subject's *representation*" (WWR2 13–14). It seems from this quote that Schopenhauer has identified a facet of Berkeleyan idealism that he wishes to take on board *in addition to* the general conclusion established by Kant that he referred to earlier. In allying himself with Berkeley, he is going beyond the 'resemblance' conclusion established by Locke and Kant, and rejecting an object beyond representation. Given this, it would appear that Schopenhauer is reacting against Kant, including both major interpretations of transcendental idealism: against the traditional 'two-object' reading of Kant, for he is stating that there is only one object, as well as the 'two aspects' view, which still holds to an underlying object that has two aspects as both appearance and thing-in-itself. I take this as a clear statement of Schopenhauer's increased sympathy for the subjective idealism of Berkeley, though revised in the light of the pioneering work of Kant.

The chapter ends with an interesting discussion on the notion of matter that may also signal something of a split from Kant.[4] Kant, in his Critical system, takes matter to be "substantia phaenomenon" (phenomenal substance, Kant, 1998, A277/B333), an empirical concept that acts as a bridge between the more abstract concept of 'substance' in general metaphysics and concrete examples in special metaphysics. Schopenhauer, on the other hand, seems to diverge from this by saying some rather un-Kantian things about matter in *WWR2*: for example, he writes "*the intellect and matter are correlatives . . .* they are in fact really one and the same thing, considered from two opposite points of view" (WWR2 18). Later on, in the chapter that Schopenhauer referred us to earlier in *FR*, namely Chapter IV entitled 'On Knowledge *a Priori*', in which he explicitly criticises aspects of Kant's idealism and epistemology, he writes about the essence of matter, stating that "[t]he essential nature of matter consists in acting; it is action itself, in the abstract, and thus action in general, apart from all difference in the manner of acting; it is through and through causality" (WWR2 55). In addition, he writes that "matter appears as the mere *visibility of the will*, so that ultimately it too can be regarded in a certain sense as identical with the will" (WWR2 52). Such an account of matter here is an implication of Schopenhauer's 'subject-object correlativity thesis', that both subject and object "has meaning and exists only through and for the other. Each is present when the other is as well and disappears when the other disappears" (WWR1 6). This thesis, a key principle of Schopenhauer's metaphysics, indicates a more thoroughgoing idealism than Kant's, one that at least points in the direction of Berkeley, in emphasising the dependency of the physical realm on the activity of the mind. It is telling, I think, that the thesis blocks the kind of 'two-aspects'[5] reading of Kant that sees transcendental idealism as either allowing for a kind of property dualism, with objects having a set of intrinsic properties that do not appear to us, or an epistemological thesis that allows for the objects of our experience to be possibly viewed from the standpoint of an 'intuitive intellect'. The 'two-object' reading begins to seem beyond Schopenhauer too, for there can be no other object other than an object that is for the subject. As such, the subject-object correlativity thesis,

I would argue, shows an important difference from Kant, and a similarity to a Berkeley-style subjective idealism. The thesis can be found in the first edition of *FR* (see FR 142), which may perhaps show latent sympathy for subjective idealism from the very early stages of Schopenhauer's philosophical reflections, before he realised it himself.

It is also well worth noting the famous castigation of Kant by Schopenhauer on the basis that he had diluted his idealism between the A and B editions of *The Critique of Pure Reason*. After noting that Kant "did not do justice" (WWR1 514) to Berkeley's philosophy, particularly the dictum 'No object without a subject', Schopenhauer states that he was delighted to see that, in the A edition, "even if Kant did not use the exact formula 'no object without subject', he nonetheless declares as resolutely as Berkeley and I have done that the external world in space and time is just a representation of the cognitive subject" (WWR1 515). As an example of Kant's commitment to a stronger idealism in the A edition, in comparison to the diluted form in the B edition, Schopenhauer quotes this passage: "If I were to take away the thinking subject, the whole corporeal world would have to disappear, as this is nothing but the appearance in the sensibility of our subject and one mode of its representations" (Kant, 1998, A383). Clearly, then, Schopenhauer is keen to preserve a strong idealism in his philosophy, and clearly wishes to distance himself at points where Kant appears to dilute his own commitment to idealism. Schopenhauer's offering of a strong idealism, keeping at least in the tradition of Berkeley, seems to have been very important to him, and something he guarded against losing in the exposition of his system.

Of course, there is still the question regarding the identification of the thing-in-itself with Will. We would do well to remember that Schopenhauer criticises Kant on his use of the notion of the thing-in-itself, stating that the latter's hypothesis in this regard is the result of a misapplication of the category of causality beyond its legitimate sphere. However, if we take the Will, understood as an essence or ground of all things, as something inherently mental (a supposition which seems at least plausible given the route through which we come to learn of it), which is something Kant would not countenance for the thing-in-itself, then we are left with something approaching the subjective idealist position that all things that exist are minds and their sensations.

It is also worth bearing in mind that Schopenhauer did not view the thing-in-itself/phenomena distinction as originating with Kant (he, for example, sees it as assumed in much Indian philosophy [see WWR1 496–497]). Hence, his use of the notion of the thing-in-itself does not necessarily indicate that Kantian transcendental idealism is being held to in Schopenhauer's system. In addition, we can take into account an early note from Schopenhauer that speaks of the thing-in-itself as the

> weak side of Kant's teaching . . . [insofar as i]t is difficult to understand why Kant did not consider this concept in greater detail and reflect

that *being*, used in the second and third persons, means nothing but *being sensuously perceived and known*, and hence that, after deducting *being sensuously known*, the remainder—or thing-in-itself—is equal to nothing.

(MR2 290–291)

It is clear, then, that Schopenhauer always feels uncomfortable with the notion of the thing-in-itself, and perhaps should suggest us that when he does at times adopt that language, he perhaps does not mean it in a wholly Kantian sense. Admittedly, in his 'Critique of the Kantian Philosophy' at the end of *WWR1*, Schopenhauer only attacks the thing-in-itself on the basis of its supposed causal relation to our empirical intuition, a context within which a subjective law of causality cannot be applied (see esp. *WWR1* 463), which does not equate to an attack on the very notion of a thing-in-itself. In line with the argument of this paper, we can note that this limited attack upon the thing-in-itself originally appears in the first edition of *WWR*, and may reflect an earlier unwillingness to step decisively away from Kantian philosophy that is weakened somewhat in later works, or we could simply state that this passage is only intended to form part of Schopenhauer's movement away from transcendental idealism. Either way, the limited attack upon the notion of the thing-in-itself here certainly does not count as evidence *against* the argument in this paper, namely, that Schopenhauer's sympathies shift from transcendental idealism, and toward subjective idealism, through the course of his philosophical career.

Schopenhauer modifies his position with regard to idealism between the publication of the first and second edition of *Fourfold Root*, in that a passage which contains a criticism of subjective idealism in removed, and another is rewritten to implicate Kant, whilst Kant is praised more for the supposed anti-theist consequences of his system, rather than for entirely doing away with subjective idealism. Further, Schopenhauer often seems to want to praise Berkeley and incorporate aspects of the Irish philosopher's thought into his system, whilst criticising Kant's approach to matter in a manner that suggests a move away from transcendental idealism. The next step will be to briefly consider possible parallels between Schopenhauer and Berkeley, with some attention to Indian thought, as well as difficulties that may face us in interpreting Schopenhauer's philosophy as advocating something approaching subjective idealism, with a view to arguing that there is good reason to believe that we can read Schopenhauer as offering a Berkeley-style subjective idealism without God. Finally, I will also resist a recent reading by Robert Wicks that offers a new approach to Schopenhauer's idealism by reading idealism and realism in his system as standing in a 'strange loop' in which neither viewpoint has primacy.

Schopenhauer, Berkeley, and Subjective Idealism

As further justification for the view that Schopenhauer could be read as more sympathetic to subjective idealism than is often supposed, we could point to certain aspects of Berkeley's philosophy that seems Schopenhauerian in tenor. Even a superficial investigation into Berkeley's epistemology and ontology suggests that it may make a great deal of sense that Schopenhauer's philosophy rests somewhere between the former's subjective idealism and Kant's transcendental idealism. The matter of interpreting Berkeley is of course up for debate, but a reasonably uncontroversial interpretation, suggested as an option by Muehlmann (1978), states that he holds that our perception is not indifferent, and that as a general rule, our perceptions are accompanied by volition. In a note from the *Philosophical Commentaries*, Berkeley states that, "[i]t seems to me that Will & understanding Volitions & Ideas cannot be severed, that either cannot be possibly without the other" (Berkeley, 1901, 54). It should be clear that Schopenhauer would be drawn to such an idea (and it is also interesting that Berkeley also denies knowledge of the subject of knowing), though at the same time rejecting Berkeley's (pre-Kantian) view that the mind is ultimately passive with regard to perception. (If that sounds inconsistent, Berkeley holds that whilst our mind is passive with respect to perceptions, it is active with regards events occurring in perception.) It seems, then, that there are certainly key ideas with regard to Berkeley's epistemology and ontology that Schopenhauer would feel drawn toward, though bearing in mind his fundamental allegiance to Kant. Of course, there will always be a major difference between Schopenhauer and Berkeley with regard to the fundamental question of the existence of God, with their respective systems being ultimately coloured by their differing approaches to the divine. However, on the level of the individual and their experience of the world, perhaps they are not as far apart as it might appear on the surface.

Schopenhauer's growing sympathies toward subjective idealism may also be attributed to the influence of Indian philosophy upon his system. Schopenhauer's engagement with Indian philosophy began in the very early years of his philosophical writing, and intensified as he grew older.[6] He clearly saw Indian philosophy as a possible source for a thoroughgoing philosophical idealism, and Cross has noted the prevalence of idealism through both Hindu and Buddhist thought, it being

> probable that the doctrine of the ultimately unreal nature of the world had been known to Indian from early times, was absorbed into both Upanisadic and Buddhist thought, was revived and developed with great force and clarity in Mahayana Buddhism, and was finally reclaimed for the Upanisadic tradition by Gaudapada and Samkara.
>
> (Cross, 2013, 84)

In *On the Will in Nature*, when speaking of the difficulties that Europeans have in understanding belief systems coming out of Asia, Schopenhauer notes,

> the essential, decided idealism of Buddhism, as well as Hinduism, a view that is known in Europe as a paradox of certain eccentric philosophers, hardly to be taken seriously, but which in Asia is even incorporated in popular belief, since in Hindustan it is generally accepted as the doctrine of *maya*.
>
> (WN 133)

In this quote, it is easy to detect Schopenhauer's sense of injustice at the way in which his own philosophy has been treated, and as such, he is clearly allying himself with the kind of idealism offered by Hinduism and Buddhism. What, then, is the kind of idealism offered by these belief-systems? Though difficult to give a definitive answer without inviting the charge of anachronism, it certainly seems that Indian thought generally looks more like Berkeley than Kant. As an example, according to Cross, the Yogacara School of Buddhism likens "the objects of the empirical world . . . to those experienced in dream: they have no true reality, no external existence outside the minds, which know them" (Cross, 2013, 153). Douglas Berger points toward the considerable influence of Vedanta and the *Upanisads* upon Schopenhauer's philosophy, a worldview which itself, I argue, seems to lend itself naturally to identification with subjective idealism. As Berger notes, "[t]he fundamental doctrine of Vedanta . . . is that all experienced objects depend essentially upon the constructive cognitive apparatus of a knowing subject" (Berger, 2004, 78), and put alongside the view that there is something false about our representations such that they obscure the true nature of the world (see esp. Berger, 2004, 84–115), it seems that Vedanta offers a plausible driving force behind a shift in sympathy toward subjective idealism.

My reading also leaves Schopenhauer with an open question regarding the 'objectivity problem' that faces any subjective idealism, a problem resolved by Berkeley and more recently, John Foster by the invocation of a personal creator God (see Foster, 2008, ch. 6). The objectivity problem arises from the worry that an idealistically created world seems more like a virtual reality than as having the sort of objectivity that we intuitively feel is necessary for it to count as a 'real world' for us. As Foster notes,

> If, as canonical idealism claims, the sensory organization makes its constitutive contribution to the existence of the world by disposing things to appear systematically worldwise at the human empirical viewpoint, it is hard to see how what (if anything) gets created could count as anything more than a virtual reality. It is hard to see how we could think of it as forming a genuine world.
>
> (Foster, 2008, 201–202)

With God controlling the course of our sensory experience, and in effect grant-ing his authentication to the idealistically created world, Berkeley and Foster argue that we can understand subjective idealism as still offering a genuine, properly objective world for us. The authority of God, who in essence provides the empirical world for us, is sufficient to give the world of appearances the objectivity it needs to avoid being a 'virtual reality'. However, Schopenhauer, within the context of a fundamentally atheistic philosophical system, does not have such a luxury. His response to the objectivity problem would be, I sug-gest, along the same lines as his response to the spectre of solipsism, which "[a]s a genuine conviction . . . can only be found in a madhouse[,] . . . treated with medication, not refutation" (WWR1 124): we simply have to assume as the most plausible state of affairs that in a substantial sense, other people share the same world as us, even given an affirmation of subjective idealism. The notion of trying to establish this kind of intersubjective objectivity within the confines of subjective idealism is an endeavour beyond the limits of this paper, but I do not see any *prima facie* reasons for thinking it an impossible one.

In addition, it may seem that sympathy on the part of Schopenhauer to subjective idealism may intensify a difficulty (noted in Wicks [2012]) regard-ing references to the physical brain in *WN* and elsewhere. Wicks notices the troubling references that Schopenhauer often makes to the brain as being the seat of experience, for example, "this perceptible and real world is obvi-ously a phenomenon of the brain; and so in the assumption that the world as such might exist independently of all brains there lies a contradiction" (WWR2 5). The difficulty here, from an idealist perspective, is obvious, for the brain is supposed to be posterior to space, time, and causality as the *a priori* forms of the world of phenomena. If the brain is in the intellect, the intellect cannot be in the brain. As Wicks writes:

> One cannot assert that space, time and causality are prior to the brain as the *a priori* conditions for the spatio-temporal world as a whole, and then maintain that they are posterior to the brain in so far as they emerged contingently from an evolutionary process that exists prior to the emergence of any animals or brains.
>
> (Wicks, 2012, 157–158)

Schopenhauer, in order to be consistent, cannot hold both to his idealist standpoint and to the view that the intellect emerged out of physical events.

In response to this potential difficulty for Schopenhauer, Wicks makes an interesting suggestion, but I think one that cannot be ultimately accepted (and certainly not if one, as I do, wishes to emphasise the idealism of Schopenhauer), by writing of a 'reciprocal containment' between idealism and realism which "involves tempering the Kantian idealistic standpoint to strengthen the realistic outlook's legitimacy, by stating that *neither* idealism *nor* realism is an absolute philosophical perspective and that each is condi-tioned by the other" (Wicks, 2012, 158). Realism and idealism are caught in a 'strange loop' that allows Schopenhauer to legitimately characterise "the brain as a function of the intellect, [and] the intellect as a function of the brain, depending upon his assumed philosophical location in the loop" (Wicks, 2012, 159). In such a looping structure, Schopenhauer is able to explain the intellect and the brain in terms of each other. Wicks reinforces his position with the following quotation from *WN*:

> Our objective standpoint is a realistic one and thus is conditioned, since it accepts the beings of nature as given, and the process overlooks that their objective existence presupposes an intellect in which they are first found as representations, but *Kant's* subjective and idealistic standpoint is similarly conditioned, since he starts with intellect, which itself certainly presupposes nature insofar as intellect can only occur as a result of the development of nature to the level of animal beings.
>
> (WN 73)

If Wicks is correct, we have to, it would appear, interpret Schopenhauer as expressing his philosophy from two equal standpoints, namely, idealism and realism, neither of which are granted primacy.

Though Wicks is undoubtedly offering us an ingenious solution to this potential difficulty, I believe we can offer a solution that does not dilute Schopenhauer's idealism to such an extent. I agree with Wicks insofar as a shift in perspective does take place with regard to Schopenhauer's references to the role of the brain in producing a human being's experience but disagree with the supposition that these two standpoints should be seen as equal within the context of his system. Rather, I claim that the intellect is a function of the brain merely from the empirical viewpoint, which is the subject of Book 1 of *WWR* (and that assumed throughout from the quasi-scientific standpoint of *WN*), a standpoint that is left aside (and far behind) in the following three books. As such, the idealist standpoint is primary, once the common-sense empirical view, in which the intellect is viewed as a function of the brain, has been left behind. Rather than seeing idealism and realism in a loop, through Schopenhauer's philosophical reflections we are able to briefly adopt the realistic viewpoint before seeing it to be ultimately false as we look behind us with new knowledge of the metaphysics of Will. Therefore, I think Wicks' model of a loop is misguided, in that Schopenhauer's system has an inherently developmental structure (seen through the developing viewpoints in Book 1 of *WWR*—the empirical, the metaphysical, the aesthetic, the compassionate, the ascetic) which simply cannot be captured in the notion of a 'strange loop'. Such a structure, I believe, is most easily preserved through an assumption of the primacy of idealism for Schopenhauer's system.

There are many other issues that would have to be considered in order to more thoroughly establish my thesis in this paper, namely, that the differences between the two editions of *Fourfold Root* can act as a signal to us of changing sympathies on the part of Schopenhauer toward subjective idealism. Given further evidence from *WWR*, the possibility of parallels between the philosophies of Berkeley and Schopenhauer, the influence of Indian philosophy upon Schopenhauer, and the ability to explain away Schopenhauer's references to the physical brain bringing about intelligence in *WN* and elsewhere, I believe we have at least a good starting-point from which we can more thoroughly investigate the thesis in further research. There is certainly a long way to go, but nevertheless such investigation would undoubtedly deepen our understanding of Schopenhauer's philosophy, even if we come to the conclusion that he remains a thoroughly committed transcendental idealist throughout his philosophical works.

Conclusion

In the current literature, the question of the nature of Schopenhauer's idealism is not often discussed, or at least, when it is, Schopenhauer is labelled as a 'transcendental idealist', and it is left at that. However, as we read the myriad ways in which Schopenhauer departs from and criticises Kant, it does beg the question whether the former should be easily labelled in such a way. I have explored reasons for thinking that Schopenhauer does shift his sympathies toward subjective idealism during the course of his philosophical career.

I would like to end this discussion with a disclaimer. In arguing that Schopenhauer drifts closer to subjective idealism toward the end of his career, I am not claiming that he is a 'subjective idealist'. Of course, Kant's influence is far too strong to even think of doing so—rather, I am talking about degrees of sympathy for both transcendental and subjective idealism on the part of Schopenhauer, and I believe that this rises for the latter position through his career. I also believe that this shift has great significance for our understanding of Schopenhauer's wider philosophical system and project, in particular the salvific and therapeutic aspect of his work—he could not achieve some of these aims within a pure framework of Kantian transcendental idealism, which necessitated a move toward subjective idealism. Moving beyond the straightforward characterisation of Schopenhauer as a transcendental idealist potentially allows us to grasp anew the more radical elements of his system, particularly those surrounding the possible changes in forms of consciousness brought about by aesthetic engagement, temporary dissolution of individuality in compassionate actions, and self-negation of the Will. Subjective idealism may give Schopenhauer the tools he requires to articulate these more unusual aspects of his philosophy.

Notes

1 The research for this paper was supported by Keele University and APRA Foundation Berlin. I would like to thanks participants at the 'Fourfold Root: 200 Years On' conference at Keele University for their useful questions and comments, particularly Dennis Vanden Auweele and Joss Walker, who offered extensive written comments on an earlier draft of this paper.

2 When scholars do approach the topic of the nature of Schopenhauer's idealism, the near-universal consensus is that he should be straightforwardly designated a transcendental idealist, along the lines of Kant: to take a couple of what could be countless examples, Barua claims that, "Schopenhauer is in total agreement with Kant. The idealism in both cases is only transcendental" (Barua, 1992, 6), whilst Hannan writes of Schopenhauer "[embracing] a modified version of Kantian transcendental idealism" (Hannan, 2009, 10). One exception to this is Snow & Snow (1991), which I shall go on to discuss. Whilst this paper is not offering a wholesale rejection of the characterisation of Schopenhauer as a transcendental idealist, we will argue that the situation is not as straightforward as is often supposed. One other possible approach to Schopenhauer is to construe him as a metaphysician who ultimately oversteps the epistemic limits laid down by Kant's Critical system, or at the very least, as a bad transcendental idealist. As an example, Copleston attacks Schopenhauer on the basis that "the proper conclusion from Schopenhauer's epistemology, as from that of Kant, is agnosticism: a metaphysic is quite out of place . . . [T]he question is, 'how, on his premises, can there be *any* knowledge of the Will at all, whether real or partial?'" (Copleston, 1947, 65) G. Stephen Neeley offers a defence of Schopenhauer against such charges (Neeley, 2003, 1–52).

3 The formulation of the philosophies of Schopenhauer and Hegel is roughly contemporaneous, so it is highly unlikely that there was any direct Hegelian influence upon Schopenhauer at the time of *Fourfold Root* and work on *WWR1*. However, despite Schopenhauer's well-known distancing from absolute idealism, it is the case that parallels are there. William Desmond, for example, explores some similarities between Hegel and Schopenhauer with regard to their respective reactions to Kant (Desmond, 2012, 89–95), and sees great "philosophical significance" in the dual movements of the philosophies of Hegel and Schopenhauer: "In Hegel a certain rational idealism reaches its culmination and yet the Hegelian hymn to ascendant reason is contemporaneous with the Schopenhauerian descent into a more ultimate darkness prior to reason. Hegel speculatively ascends to thought thinking itself, Schopenhauer philosophically descends to what is other to thought thinking itself, the Will willing itself" (Desmond, 2012, 89).

4 We can also consider the discussion of Locke and Kant here in WWR2, who are evaluated on the basis of their philosophical investigations into the origin of concepts (in contrast to so-called "mind-destroying Hegelism" [WWR2 46]). Despite Schopenhauer's praise for such a project, he also criticises the latter for "neglecting empirical perception too much in favour of *pure* perception", further stating that "[w]ith me perception is throughout the source of all knowledge" (WWR2 47). We can certainly find in the second volume of WWR a great deal of unhappiness with regard to Kant's construal of the phenomenal realm, as well as his explanation of the origins of concepts.

5 For more on the distinction between the two-aspects and two-objects readings of Kant's transcendental idealism, see Rohlf (2016), esp. 3.1 and 3.2.

6 As Cooper notes, "The wealth of Schopenhauer's references to these traditions attests to his considerable familiarity with both the translated Indian texts and the commentaries on these by Western scholars . . . By 1815, moreover, he was acquainted with leading figures in the new field of 'orientalism' . . . The first volume of *The World as Will and Representation*, published four years later, displays considerable knowledge of Hindu thought, while the second volume, published a quarter of a century later, indicates the author's growing acquaintance, during those years with Buddhism" (Cooper, 2012, 266).

Bibliography

Barua, A. *The Philosophy of Arthur Schopenhauer*. New Delhi: Intellectual Publishing House, 1992.

Berger, D. *The Veil of Maya: Schopenhauer's System and Early Indian Thought*. Binghamton, NY: Global Academic Publishing, 2004.

Berkeley, G. *The Works of George Berkeley: Volume 1, Philosophical Works 1705–21*, ed. A. C. Fraser. Oxford: Clarendon Press, 1901.

Cooper, D.E. 'Schopenhauer and Indian Philosophy', in B. Vandenabeele (ed.), *A Companion to Schopenhauer*. Chichester, UK; Malden, MA: Wiley-Blackwell, 2012, 266–279.

Copleston, F. *Arthur Schopenhauer: Philosopher of Pessimism*. London: Burns, Oates and Washbourne, 1947.

Cross, S. *Schopenhauer's Encounter with Indian Thought: Representation and Will and Their Indian Parallels*. Honolulu: University of Hawai'i Press, 2013.

Desmond, W. 'Schopenhauer's Philosophy of the Dark Origin', in B. Vandenabeele (ed.), *A Companion to Schopenhauer*. Chichester, UK; Malden, MA: Wiley-Blackwell, 2012, 89–104.

Dunham, J., Hamilton Grant, I., & Watson, S. *Idealism: The History of a Philosophy*. Durham: Acumen, 2011.

Foster, J. *A World for Us: The Case for Phenomenalistic Idealism*. Oxford: Oxford University Press, 2008.

Hannan, B. *The Riddle of the World: A Reconsideration of Schopenhauer's Philosophy*. Oxford: Oxford University Press, 2009.

Kant, I. *The Critique of Pure Reason*, trans. and ed. Guyer & Wood. Cambridge: Cambridge University Press, 1998.

Muehlmann, R. 'Berkeley's Ontology and the Epistemology of Idealism', *Canadian Journal of Philosophy* 8(1), 1978: 89–111.

Neeley, G.S. *Schopenhauer: A Consistent Reading*. Lewiston; Queenston; Lampeter: Edwin Mellen Press, 2003.

Rohlf, M. 'Immanuel Kant', in Edward N. Zalta (ed.), *The Stanford Encyclopedia of Philosophy*. (forthcoming Spring 2016 Edition), URL = http://plato.stanford.edu/archives/spr2016/entries/kant/, 2016.

Snow, D.E. & Snow, J.J. 'Was Schopenhauer an Idealist?', *Journal of the History of Philosophy* 29(4), 1991: 633–655.

Wicks, R. 'Schopenhauer's *On the Will in Nature*—The Reciprocal Containment of Idealism and Realism', in B. Vandenabeele (ed.), *A Companion to Schopenhauer*. Chichester, UK; Malden, MA: Wiley-Blackwell, 2012, 147–162.

4 "The World Knot"

Schopenhauer's Early Account of the Subject of Knowing and Willing in the Historic and Systematic Context of German Idealism

Günter Zöller

The New Schopenhauer

Schopenhauer's fame and reputation as a philosopher with influence worldwide (from Europe to South America) and in many fields (from music through literature to the arts) dates from the second half of the nineteenth century. The historiography of philosophy, too, has tended to locate Schopenhauer in that era, treating him as an important influence on Nietzsche and typically pairing the two as radical renewers of philosophical thought after Kant and Hegel and as advocates of an anti-intellectualist attitude focused on life and existence with lasting repercussion in twentieth-century thought, from the philosophy of life (*Lebensphilosophie*) to existentialism.[1] Viewed in that context, Schopenhauer appeared as an irrationalist in deep opposition to previous philosophy and as the originator of an entirely novel manner of looking at self and world.

More recently, though, an alternative assessment of Schopenhauer has emerged from two directions, each of them intent on locating Schopenhauer squarely in the first, rather than the second half of the nineteenth century. In terms of general intellectual history, Schopenhauer has come to be seen as part of the larger movement of European Romanticism with its sustained stress on longing, yearning, and regret—as embodied by such diverse poets and writers as G. Leopardi, Lord Byron and F. Grillparzer with their aesthetics of creative suffering (*mal du siècle*, *Weltschmerz*).[2] Schopenhauer's emphasis on the drivenness of willful existence, along the latter's fundamental frustration, puts him squarely in the camp of Romanticism in literature, music, and the visual arts, which, after preparations in the late eighteenth century, came to the fore Europe-wide in the opening couple of decades of the nineteenth century.

Moreover, from a more narrowly philosophical perspective, Schopenhauer's double philosophy of the affirmation and the negation of the will more recently has been relocated from its later reception toward the end of the nineteenth century to its actual circumstances of origin in the early nineteenth century. Accordingly, the reference authors for assessing Schopenhauer's status and standing in philosophy have shifted from his heirs and followers, chiefly among them R. Wagner and Nietzsche, to his predecessors and teachers, most of whom belong entirely into the first half, even into the very first decades of the nineteenth century. The alternative context into which Schopenhauer has been placed by these new looks at his life and works is that of classical German philosophy from Kant through Fichte and Schelling to Hegel.[3]

To be sure, Schopenhauer was always eager to distance himself from the concrete circumstances of his philosophical upbringing in post-Kantian philosophy and from the closer context of his philosophical emergence out of German idealism. More yet, he cultivated an attitude of disregard, hostility, and even contempt toward the chief representatives of German idealism— Fichte, Schelling, and Hegel. Even his proud self-proclamation as Kant's authentic heir, as opposed to the German idealists' merely alleged and vain claim to that title, went together with serious criticisms of the Kant's moral philosophy in general and his ethics of categorical obligation in particular.

Still the biographical facts place Schopenhauer squarely in the philosophical environment of Kantian and post-Kantian philosophy. He completed his university studies in Berlin, where he attended Fichte's lectures, and he qualified for the function of university lecturer (*Privatdozent*) at the same university, effectively becoming an (unsalaried) colleague of Hegel's. Most importantly, though, his main work, *The World as Will and Representation*, upon its first publication in 1818 (with the year 1819 indicated on the title page), provided the first completely executed system of philosophy in the age of German idealism—an integral presentation of professional philosophy already aimed at by Kant and attempted in various partial, incomplete, abandoned, or sketchy ways by Fichte, Schelling, and Hegel alike.

But the recent reintegration of Schopenhauer's life and works into the broader context of classical German philosophy concerns not only his main work and subsequent publications. Schopenhauer's body of early work, published or penned prior to *The World as Will and Representation*, contains particularly poignant evidence for Schopenhauer's philosophical upbringing and sojourn under the shaping conditions of contemporary German philosophy. Moreover, Schopenhauer's early writings contain clear indications of the specific points of departure for the development of his own philosophical position—a position at once informed by and alienated from the philosophical views taken and taught by his older contemporaries, actual teachers, or philosophical mentors.

A particularly telling example of the revelatory character that Schopenhauer's early work possesses both with regard to the origins of his thought in Kantian and post-Kantian philosophy and with respect to his own emerging diverging views is his doctoral dissertation from 1814, submitted *in absentia* at the University of Jena, while Schopenhauer was living near Weimar. The wider significance of the work, beyond its narrow purpose as a publication for academic qualification, is attested by two facts. For one, Schopenhauer later recommended *On the Fourfold Root of the Principle of Sufficient Reason* as the ideal introduction into his subsequently developed and published *magnum opus, The World as Will and Representation.* Moreover, he revised portions of the doctoral dissertation, adding substantial sections to it in light of his main work, for a second edition that appeared in 1847, only a few years after the main work itself had come out in a second, substantially enlarged edition—the additions consisting chiefly in an entire additional volume designed to supplement each chapter of the previously published single-volume edition.[4]

The special status of the doctoral dissertation as a connecting link between Schopenhauer's classical German philosophical upbringing, under the twin influence of Kant and the post-Kantians, and his post- and anti-classical emergence as a philosopher *à part*, is particularly striking in the final, fourth form of the principle of sufficient reason, which treats of the will under the law of motivation. A closer look at the principle of sufficient volitional grounding and the corresponding class of objects affords a fascinating glimpse into the historical underpinnings, the conceptual inventory, and the doctrinal arsenal that links Schopenhauer's early systematic philosophizing with the philosophical system that was to result from it.

In order to better appreciate and properly assess the status and significance of the concluding perspective of the dissertation, the remaining sections of this essay will present, first, the basic features of classical German philosophy which were to serve as preludes and overtures to Schopenhauer's own emerging position; second, Schopenhauer's specific uptake on those features in his overall philosophical project; and third, the specific take on classical German philosophy to be found in Schopenhauer's distinctly post-Kantian account of the subject of cognition and volition in the dissertation. The comparison and contrast with classical German philosophy that is to illuminate Schopenhauer's critical contribution to this tradition will be effectuated primarily with regard to Kant and Fichte as the main authors who provided the inspiration behind Schopenhauer's own original contribution to post-Kantian philosophy. By contrast, Schopenhauer's critical engagement with Schelling and Hegel proves less productive and more marked by polemics and rejection than by the clandestine continuity and the productive transformation that characterizes Schopenhauer's constructively critical relation to Kant and Fichte.

The point of the parallels to be drawn between Schopenhauer and his main sources of inspiration (and irritation) is not a historical study of influence and dependency but a philosophical examination of the shape, *Gestalt* or *eidos* that Schopenhauer's thinking assumes in the light of classical German philosophical thought. The frame of reference will be provided by the first edition of *On the Fourfold Root of the Principle of Sufficient Reason*, with additional consideration given to the second edition of the dissertation and to the first and second edition of *The World as Will and Representation.*

German Real-Idealism

Schopenhauer's extended membership in the movement known as "German idealism" becomes apparent upon a closer examination of that movement's core character. The traits to be gathered in that regard can be seen to serve as preludes and overtures to the further and farther steps taken, on their basis, in the work of Schopenhauer. The national identifier employed in the phrase "German idealism" is meant to set off the idealism espoused by Fichte, Schelling, and Hegel from alternative versions of idealism, chiefly the immaterialism of George Berkeley, for whom there are but minds (including the divine mind) and their ideas ("perceptions"). In addition, the modern idealism introduced by Kant and espoused by the German idealists is to be distinguished from the ancient idealism of Plato, for whom the only true kind of being are the Forms or Ideas (German *Ideen,* hence the German term for idealism, *Idealismus*) in the sense of mind-independent supranatural entities.

By contrast, the idealism maintained in various ways and under different forms by classical German philosophy is an idealism of non-empirical, "a priori" forms and norms governing the natural and cultural world as their embedded principles of order and meaning. Unlike Berkeley, the German idealists maintain the empirical reality of material objects, even if that reality is neither original nor ultimate but derived and to be superseded. Unlike Plato, the German idealists do not disengage the ideal, intelligible, or noumenal from the real, sensible, and phenomenal (*chorismos*) but consider the former as the latter's chief source and the latter as the former's main manifestation.

So close is the linkage between specifically idealist and specifically realist features in the German-idealist accounts of self and world that the movement's main representatives coin concepts designed to convey the intrinsic connection between the two. Thus Kant pairs (transcendental) ideality with (empirical) reality when it comes to characterizing the status and function of space and time as forms of sensible intuition and of all (empirical) objects so intuited. Fichte refers to his position of a radicalized Kantianism as "real-idealism" or "ideal-realism." Schelling maintains the equiprimordiality of mind and nature as alternative manifestations of some undifferentiated, "indifferent" originary being. Hegel introduces the notion of spirit as an overarching principle capable of reintegrating its own opposite, which thus proves to be as much other than itself as it proves to be its own other.[5]

In a related development, Kant, as well as the chief representatives of German idealism that succeed him, each in their own way, recognize the presence of some originary or ultimate stratum or dimension of reality that precedes, exceeds, or eludes cognitive capture. In Kant this is the inscrutable source of sensory affection, viz., the thing in itself (*Ding an sich*). In Fichte, the latter is systematically reduced to a minimal moment of foreign force (*Anstoß*). For Schelling nature in its productive potential (*natura naturans*) underlies even the development of the mind. In Hegel nature is the presupposition of mind or spirit, which emerges from it as much as it departs from it.

Even the focus on freedom that pervades German-idealist thought is not without a sustained regard for resistance, restriction, and regulation that condition as much as enable freedom and make it different from arbitrary choice. In Kant there is the identification of freedom *qua* autonomy with the rule of reason. Fichte ties freedom to radical and complete self-determination. Schelling identifies freedom—human freedom, to be precise—with the alternative capacity for good as well as evil. Hegel subjects freedom to the historically varying conditions of its realization.

In addition, Kant and his successors take into account external factors and foreign forces that enable as much as restrict the realization of freedom. Kant countenances inclinations in general and the striving after happiness in particular as rivals to rational freedom's reign. Fichte introduces the natural drive (*Naturtrieb*) as a functional complement to the pure drive for sustained self-identity. Schelling locates a dark and destructive longing beneath the constructive workings of mind and spirit. Hegel features the negativist nature of reality, which involves annihilation (*Vernichtung*) and going under (*Untergang*) as much as continued progress and further development.

Even the principal identity and the formal unity that Kant and the German idealists programmatically pursue as the basis for the distinctions and differentiations permeating self and world alike is not simple and single, but complex and plurally structured. Kant envisions the unity of theoretical and practical reason to reside in the infinitely remote final fusion of freedom and nature under the guise of the highest good, which conjoins morality and happiness. Fichte considers the unity of thinking and willing to involve an "original duplicity" at the root of human subjectivity. Schelling introduces the divisive features of fall and abyss into the constitution of mind and world. For Hegel identity consists in the complex identity of simple identity and opposed difference.

Moreover, even the absolute, which stands at the center of the vaulting ambition of the German idealists to advance from everything conditioned to the unconditioned condition of it all, is typically conceived as an end to be pursued rather than an entity obtained. In Kant, the absolute figures as an idea or a concept of reason with a merely regulative rather than constitutive function for purposes of cognition. In Fichte, the absolute is as much a product of thought as the precondition of all thinking. Schelling introduces the absolute as the evasive, pre-disjunctive prerequisite ("indifference") for subsequent distinction and differentiation. For Hegel, the absolute resides in human cultural productions, which, while being historically based and conditioned, tend to transgress temporal and spatial limitations through art, religion, and science.

There are several further features that link the chief representatives of German idealism both back to Kant but also forward to Schopenhauer. To begin with, the German idealists typically take recourse to a non-sensory source of insight that is to surpass the confines of sensory intuition, discursive understanding, and inferential reasoning previously delineated by Kant. Claiming to extend Kant's own insights into the immediate yet intellectual nature of theoretical and practical consciousness ("transcendental apperception," "fact of pure practical reason"), Fichte, Schelling, and Hegel introduce intellectual intuition, an intuitive intellect and speculation as genuine modes of philosophical insight.

Moreover, Kant and the German idealists (along with Schopenhauer) share the architectural project of erecting a comprehensive system of philosophy. Kant mainly concerns himself with the preparation of the system (of philosophy) through a comprehensive critique (of reason) that is to ground the twofold system of nature and freedom. Fichte erects a comprehensive system of freedom that integrates nature, in terms of the latter's principles as well as objects, into the systematic elaboration of the formal and material conditions of freedom at the individual and social level. Schelling's multiple attempts at a system of philosophy range from the alternative recourse to nature and to spirit as co-original principles of philosophy through the reliance on an undetermined, "indifferent" absolute as the principle of philosophy to the eventual abandonment of systematically constructed and rationally ruled philosophy in favor of the sustained reference to mythical and religious sources of insight ("positive philosophy"). Hegel considers the system the only presentational form adequate for philosophical knowledge ("idea") and subjects the latter to a three-stage procedural system of logical, natural, and spiritual forms or "shapes".

Furthermore, again following Kant, the German idealists maintain, albeit in various ways, the prominence, even the primacy of the practical over the theoretical, of practice over theory and of volition over cognition in a sustained focus on key conceptions such as practical reason, choice, will, and action. The primacy of the practical holds for Fichte, who outright subordinates knowing under willing, but also for Schelling, who treats the state as the worldly absolute, and even for Hegel, who identifies spirit in its outward manifestation ("objective spirit") with moral, legal, social, and political action.

Finally, and consistent with its overall practical orientation, classical German philosophy in and after Kant shows a keen awareness of the limits of knowledge and the boundaries of reason, without yet succumbing to unprincipled irrationalism and to what Kant had termed "hatred of reason" ("misology") (AA 4:395; 9:26). Conceptions such as faith (*Glaube*), feeling (*Gefühl*), and life (*Leben*) are explicitly designed and pointedly deployed by Kant and the post-Kantians to indicate an attempted or accomplished self-transcendence of knowledge in the course of which the completed circle of cognition indirectly and limitatively is to point beyond itself.

Parodic Idealism

Placed against the background of the main themes and the major tenets of Kantian and post-Kantian, "idealist" philosophy, Schopenhauer's thought seems at once familiar and alien: familiar in terms of the shared concepts and common concerns; alien in terms of the meaning and use those concepts and concerns acquire in an altogether altered context. Formally speaking, Schopenhauer's work stands to that of the German idealists in a parodic relation, provided the term "parody" is not taken in its current comic sense but as a technical term, still familiar in music, for designating the refilling of a more or less identical form with an altogether different, even contrary content. Schopenhauer's parodic idealism picks up on the chief forms and main features of standard German idealism by lending them a completely changed orientation and alternative assessment. Again, the claimed parodic nature of Schopenhauer's thought in relation to standard German idealist thought is not meant to suggest that Schopenhauer is making fun of Fichte, Schelling, or Hegel, or to imply the comic character of Schopenhauer's own thought. Rather the point and purpose of the analogy is to highlight the strange constellation of extensive formal convergence and considerable material divergence to be found between Schopenhauer and the German idealists.

The basis for Schopenhauer's peculiar, parodic relation to German idealism is a curious mix of proximity and distance. On the one hand, Schopenhauer is sufficiently familiar with the particular problems posed and the specific solutions sought in Kantian and post-Kantian philosophy to share the language, terminology, and conceptuality of its body of work. On the other hand, Schopenhauer is sufficiently removed from the immediate circle and close circumstances of that work to have gained the space for a freer and less predictable approach to the common concerns and shared suppositions.

In particular, there is a distinct biographical basis for Schopenhauer alienated proximity, or close remoteness, with regard to the German idealists. In generational terms, Schopenhauer's year of birth (1788) places him outside the generation of Hegel (born 1770) and Schelling (born 1775), much more so that of the significantly earlier Kant (born 1724) and even of Fichte (born 1762), whose chief intellectual background is the European Enlightenment and who all experienced its culminating event, the French Revolution, in their student years or as mature men. By contrast, the age in which Schopenhauer grew up was the post-revolutionary world of Napoleonic Europe and of European Romanticism.

In addition, there is a significant difference in socioeconomic background and educational career that sets Schopenhauer off from the German idealists. Rather than having grown up in more modest or even deprived financial circumstances with little personal exposure to the wider world and with the constant need to earn a living, as had been the case with Kant, Fichte,

Schelling, and Hegel, Schopenhauer grew up in a wealthy trading family, benefitted from international travels and schooling, and started training for a career as a Hanseatic overseas merchant in the family business. It was only upon the sudden and unexpected death of his father (probably from suicide) that Schopenhauer became free to pursue academic studies and a university career.

Moreover, Schopenhauer's belated university studies initially did not take place in the context of Kantianism and post-Kantianism, such as Jena, where Fichte, Schelling, and Hegel had taught or worked, but in British-influenced Göttingen and its milieu of neo-skepticism and neo-empiricism. Schopenhauer's acquaintance with post-Kantian idealism came comparatively late, through a few further years of university studies in Berlin, where he attended, among others, the lectures of Fichte. In addition, while seeking to pursue a university teaching career, Schopenhauer was not in financial need of the income from it and consistently cultivated a degree of detachment from the requirements and practices of professional and collegial life, both in terms of lifestyle and manner of thinking, that effectively excluded him from the standard forms and paths of academic success, chiefly among them a salaried position and well-received publications.

There are further factors that contributed to Schopenhauer's continuing status as an outsider in the field of professional philosophy. His early and increasing familiarity with and philosophical affinities to non-Western philosophy, especially Indian thought (Hindu as well as Buddhist philosophy), alienated Schopenhauer from the mainstream of contemporary philosophy with its primary historical fixation on Classical Greek philosophy. Also his deep affinities for literature, music, and the arts that thoroughly saturated his philosophical thinking set him apart from the professional mainstream of academic philosophy. Finally, Schopenhauer's writing style, which was at once innovatively engaging and thoroughly polemical and was to assure his later worldwide fame as a modern writer of philosophical prose, diverged dramatically from the either quite sober or else excessively speculative standard style of philosophical publications at the time.

A further feature that kept Schopenhauer apart from the German idealists was the distance he himself sought to establish between his work, for which he claimed absolute originality, and the philosophical predecessors and contemporaries who had influenced him. By sharply criticizing, outright maligning, and even insulting Fichte, Schelling, and Hegel, charging them with conceit and deception, with lies and plagiarism, Schopenhauer effectively isolated his own work from the influences it had undergone in its original formation and further development, thus severing it from the intellectual contexts in which it had arisen and continued to stand.

Schopenhauer's strategic self-alienation from the other post-Kantians is especially striking given the chronology of his early and only *magnum opus*, the writing and publication of which fell into the second half of the second decade of the nineteenth century. This makes him not a successor but a contemporary of the German idealists in general and even a precursor of Schelling and Hegel in their later works in particular. It is an irony of the history of modern philosophy that it was Schopenhauer, and not one of the three German idealists, who produced and published the first (and only) completely executed philosophical system from the era of German idealism. The *World as Will and Representation*, in its first edition from 1818, offered a four-part philosophical system, with the theory of knowledge ("gnoseology") contained in Book 1 drawing chiefly on Kant's critical philosophy, the account of nature given in Book 2 showing the influence of Schelling's early philosophy of nature (*Naturphilosophie*), the philosophy of art, including music, featured in Book 3 evincing strong Platonic influences, and the ethics set out in Book 4 reflecting the influence of classical Indian thought.

Schopenhauer's substantial debt to antecedent authorities and concurrent competitors in German idealism is particularly apparent in the case of Kant and particularly striking in the case of Fichte. By contrast, the influence of Schelling and Hegel is more confined to single conceptions taken over from them in suitably modified form, such as Schelling's comprehensive conception of nature, and, moreover, is characteristically combined with severe and sharp criticism of their overall contributions to contemporary philosophy.

In the case of Kant, Schopenhauer's intellectual debt to the critical philosophy in general and to critical theoretical philosophy ("transcendental philosophy") in particular is not even kept a secret but openly admitted by him. Still Schopenhauer adds an entire lengthy appendix to the four books of his main work, taken over into its second edition, that contains a comprehensive critique of the "Kantian philosophy." Schopenhauer's chief debt to Kant is the doctrine of transcendental idealism, with its "critical distinction" between things in themselves and appearances, which serves as the template for Schopenhauer's twin take on the world as will and as representation.

In the case of Fichte, the formative influence, while present, is not documented by Schopenhauer himself and is even concealed under attacks and rejections addressed at key features of Fichte's philosophy. Still the role played by intellectual intuition in the constitution of experience and the foundational function exercised by the will, both to be found in Schopenhauer, have their distinct precedent in Fichte. In particular, Book 2 of Fichte's most widely read work, *The Vocation of Man* (1800), entitled "Knowledge," provides an account of objective knowledge that supplements the dual deliverances of sensible intuitions and discursive concepts, recognized in Kant, with the further function of intellectual intuition for providing the mental space, so to speak, for the eventual insertion of given intuitions and made concepts for purposes of the determination of the objects in space and time. The same tripartite set-up, with the essential mediating function of intellectual intuition, is subsequently detailed in Book 1 of the *World as Will and Representation*.

In a similar vein, Schopenhauer's identitarian account of mind and body and by extension, of willing and acting, according to which the distinctions in questions are but different sides or aspects of the very same underlying entity, is deeply informed by the account of mind and matter to be found in Fichte's version of transcendental philosophy (*Wissenschaftslehre*) generally speaking and in Fichte's chief work in moral philosophy, *The System of Ethics* (1798), in particular. In his own account of the essential as well as numerical identity of mind and body and of willing and acting, provided in the *World as Will and Representation*, Schopenhauer closely follows Fichte's earlier account of the matter, albeit without citing him as a source. Even Schopenhauer's seemingly novel account of ethical de-individualization, according to which ethical life aims at the altruistic overcoming of selfish individuality, has its precursor in Fichte's ethics, which considers individuality but the instrument and vehicle for a communal life form beyond the confines of individuality and particularity.[6]

To be sure, the move from original German idealism to its parodic retake in Schopenhauer, in addition to exhibiting continuity at a more formal and general level, also involves substantial changes and significant modifications in the particulars of the passage from Kant and Fichte, along with Schelling and Hegel, to Schopenhauer. The decisive divide runs along the conception of reason. For Kant and, following him, Fichte—and by extension also for Schelling and Hegel—reason is not only theoretical or involved in cognition but essentially, if not primarily practical and engaged in volition. By contrast, Schopenhauer recognizes no such separate power, or at least employment or usage, of reason. Accordingly, Schopenhauer's affirmative reception of Kant's critical philosophy is strictly limited to the latter's theoretical philosophy, at the explicit exclusion of Kant's moral philosophy in general and his deontological ethics ("categorical imperative") in particular.

For Schopenhauer there is no pure practical reason as the mind's genuine faculty or capacity for determining the will through reason alone. In that regard, Schopenhauer follows Hume, for whom reason—including practical or action-geared reason—is but the "slave of the passions," which dictate the ends for reason's prudential pursuits. Accordingly, the Kantian core conceptions of an autonomous will and purely moral motivation, which make reason the form as well as the ground of morality, are entirely absent from Schopenhauer's account of morality, which instead issues in a quietist ethics of non-volition and inaction. The main trait that results from this crucial discrepancy between the Kantian and post-Kantian account of genuinely practical reason, on one side, and Schopenhauer's denial of such a special form of reason altogether, one the other side, is the disengagement of the will as such from rational rule and a priori principles.

It is on the basis of Schopenhauer's unprecedented separation of unruly, merely "blind" willing from a reduced reason that as such is normatively void and practically ineffective—a merely cognitive and contemplative reason with no practice to match it—that the disengaged, reason-free will in Schopenhauer can assume its further function, which extends it from an irrational psychic force or drive to a cosmic such force ("world as will").

Yet rather than constituting a novel first principle or alternative absolute ground, in the manner of the absolute of the German idealists and akin to "the I" or to "spirit" featured in Fichte, Schelling, or Hegel, the will in the novel meaning it receives in Schopenhauer can no longer be considered a principle or ground (*ratio*) at all. Given its constitutive lack of rationality and its ensuing exemption from the rational pattern of ground and consequent, the will in Schopenhauer is no ruling principle but an unprincipled, endlessly striving field of forces beyond all reason and any rationality.

The Knot and Bond of the World

Considered in the twofold context of German idealism in general and of Schopenhauer's marginal membership in the movement in particular, his dissertation *On the Fourfold Root of the Principle of Sufficient Reason* takes on a new status and function as the mediating link between Schopenhauer's German-idealist beginnings and his post-idealist later stance. The core concerns that unite as much as divide the German idealists and Schopenhauer's early dissertation work as well as his only slightly later main work are the nature and the boundaries of reason.

To be sure, in choosing the principle of sufficient reason (*principium rationis sufficientis*) as his dissertation topic, Schopenhauer seems to be following and in effect continuing an older tradition in logic and metaphysics going back to Leibniz and his successors in German scholastic philosophy (*Schulphilosophie*), chiefly among them Christian Wolff. But beyond its surface appearance as an exercise in formal ontology, Schopenhauer's dissertation furnishes an account of reason marked by a Kantian inspiration and a critical intent. The focus on the principle of sufficient reason allows Schopenhauer to examine and assess reason in its basic function of providing grounds, or reasons, of all kinds for consequences of all kinds. The principle under investigation thus encompasses the extent as well the limits of reason's generic capacity for providing the reasons that make it that something rather than something else obtains or is the case. Moreover, as indicated by the qualification "sufficient," added to the operative mode of reason in the naming of the principle, the reasons in question are not merely contributing to something obtaining or being case. They alone, merely by themselves, are responsible for it obtaining or being the case.

In Leibniz the principle of sufficient reason had figured as the supreme metaphysical principle, supplementing the principle of contradiction as the supreme logical principle. According to Leibniz, the logical principle of contradiction covers logical truths ("truths of reason"), while the ontological principle of sufficient reason serves as the covering principle for factual truths ("truths of fact"). Subsequent to Leibniz's introduction of the two "great principles," Wolff even had attempted to derive the principle of sufficient reason from the principle of contradiction by means of a logical proof.

When Schopenhauer revisits the traditional topic of the principle concerning sufficient reason (*Satz vom zureichenden Grund*) in his dissertation, he does so against the background of Kant's *Critique of Pure Reason* with its influential distinction between general pure logic ("formal logic"), which abstracts from all content, and a materially specific logic of objectively valid cognition ("transcendental logic").[7] In addition, Schopenhauer takes into account Kant's equally original distinction between the forms of thinking ("transcendental logic") and the forms of intuiting ("transcendental aesthetics") as the twin set of universal as well as necessary, "a priori" conditions governing objective cognition.

In a more general vein, Schopenhauer follows Kant's critical insight into the inscrutability of a possible common root of sensibility and understanding, maintaining a strict division between the aesthetic or sensory and the logical or intellectual mode of human cognition. Accordingly, Schopenhauer's project in the dissertation is not the reduction of the principle of sufficient reason to a unitary, single principle. Instead the dissertation aims at articulating the plural basic forms of rational relations in the specifically different domains of the principle's manifold modes of application. Accordingly, the nominally identical and generically vague principle of sufficient reason as such, according to which everything that obtains or is the case has a sufficient reason that makes it so by contributing the very reason why it obtains or is the case, has a plural basis ("root") rather than a single basic form from which the others might be derived.

In a further move beyond the traditional treatment of the principle of sufficient reason and under the inspiration of Kantian and post-Kantian philosophy, Schopenhauer's dissertation recognizes the specifically different function and the special status of the grounding relationship involved in volition and action, in which the cognitive character and the theoretical purpose of the principle of sufficient reason, as previously treated, is enlarged to include the specifically different deployment of the principle for the practical cognition of ends to be pursued by means of reason-guided action.

Finally, Schopenhauer's dissertation partakes in the general project of Kant's critical philosophy, along with its various successor projects in Fichte, Schelling, and Hegel, to assess the extent but also the limitation of reason's principle-governed use. In that regard, providing a comprehensive inventory of the plural basic types of sufficient rationality serves to delineate the overall sphere and the comprehensive conditions under which rule-governed relations between a given ground ("reason") and its consequent obtain. Independent of that plural principle and outside of its multiple spheres, reason *qua* ground (*ratio*) does not come into effect at all.

The plural basic forms of the principle of sufficient reason recognized in Schopenhauer's dissertation are so many modes in which something may function as the (sufficient) ground for something else as its consequent. In particular, in the dissertation Schopenhauer distinguishes four basic types of ground and their corresponding specifically different relations of (sufficiently) grounding their consequent. In addition, the four forms of sufficient grounding distinguished in the dissertation are supposed to be the only such forms and moreover, to be irreducible to each other or to any other principle.

The fourfold scheme provided by Schopenhauer for the principle of sufficient reason countenances the following four classes of ground: the ground of becoming (*Werdegrund*), the ground of cognition (*Erkenntnisgrund*), the ground of being (*Seinsgrund*), and the ground of action (*Handlungsgrund*).[8] Moreover, each of the four classes of ground is exclusively correlated with a class of objects governed by the respective version of the generically conceived principle of sufficient reason.

The objects of the first class comprise the sum total of objects in space and time, idealistically conceived—along Kantian lines—as "empirical representations" (FR 28). The objects of the second class are concepts and judgments as logical entities, idealistically conceived as "representations of representations" (FR 75). The third class of objects comprises the formal sensory features of empirical representations, idealistically conceived as "pure intuitions" and as merely subjective "forms of inner and outer sense" (FR 91). Finally, the fourth class of objects, under the principle of the sufficient reason of willing, comprises but one object, a given human being's will, idealistically conceived as the "immediate object of inner sense" (FR 105).

In the dual perspective of the origins of Schopenhauer's early thought in German idealism and of its subsequent development into a distinct variant of German real-idealism, the fourth and final form of the principle of sufficient reason and its associated class of objects deserves special attention. For one, this part of the dissertation (Chapter 7) contains an early account of the status and function of willing in Schopenhauer and can be considered a starting point for the mature philosophy of his main work. Moreover, the chapter provides an early account of the close connection between cognition and volition in Schopenhauer, which also was to become a main issue in the main work only a few years later. Most importantly, though, the chapter furnishes an early indication of the special link between psychological and cosmological considerations regarding the will—a linkage that was to form the very core of Schopenhauer's soon-to-emerge philosophical system.

To begin with, in discussing the fourth form of the principle of sufficient reason and its associated class of objects, Schopenhauer operates with a basic distinction between the two fundamental functions of the human being—abstractly referred to as "subject"—as the bearer of knowing ("subject of knowing") and as the bearer of willing ("subject of the will") (FR 105). In particular, the subject of willing is to function as the only immediate object of the subject of willing. Schopenhauer here takes up the Kantian and post-Kantian position that introspection ("inner sense") affords direct access, unmediated by any other representation, of one's own state of mind.

Yet Kant had limited inner sense to an immediate cognitive self-awareness under the guise of (sensory) self-intuition and delegated the self-awareness of one's own feelings and inclinations to other modes of immediate self-awareness ("feeling"). By contrast, Schopenhauer, who here follows the lead of the post-Kantian affirmative introduction of intellectual intuition, extends the scope of immediate self-cognition to encompass one's entire mind-set, specifically including volitions. Accordingly, the immediate, inner object of the subject of knowing is the subject in its entire affective and volitional constitution ("subject of the will").

In a further move inspired by his philosophical predecessors, in this instance chiefly Kant and Fichte and perhaps Hegel with their analyses of the immediate self-relation involved in the "I think," the "I" and the "subject-object," Schopenhauer goes on to outright identify the subject of willing and the subject of knowing. As an object unlike any other, the subject of willing serves as immediate object for the subject of cognition. So close is the supposed cognitive linkage in question that no external relation on the model of ground and consequent and hence no form of causal relation either is involved in the relation in question. Rather, on Schopenhauer's account in the dissertation, the subject of knowing and its cognitive counterpart, the subject of willing, are strictly speaking one and the same being—a subject that is at once the site of cognition and the site of volition, and the site of the cognition of volition at that.

To be sure, on Schopenhauer's account in the dissertation, knowing and willing remain distinct faculties in a complexly structured being that serves as their numerically identical but essentially diverse subject. Accordingly, one and the same subject is considered to exhibit two distinct sides or aspects, each coming into view under specifically different perspectives. In particular, the subject of knowing comes in as the universal underlying condition of all cognition of objects, while itself not being the object of any possible cognition (FR 105f.). By contrast, the subject of volition comes in as the sole immediately and inwardly known object of the cognitive subject and hence as involving a subject that stands in an immediate relation of cognition to its own willing.

Schopenhauer's account of a unitary subject with a twofold and, moreover, closely connected functionality (knowing and willing, knowing one's willing) builds on Kantian and post-Kantian portrayals of the human subject as at once unitary and complex, or rather duplex, and as displaying an internal structure of reciprocal supplementation and mutual complentarity. In particular, the numerical identity of the subject of knowing and the subject of willing in the early Schopenhauer can be seen to build on the unity of theoretical and practical reason maintained, in characteristically different ways, by Kant and Fichte, for both of whom the unity and identity of the subject is not reductive and monistic but structurally and functionally complex.

Schopenhauer also shares with his Kantian and post-Kantian idealist predecessors the assessment of the subject's unity amidst difference as a matter of certainty that yet remains inexplicable and leads all of them to treat the ultimate unity of the subject as a quality *sui generis* calling for its very own conceptuality, such as that of "transcendental apperception" (Kant) or of "intellectual intuition" (Fichte, Schelling). In the early Schopenhauer the elusive basic build of the dually unitary subject finds expression in its designation as a "miracle," even as the "miracle *par excellence*" (FR 113). The term "miracle" is aptly chosen by Schopenhauer, considering the exempt status that the complexly unitary, thinking-willing subject possesses with regard to any relation of ground and consequent covered by the principle of sufficient reason.

According to Schopenhauer, the subject of knowing (and by extension its twin, the subject of willing) is the structural preconditions of any and all thinking (and willing) and as such not itself subject to the laws of thinking (and willing) that issue from them. Even the fourth form of the principle of sufficient reason—the "principle of the sufficient reason of acting" (FR 115)—does not rule over the subject of the will but only over the latter's mental manifestations, viz., particular acts of willing (and feeling). It is the latter that are subject to the "law of motivation" (FR 114), according to which an action ensues upon the presence of a volitionally relevant cognition ("motive") and on the basis of the human being's underlying, fixed though essentially inscrutable practical disposition ("character").

On Schopenhauer's view in the dissertation, the structural impossibility of turning the subject of knowledge into its own object has its exact counterpart in the impossibility of ascertaining the precise character on the basis of which a given subject of willing responds to given motives in a law-governed manner, covered by the principle of sufficient reason (FR 116–125). For the early Schopenhauer, the cognitive gap between given motives and the hidden basic character amounts to the absence of sufficient determination, leads to the end of mere nature and opens up the "domain of freedom" (FR 123). With the final perspective of his dissertation on freedom as freedom from the principle of sufficient reason, the early Schopenhauer takes up Kant's account of transcendental freedom in the Third Antinomy of the *Critique of Pure Reason*, which also was to remain the chief source of inspiration behind his later treatments of the freedom of the will in the *World as Will and Representation* and in the late *Prize Essay on the Freedom of the Will* (1839).

But Schopenhauer's dissertation contains not only a prefiguration of the dual composition of the self as willing and as knowing ("will and representation") to be found in the main work only a few years later. In its second edition, revised in light of the main work written and published since, Schopenhauer additionally links the dual disposition of the self ("subject") under the principle of sufficient reason in its fourth form to an analogous twin character of all reality ("world") as will and as representation. In the later edition of the dissertation, in addition to labeling the absolute identity of the subject of cognition and the subject of the will a "miracle," even the "miracle *par excellence*," Schopenhauer addresses the dual unity or the unitary duality of the cognitive-*cum*-conative subject as the "world knot" (*Weltknoten*), which he immediately proceeds to declare being "inexplicable" (FR first edition 153).

Typically readers and interpreters of the later passage about the absolute identity of the subject of knowing and the subject of willing have taken the newly introduced appellation "world knot" as a variation on the earlier designation "miracle," serving to indicate something so out of the ordinary that it lacks explanation in general and a narrowly causal account of the relation between the subject-subject of knowing and the object-subject of willing in particular. But as suggested by the explicitly appended characterization of the miracle as "inexplicable," the term "world knot" all by itself does not yet convey miraculous inexplicability. On the contrary, the term is suited to indicate the positive status and the actual function that the identity of the dual subject possesses independent of its narrowly epistemic character as miraculous and inexplicable.

To be sure, the significant further meaning carried by Schopenhauer's choice of the term "world knot" for designating the identity of the dually functional subject is not captured by the current meaning and use of the term "knot," which has it refer to the identity in question as posing a thorny problem and an issue hard to untangle or untie. But the specific sense of the word "knot" figuring in the novel designation of the identity of the twin subject as "world knot," to be found in the second edition of the dissertation, is not simply that of a knot tied into a rope, and perhaps hard to untie, but that of a nodal point in a net that serves to connect and hold together the different directions or dimensions of a complexly organized structure or web.

There is a historical precedent for the meaning of "knot" as "nodal point" in general and for its use in that meaning and use in the phrase "world knot" in particular, to be found in a famous founding text of Italian Renaissance thought: Giovanni Pico della Mirandola's Latin *Oration on the Dignity of the Human Being* (1486), in which the cosmic position of the human being is described as constituting the "knot and bond of the world" (*nodus et vinculum mundi*). As the pairing of "knot" or "nodal point" with "linkage" and "bond" in Pico's phrase indicates, the carefully chosen term serves to designate the connecting function that the human being exercises, due to its unique cosmic position, in the network of interconnections that is the world or the universe. In particular, the poignant phrase employed by Pico refers to the special status and exclusive function of the human being as a microcosm with respect to the macrocosm and hence as a clue for disclosing the world at large.

Transposed into the context of Schopenhauer's distinctly Kantian and post-Kantian account of self and world, Pico's phrase about the nodal role of the human being within the cosmos serves to convey the disclosure of the world at large by the miniature world that is the self. The latter's dual composition—as will (willing) and as representation (knowing)—is the clue for unlocking the analogous composition of the "world as will and representation." Where Pico, and others before him, referred to the human being as a mirror and an abbreviation of sorts for the cosmic order, Schopenhauer, under the influence of Kant and post-Kantianism, takes his point of departure from the human constitution in order from there to gain insight, by way of analogy, into the overall constitution of world. With the former authors the human being was a microcosm; with Schopenhauer the world becomes the human being writ large (*"macranthropos"*).

By inserting the formula of the "word knot" into the second edition of his dissertation, Schopenhauer supplements the premonitions of the later developments of his philosophical thought already contained the work's original version with the early work's subsequent integration into the maximally widened application that the identity of the subject of knowing and the subject of willing first maintained in the dissertation had received in the main work, where it had served to disclose the unitary and dynamically related overall structure of the world.[9] Thus the move from the characterization of the absolute identity of the subject in terms of a miracle in the first edition of the dissertation to its characterization as the "world knot" in the second edition succinctly summarizes the trajectory of Schopenhauer's philosophical project, both at the biographical and at the systematic level, from the self as will and representation to the world as will and representation.

Notes

1 See Simmel (1991).
2 See Safranski (1991).
3 See Malter (1991).
4 For a schematic comparison of the two editions of the dissertation, see Schopenhauer (1959, XXXV–XLIII).
5 For a more detailed account of the realism inherent in German idealism, see Zöller (2000).
6 For a closer examination of Schopenhauer's unacknowledged intellectual indebtedness to Fichte, see Zöller (2006) and Zöller (2012).
7 On Kant's conception of transcendental logic, see Zöller (2016).
8 For the German terminology in classifying the four kinds of ground, see FR VI f.
9 On the systematic connections between the self and the world as both will and representation, see Zöller (1999).

Bibliography

Malter, R. *Arthur Schopenhauer. Transzendentalphilosophie und Metaphysik des Willens*. Stuttgart-Bad Cannstatt: Frommann-Holzboog, 1991.
Safranski, R. *Schopenhauer and the Wild Years of Philosophy*, trans. Ewald Osers. Cambridge, MA; London: Harvard University Press, 1991.
Schopenhauer, A. *Über die vierfache Wurzel des Satzes vom zureichenden Grunde*, eds. Michael Landmann and Elfriede Tielsch. Hamburg: Felix Meiner, 1959.
Simmel, G. *Schopenhauer and Nietzsche*, trans. Helmut Loiskandl, Deena Weinstein and Michael Weinstein. Champaign, IL: University of Illinois Press, 1991.

Zöller, G. 'Schopenhauer on the Self', in C. Janaway (ed.), *The Cambridge Companion to Schopenhauer*. Cambridge: Cambridge University Press, 1999, 18–43.

Zöller, G. 'German Realism: The Self-Limitation of Idealist Thinking in Fichte, Schelling and Schopenhauer', in K. America (ed.), *The Cambridge Companion to German Idealism*. Cambridge: Cambridge University Press, 2000, 200–218.

Zöller, G. 'Kichtenhauer: Der Ursprung von Schopenhauers *Welt als Wille und Vorstellung* in Fichtes *Wissenschaftslehre 1812* und *System der Sittenlehre*', in L. Hühn with Ph. Schwab (ed.), *Die Ethik Arthur Schopenhauers im Ausgang vom Deutschen Idealismus (Fichte/Schelling)*. Würzburg: Ergon, 2006, 365–386.

Zöller, G. 'Schopenhauer's Fairy Tale about Fichte: The Origin of the World as Will and Representation in German Idealist Thought', in B. Vandenabeele (ed.), *A Companion to Schopenhauer*. Oxford: Blackwell, 2012, 385–402.

Zöller, G., 'Conditions of Objectivity. Kant's Critical Conception of Transcendental Logic', *Yearbook of German Idealism/Jahrbuch des deutschen Idealismus* 14, 2016: forthcoming.

5 Schopenhauer's Early *Fourfold Root* and the Ghost of Kantian Freedom

Sandra Shapshay

There is an important reason why Schopenhauer has been rather neglected as an ethical theorist, namely, it is widely held that despite his invocations of transcendental freedom, Schopenhauer's view really amounts to a *hard determinism*, the view that human beings (in addition to non-human animals) are determined to act as they do on the basis of psycho-physical laws. Dale Jacquette, for one, acknowledges Schopenhauer's discussion of "transcendental freedom" but in the final analysis holds that "there can be no meaningful human freedom in Schopenhauer's system." He cites two main reasons why Schopenhauer's view amounts to hard determinism: "First, the actions undertaken by moral agents, like all events in the phenomenal world, are governed by the fourfold root of the principle of sufficient reason, and in particular by causal laws . . . [and second] Schopenhauer regards the character of each willing subject . . . [as] unalterable, incapable of change" (Jacquette, 2005, 186). Similarly, Günter Zöller maintains that while Schopenhauer holds onto a "transcendental freedom" founded on his metaphysics of will, "freedom is not to be found in the world as representation or the world known under the forms of space, time and causality. In that case freedom would be the miraculous suspension of the natural order . . . freedom is a mystery but not a miracle" (Zöller, 2004, xxix). Most recently, Christopher Janaway has argued that despite Schopenhauer's invocation of a Kantian intelligible character on which to ground the freedom of the human will, "a more consistent position would have been to deny freedom of the will to the individual" (Janaway, 2012, 431). This is because, according to Janaway, the differences between Schopenhauer's account of the intelligible character and Kant's are so stark (viz. its rationality and causal efficacy) that Schopenhauer *should* have dropped his talk of the intelligible character, and should have recognized that his "picture of human existence . . . has no room for genuine individual freedom at all" (Janaway, 2012, 455).

For normative ethical theory, this view that there is 'no genuine individual freedom' and that freedom as 'not to be found in the world of representation' is a nonstarter: Insofar as human beings *cannot* act other than they do, it makes little sense to hold that they *ought* to act differently. In other words,

without the presumption of freedom, it makes little sense to offer a normative ethical theory.[1] Consistent with these views, Schopenhauer does at times
assert that his philosophy as a whole, including his ethical thought, is merely
descriptive not prescriptive, and that "mature insight should encourage us
to give up" the demands for philosophy to become "practical, guide action,
[and] shape character" (WWR1 319). Yet, sustained reflections on ethics
where he does prescribe complicate this determinist picture. For instance,
he offers the following command as *the* ethical principle: "Harm no one;
rather help everyone to the extent that you can [*Neminem laede; imo omnes,
quantum potes, iuva*]" (BM 137), and while Schopenhauer does not hold
that this principle has the source or force of Kant's categorical imperative,
nonetheless it is supposed to encapsulate the guiding principle of the *good*
person. Schopenhauer is not content merely to describe how the person we
generally call 'good' acts, but further argues in the final section of BM (section 22) that the good person's conduct is normatively preferable to that
of the egoist or malicious person, for the former perceives the world aright
and the latter two are in metaphysical error (BM 270).[2]

In this essay I shall argue against the prevailing scholarly view that
(a) regards Schopenhauer's views on freedom as amounting to hard determinism, (b) treats Schopenhauer's views on freedom as *static*, and (c) sees his ethics
as entirely descriptive. By contrast, I shall argue that there is significant intellectual development in Schopenhauer's views on freedom, and second, that his
view never does or should amount to hard determinism; rather, from his early
Fourfold Root to his final writings on freedom, Schopenhauer firmly espouses
a Kantian-style compatibilism interwoven with mysterianism.[3] Ultimately, I
hope to show that Schopenhauer's evolving theory of freedom, then, makes
his commitment to Kantian compatibilism far from a careless relic of his early
view, but rather an important and abiding facet of this thought.

The 1813 Dissertation View on Freedom

One of the areas of major revision between the 1813 dissertation version of
Fourfold Root of the Principle of Sufficient Reason and the 1847 version is
Chapter 7 'On the fourth class of objects for the subject and the form of the
PSR governing it'. This chapter concerns only one object for the faculty of
representation, namely, "the subject of the will" (EF 50). In the dissertation
version of this section, Schopenhauer holds that the subject of willing, *considered* as distinct from the subject of knowing—the 'I'—but nonetheless,
mysteriously *identical* to it, is only knowable in introspection via particular
acts of one's own willing. The "I" constitutes "a perduring state" independent of time and space, and identifiable as the Kantian "intelligible character" (EF 55–56). In this early work, Schopenhauer holds that the intelligible
character is *causally related* to bodily acts in time and is also able to "exert
a causal influence . . . on the knowing self" in mental acts of attention and
memory (EF 58).

Thus, in the dissertation, one sees that Schopenhauer employs a broadly Kantian, two-worlds view of freedom, attributing *a causally efficacious spontaneity to the subject of willing/knowing or the intelligible character.* Furthermore, in the early *Fourfold Root*, he clearly regards the "phenomenon of freedom [as] having its roots in reason and possessed by humans alone" (EF 57). Thus, he is explicit in his allegiance to Kant's view of freedom not only as noumenal causality, but also as *rational spontaneity,* and lauds Kant's treatment as "an incomparable and wholly admirable masterpiece of profound human thought" (EF 56).

This espousal of the Kantian view of freedom as rational spontaneity in EF is consistent with his 1812–3 manuscript entries from Berlin in which he holds that theoretical reason is "conditioned by the life of man" but that practical reason "is not" (MR1 fr. 44), for the "motive of a purely moral resolve is a supersensuous one" (MR1 60). Unlike Kant, however, Schopenhauer holds that the motive to act on a moral principle does not *derive* from pure practical reason, but rather from what he calls the "better consciousness" (MR1 80). Nonetheless, the faculty of reason, for Schopenhauer, is still a necessary condition for freedom and enables a human being to act according to the motives of the "better consciousness." Accordingly, he holds that "animals cannot be called free, and this is due to the fact that they lack *reason* . . . [which in its practical mode] enables us to consider and survey always in association the whole of life . . . and therefore to act *generally in accordance with maxims*" (MR1 87).

After the completion of his dissertation, however, it seems that Schopenhauer realized he must deal with a criticism leveled famously by F.H. Jacobi and G.E. Schulze (who was Schopenhauer's teacher at Göttingen and advised him to focus his studies on Plato and Kant). The objection goes as follows: In the *first Critique*, Kant had applied the category of causality to things in themselves in order to derive their existence from appearances, but this move is illegitimate since the principle of causality, by the lights of the Critical system itself, may only be applied intra-phenomenally. In Jacobi's much-quoted synopsis of the objection, without the assumption of things in themselves as causally related to phenomena "I could not get into the system; with it, I could not stay."[4] Although the objection had been leveled in print as early as Schulze's *Aenesidemus* in 1792, it seems from EF and the *Early Manuscripts* of 1812–3 that Schopenhauer did not fully recognize until after writing his dissertation that the objection also implicated Kant's rational spontaneity view of freedom, for it too involves an ascription of causal efficacy extra-phenomenally to a thing-in-itself (in this case, to the 'intelligible character').

Schopenhauer explicitly invokes Schulze and Jacobi's objection to Kant's manner of introducing things in themselves (WWR1 516) and it seems to have led him to revise his EF allegiance to a broadly Kantian view of freedom as rational spontaneity in his *Prize-Essay On the Freedom of the Will* (1839/41, hereafter FW). Accordingly, in his revision of FR in

1847, Schopenhauer excises the view that the intelligible character is a spontaneous cause of mental and bodily actions, and that the intelligible character exerts a spontaneous causal influence in the phenomenal world holding instead that "[t]he influence that the will exercises on cognition is not based on causality strictly speaking, but on the identity of the cognizing with the willing subject . . ." (FR 145). Willing, on the one hand, and mental and bodily actions, on the other, are now regarded as two metaphysical *aspects* of the same event, and Schopenhauer no longer holds that in cases of free will, the rational spontaneity of the intelligible character plays a causal role.

Given this revision, the natural question to ask is then is *what becomes of the role of the intellect or the faculty of reason* in this new picture? Focusing on this question is quite revealing, for Schopenhauer's official pronouncements on the role of the faculty of reason, which are generally quite deflationary, *belie the actual role the faculty of reason continues to play* on Schopenhauer's picture in cases where the subject seems to exercise transcendental freedom. Schopenhauer's official pronouncement on the faculty of reason (after the 1813 FR through FW) is that reason:

(a) is distinctive to human cognition
(b) is the faculty that abstracts concepts from experience and imposes four modes of explanation—the four roots of the principle of sufficient reason—onto experience as well as onto our judgments.

(see esp. FR chapter 5 and WWR1 section 3)

(c) can shape human action only in the sense of helping us to achieve what it is that we will in a more effective manner, though reason cannot determine or change *what* we will.
(d) is *not* purely practical in the sense of giving or motivating a rational being to follow the moral law.

Certainly, Schopenhauer's mature writings explicitly demote the power of reason or more generally, 'the intellect' from a transcendent, spontaneous cause in the phenomenal world and the giver of the moral law, to merely the faculty of concepts and ratiocination that came into being to serve the individual will-to-life and is enlisted generally in that service.

Yet, as I shall detail below, Schopenhauer's official position on the power of reason or the intellect conflicts with his 'unofficial position,' which reveals itself most clearly in his theory of the sublime and in his discussion of ascetic renunciation of the will-to-life. Here, he implicitly retains his early Kantian, dissertation position, namely, the view that *the spontaneous intellect can exert freedom in the phenomenal world*. I shall refer to this unofficial position as the 'ghost of Kantian freedom.' Although Schopenhauer buried the Kantian freedom view shortly after writing his dissertation, its ghost haunts Schopenhauer's writings on freedom up through his final major writings on the subject.

Determinism

In FW (1839/published 1841), Schopenhauer grants that human beings may possess both physical and intellectual freedom, but he construes these in purely negative terms: in the case of physical freedom, it is freedom *from* material obstacles that would prevent one from doing what one wills; in the case of intellectual freedom, it is freedom *from* cognitive impairments, both internal (such as madness or intoxication) and external (such as deception or illusion grounded in extra-subjective factors). However, the key philosophical question Schopenhauer sets out to answer in this essay is not whether I can *do* what I will, but rather whether I can *will* what I will (FW 6). In other words, is my will motivationally constrained such that I could not possibly will but in the manner that I do? This is the question of whether we are free in a moral sense, the question of whether human beings are endowed with *liberum arbitrium indifferentiae*, and this is the primary question he sets out to answer in his prize-winning essay.

In sections 1–4 of FW, Schopenhauer's answer is that one is *not* free to choose *what* one wills. The grounds for this conclusion rest largely on his epistemological doctrine of FR, namely that the principle of sufficient reason is the *a priori* form of all human experience. Accordingly, the natural world is universally causally determined. As he puts it, "all *alterations* that happen to objects . . . situated in the real external world, are therefore subordinate to the law of *causality*, and so always occur . . . as *necessary* and inevitable.—There cannot be an exception to this, because the rule stands firm a priori for all possibility of experience" (FW 28). The psychological realm is also entirely subject to the causal nexus: in this regard, the only difference between a rock and a rabbit, for example, is that the rabbit's behavior is governed by the causality of *motives* on the rabbit's nature. Schopenhauer defines "motivation" as "causality that goes through cognition" (FW 31). Thus, given the nature of the rabbit, the presentation of a certain perception—say, that of a fox bounding toward it—provides a sufficient motive for the rabbit's flight, which follows with strict necessity.

The same holds true for human beings, though with two notable differences. First, unlike the rabbit, the motives that operate in human psychology are typically presented in consciousness in conceptual and linguistic form. And second, Schopenhauer holds that human beings have unique, individual characters, not just the character of their species. Schopenhauer does moreover allow that in more cognitively complex animals such as dogs or elephants individuals may show a greater degree of individuality as well. These differences notwithstanding, given the particular empirical character of a human being (empirical inasmuch as it is known *a posteriori*), should that human being be presented with certain motives, Schopenhauer holds, the resulting action would follow with necessity.[5]

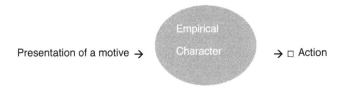

Figure 1

It is crucial to Schopenhauer's conception of the matter that for human beings, "the individual character is *inborn*; it is no work of art or of circumstances subject to chance, but rather the work of nature itself" (FW 53), and further, that individual character is *unchangeable*. He offers two *a priori* reasons in support of this position. First, given his view of the principle of sufficient reason and recapitulating the Schulze objection, he holds that any spontaneous action, one that actually *formed* character from nothing rather than one which merely *flowed from* a character, would constitute an "inexplicable miracle—an effect without a cause" (FW 45–46). Since the mind has no form for conceiving an effect without a cause, the idea of a truly spontaneous action lacks real sense. This leaves open the possibility of modification of character through habituation in a manner that is not entirely spontaneous, but this option is foreclosed in Schopenhauer's thought by his second main reason for accepting determinism, namely, the *a priori* law that every *existentia* presupposes an *essentia,* that is, "everything that is must also be *something,* have a definite essence" (FW 57). Human beings, like everything else in nature, have essential qualities with which they are born.[6]

Although Schopenhauer takes the empirical character to be fixed, individuals may learn through experience "what we want and what we can do" as well as "the dimensions and directions of our mental and physical abilities" and our "total strengths and weaknesses" (WWR1 359–60). If people acquire "knowledge of the invariable qualities of [their] own empirical character" then, he suggests, they have developed "acquired character" [*den erworbenen Charakter*]. Schopenhauer's terminology here is somewhat misleading inasmuch as it suggests that an individual can 'acquire' a different character from her empirical one. What is really being 'acquired' here is empirical *self-knowledge*. Schopenhauer's point is that a person may learn how most effectively (i.e., in a manner that is socially acceptable and in keeping with his physical and mental abilities) to achieve what he inevitably wills if he acquires empirical self-knowledge.

To illustrate: imagine a heavy drinker, Bill, who has ruined his personal life by mistreating his family when drunk. In Schopenhauer's terms, one of Bill's empirical character traits is that he is an 'alcoholic'. After hitting rock bottom, Bill joins Alcoholics Anonymous to work its twelve-step program. In doing so, he may come to recognize a fact about his empirical character, namely that he is *essentially* alcoholic. In Schopenhauer's terms, if he acquires such knowledge, he now has 'acquired character.' What this really amounts to, however, is the possibility of a difference in his behavior, on the basis of his acquired 'empirical self-knowledge,' despite the fact that his empirical character remains unchanged. Bill no longer believes that he can go to the bar and have 'just one little drink.' He realizes that this former belief of his is false and was perhaps all along self-deceptive, and knows that, as soon as he puts himself in that situation, motives will act on his empirical character with the force of necessity, and he will arrive home drunk. Once he has 'acquired empirical self-knowledge,' however, he can refrain from putting himself in situations where he will be tempted to drink. He can consciously avoid bars and parties where alcohol is being served. Note, on this picture, he still *wills* to drink but he also wills to be a good father and husband too, and he realizes that the former desire is incompatible with the latter. By acquiring empirical self-knowledge, he can utilize his intellect or faculty of reason to avoid the situations where he will, necessarily, get drunk—for he is essentially, alcoholic—as this behavior conflicts with what he also wills, namely, to have a happy family life.

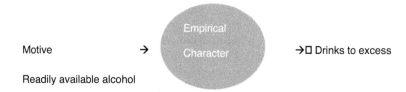

Figure A Bill, pre-AA—wills incompatible things (1) to get drunk and (2) wills to have a good family life

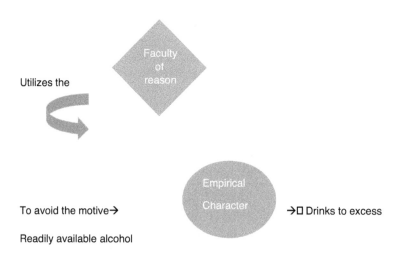

Figure B Bill, post-AA: Uses his intellect to achieve (2) at the expense of (1)

A similar but more extreme use of reason to govern our practical affairs in order better to attain what we desire is evidenced on Schopenhauer's account by the Stoic sage who "presents in an ideal form the most complete development of practical reason in the true and authentic sense of the word" (WWR 1, 103). The Stoic sage desires happiness but recognizes that desire and attachment are the chief obstacles thereto, and so he looks to reason to detach from desire in order to achieve peace of mind (*ataraxia*).

Indeed, for Schopenhauer, rational human beings—unlike nonhuman animals—can attain a measure of relief from suffering in this way, for if we can retreat into reflection we become "like actors who have played our scene, and now take our seats among the audience before we have to return to the stage; anything may now happen on the stage, even the preparation of our own death, and, looking out from the audience, we view it with equanimity [*Gelassenheit*]" (WWR1 102).

It is important to note, however, that Schopenhauer does not equate the ability to achieve equanimity [*Gelassenheit*] through rational reflection with true moral virtue, as did the Stoics. In fact, he believes that this use of reason to achieve equanimity can be put in the service of great virtue or great wickedness. Crucial for this inquiry, this sort of 'practical reason' does not constitute freedom of the will for Schopenhauer. The stoic sage does not actually, self-consciously change *what* he wills, namely, to achieve happiness. Rather, he uses reason to detach from his desires in order better to attain what he has always willed, namely, happiness. Thus, reason is used in the Stoic case in a manner akin to (albeit more extremely than) the case of Bill the recovering alcoholic—that is, practical reason is employed better to achieve what one happens to will. In other words, reason is used as a means for managing our lives in a more enlightened, self-interested manner. In stark contrast to Kant, then, Schopenhauer holds that the only "true and authentic sense" of pure practical reason is the ability to "retreat into reflection" in order to manage one's affairs more efficaciously or even to gain some measure of tranquility. Notwithstanding, Schopenhauer does hold that this ability lends human beings a kind of dignity that animals cannot have, but he underscores that "there is no other sense in which we can talk of [human] dignity" (WWR1 107).

Freedom in Aesthetic Experience and Resignation

On the basis of the thoughts outlined above—that human beings have inborn, unalterable empirical characters and that the law of causality operates with strict necessity in the psychological as well as the physical realm—Schopenhauer declares that "we have entirely removed all freedom of human action and recognized it as thoroughly subordinate to the strictest necessity" (FW 93). Small wonder that most commentators would say that Schopenhauer's theory of freedom amounts to a hard determinism!

Yet, as I shall detail below, this official pronouncement conflicts with Schopenhauer's characterization of the subject of aesthetic experience and of the person who renounces the will-to-life, for these subjects seem to be possessed of spontaneous intellectual freedom, a freedom not only to deal with one's 'unalterable' empirical character more efficaciously (e.g., in the case of Bill and the Stoic sage above), but also actively to alter—even if temporarily—that supposedly 'unalterable' character. In short, in descriptions of certain aesthetic and ascetic experiences, Schopenhauer suggests that people can somehow voluntarily and self-consciously *change their empirical character*.

In aesthetic experience, as he understands it, a subject "loses himself" in his contemplation of an object in such a way that "what we cognize is no longer the individual thing as such, but rather the *Idea*, the eternal form, the immediate objecthood of the will at this level" (WWR1 210). In this way, the subject loses herself as a willing subject, and her desires and strivings are put on hold by the absorption of the intellect in the aesthetic object. More starkly, for the denier of will, "a recognition of the whole, of the essence of things in themselves . . . becomes the *tranquillizer* of all and every willing." (WWR1 448). Implicit in these pictures of aesthetic and ascetic experience, it would appear, is a conception of the subject who is not merely an instrumentally enlightened willing being (like Bill, the alcoholic), but is further a subject who can choose to varying degrees to deny that will, and who can act in a manner that is different from the ordinary dictates of her empirical character. For in contrast to the post-AA Bill and the Stoic sage, the aesthetic contemplator and the ascetic renouncer are not utilizing the intellect in enlightened service to the will-to-life to attain happiness. Rather, these seem like cases where the intellect actually opposes the will-to-life and its myriad desires and causes the person to act out of empirical character.

One might think, however, that the way I have put things here is too voluntaristic—perhaps we simply undergo these experiences, we do not really choose them.[7] And indeed, Schopenhauer does sometimes describe these experiences—especially the experience of the beautiful—as simply 'happening to' a subject, rather than involving a voluntary intellectual act. But at other times, Schopenhauer describes these experiences as involving a distinct, intellectual effort even *a struggle* on the part of the subject to overcome one's typical empirical-character driven responses. Consider, for example, Schopenhauer's account of what he describes as "the transition that is possible, but to be regarded only as an exception" from ordinary experience to aesthetic experience. He writes:

> When elevated by the strength of mind [*die Kraft des Geistes*], to stop viewing things in the ordinary way . . . if we stop considering the Where, When, Why and Wherefore of things but simply and exclusively the *What*, if we do not allow our consciousness to become engrossed by abstract thinking, concepts of reason; but if instead of all this, we devote the whole power of our mind [*die ganze Macht seines Geistes*] to

intuition and immerse ourselves in this entirely, . . . We *lose* ourselves in this object completely, i.e. we forget our individuality, our will.

(WWR1 210)

Schopenhauer's language here would seem to imply that the subject of aesthetic experience becomes such by virtue of a *deliberate intellectual act* that breaks the normal, will-driven, conditioned course of experience: we are "elevated by the strength of mind," we "do not allow our consciousness to become engrossed by abstract thinking," and we "devote the whole power of our mind to intuition." A few lines later, he suggests that "a cognizing individual raises himself to a pure subject of cognition" and thus "raises the object observed to an Idea" (WWR1 211). These remarks suggest that in making the transition from ordinary to aesthetic experience the subject *deliberately chooses* to break free of the demands of his will and the grip of the principle of sufficient reason.

When he turns to a discussion of resignation, Schopenhauer again appears to be working with a conception of the subject as potentially free from the law of motivation, a subject with the capacity *to choose* whether to affirm or to deny the will-to-life. The latter option is modelled most clearly, he suggests, in certain works of tragedy, such as Calderón's *La vida es sueño* and Shakespeare's *Hamlet*, where we see that "the noblest people eventually renounce forever the goals they had, up to that point, pursued so intensely, as well as renouncing all the pleasures of life, or even willingly and joyfully giving them up" (WWR1 299). "Willingly giving up" sounds very much like something that one wilfully decides to do. And Schopenhauer is clear that while such renunciation of the will-to-life, initiated by a subject's recognition of the "contradiction of the will-to-live with itself," is often accompanied by great personal suffering such that renunciation "does not follow from suffering with anything like the necessity of an effect from its cause, but rather the will remains free" (WWR1 467). In other words, in these cases we seem to have a subject *choosing what he or she wills—willing out of empirical character*—and not merely changing how he attains what he wills by virtue of his so-called unalterable empirical character.[8]

One might object that I am reading Schopenhauer's accounts here too literally. And as mentioned above, it is true that the experience of beauty is often characterized as entirely passive. So too will be the experience of many of those who attain denial of the will-to-live via great personal suffering, which, although it "frequently leads to a full resignation," Schopenhauer suggests, does so "often not until the presence of death" (WWR1 463–4). But even if the experience of beauty seems more passive and is the most common kind of aesthetic experience, it is not the only kind; and even if the most common route to renunciation is one along which the denier of the will-to-live is carried passively, again, it is not the only kind that Schopenhauer describes. In the following description of ascetic renunciation, for instance, the activity of the intellect is especially notable:

> [W]e must not think that, after cognition has become a tranquillizer of the will and given rise to the negation of the will to life, it will never falter and that it can be relied upon like inherited property. Rather, it must constantly be regained by steady struggle. . . . Thus we find that the peace and blissfulness we have described in the lives of saintly people is only a flower that emerges from constant overcoming of the will, and we see the constant struggle with the will to life as the soil from which it arises.
>
> (WWR1 462–3)

This passage suggests that even if the initial transition into denial of the will-to-live is something with respect to which the subject is passive, *maintaining this state* requires "steady struggle". And so it seems that the ascetic path to renunciation is one that requires agency—specifically, agency on the part of the intellect.

In a similar vein, sublime experience involves a "conscious" and "violent" struggle for will-lessness, in response to objects or states of affairs that stand in "a hostile relation to the human will in general" (WWR1 237). Sublime objects and environments are recognised by the subject as threatening in some sense, and that recognition is an impediment to transition into will-less contemplation of them. Despite this, Schopenhauer insists, such contemplation of the sublime is possible. He writes,

> with the sublime . . . that state of pure cognition is gained only by means of a conscious [*bewußtes*] and violent tearing free from relationships between the same object and the will (relationships that are recognized as unfavourable) by means of a free and conscious elevation over the will and the cognition relating to it [*ein freies, von Bewußtseyn begleitetes Erheben über den Willen*] This elevation must not only be achieved consciously, it must also be sustained and is therefore accompanied by a constant recollection of the will.
>
> (WWR1 238)

Thus, experience of the sublime requires *active sustenance or maintenance,* and the best candidate for pulling off this active feat is the intellect, which is apparently capable of tearing the subject's *attention* free from the threat posed by the object to her individual will (WWR1 238).

These remarks concerning the possibility of aesthetic experience and renunciation of the will-to-life are, on the face of it, in clear tension with the determinist position that Schopenhauer defends in the first four sections of FW. Paul Guyer, for one, has recognized the same tension here with respect to Schopenhauer's aesthetic theory. He construes Schopenhauer as holding that the transition from ordinary to aesthetic experience must be "the consequence of an active, even violent adoption of a cognitive attitude by the individual mind," so that "we actively will [. . .] to free ourselves from the will." Thus he notes quite rightly that there is "something unsettling" and "an air of paradox about Schopenhauer's account" (Guyer, 1996, 116).

Far from hiding from this tension, Schopenhauer draws our attention precisely to "the contradiction between our claim, on the one hand, that there is a necessary determination of the will through motives in accordance with character, and our claim, on the other hand, that it is possible to completely [or temporarily] abolish the will" (WWR1 477). He holds that the "key to reconciling these contradictions" is to acknowledge the power of an "altered mode of cognition" (WWR1 477), namely, cognition of the Ideas. This "altered mode of cognition" breaks the ordinary causal-motivational chain, and allows "the character itself [to be] fully abolished" (WWR1 477).

In short, his view seems to be that a certain mode of cognition—namely, one that sees to the essential features of the world—actually enables a change in empirical character. Schopenhauer's phenomenological descriptions of temporary will suppression (in the sublime) and will denial (in ascetic renunciation) both seem to involve this altered, aesthetic mode of cognition that is capable of altering or even abolishing the empirical character. Since the intellect in these cases is acting in a manner that is *not* in the service of the empirical character but rather allows and/or effects some kind of change or even complete abolition of that empirical character, this is certainly reminiscent of the spontaneous, unconditioned intellectual agency view that he supposedly jettisoned after the dissertation.

Given Schopenhauer's own manner of resolving this apparent contradiction between determinism and the evidence of actual transcendental freedom—one that centrally involves the power of the intellect—we thus have reason to question whether Schopenhauer has really left the Kantian rational spontaneity view behind, for the intellect or reason in aesthetic-cognition does seem capable, on his account, of exercising some voluntary control over the empirical character. How else to illuminate the transition between attainment of a certain kind of insight into the world and the corresponding radical character change that people then display in the world of representation?

Pointing further to the remnant of the Kantian view, Schopenhauer locates the apparently spontaneous control over character in reason, writing that "[t]he possibility of a freedom that expresses itself in this way is the greatest advantage of being human, and one that animals will always lack because it requires a careful and deliberate reason [*Besonnenheit der Vernunft*] that can survey the whole of life, abstracted from any present impression" (WWR1 478). He continues, "[a]nimals lack any possibility of freedom, just as they lack any possibility of an authentic, which is to say a careful and deliberate ability to choose following a complete conflict of motives, which must be abstract representations for this to happen" (WWR1 478).

Thus, I suggest that in Schopenhauer's account of the active ascetic and the active subject of sublime experience in WWR1, we see unmistakable remnants of the Kantian rational spontaneity view, a view as I have outlined above that he officially repudiates in his post-dissertation writings. In the next section, I shall argue that this 'ghost of Kantian freedom' also haunts his later FW where it makes a dramatic and unexpected appearance in the final section, and thus should not be discounted as a careless relic of his former view.

The Limits of Determinism

As described above, the bulk of Schopenhauer's FW is devoted to establishing the truth of determinism. However, in the essay's all-important concluding section, he changes tack. Having "entirely removed all freedom of human action and recognized it as thoroughly subordinate to the strictest necessity," he suggests, he has taken us to "the point where we will be able to grasp *true moral freedom*, which is of a higher kind" (FW 93). He goes on: "For there is one more fact of consciousness that I have entirely neglected so far. . . . This is the wholly clear and sure feeling of *responsibility* for what we do, of *accountability* for our actions, which rests on the unshakeable certainty that we ourselves are *the doers of our deeds*" (FW 93). In the last few pages of the essay, Schopenhauer suggests that the existence and indeed the character of "true moral freedom" can indeed be inferred from this "fact of consciousness," allowing him to answer in the affirmative the question set by the Royal Norwegian Society of Sciences: "Can the freedom of the human will be proved from self-consciousness?"

The argument of these last few pages goes, in essence, as follows:

(1) We have an "unshakeable certainty that we ourselves are *the doers of our deeds*.

(FW 93)

(2) This feeling is based on the recognition that with respect to any individual's action, "quite another action, indeed the action directly opposed to his own, was after all entirely possible and could have happened, *if only he had been another.*"

(FW 93)

(3) Thus, "the *responsibility* he is conscious of relates only provisionally and ostensibly to the deed, but fundamentally to his *character*; it is for *this* that he feels himself responsible."

(FW 93)

(4) "And it is for *this* that others hold him responsible, as their judgment forsakes the deed at once in order to discover the qualities of the doer . . . their reproaches go back to his *character.*"

(FW 93–4)

(5) "Where *guilt* lies, there must *responsibility* lie also: and since the latter is the sole datum from which the conclusion to moral freedom is

justified, *freedom* must also lie in the very same place, that is in the *character* of the human being."

(FW 94)

At this point, Schopenhauer in effect faces a dilemma. On the one hand, he takes himself to have "disclosed" the fact that we are in some sense free, appealing to "data" that amount to "a fact of consciousness," and to have identified the "location" of that freedom in character (FW 94). On the other hand, as he takes himself to have demonstrated earlier in the essay, the character is inborn and unalterable. To escape the dilemma—as one might expect given his discussion of the sublime, ascetic renunciation and his EF—he appeals to Kant's account of the relation between empirical and intelligible character "and thereby . . . the compatibility of freedom with necessity, which belongs among the most beautiful and most profoundly through products of this great mind, and indeed of human beings ever" (FW 95). Following Kant, he writes,

> as an object of experience the empirical character is, like the whole human being, a mere appearance, and so bound to the forms of all appearance, time, space and causality, and subordinate to their laws; by contrast, that which is thing in itself is independent of these forms and so subordinate to no time distinction, and is therefore the enduring and unalterable condition the foundation for this whole appearance, is *his intelligible character*, i.e. *his will* as thing in itself, to which, in this capacity, there certainly also pertains absolute freedom.
>
> (FW 96, emphasis added)[9]

On this picture then, while the empirical character is determined, the intelligible character has "absolute," "transcendental" freedom, and in virtue of the fact that each human person has an intelligible character "all deeds of the human being are his own work, however necessarily they issue from the empirical character upon its coincidence with motives" (FW 96).

At this point, commentators tend to identify the "intelligible character," with the metaphysical will (Zöller, 2004, xxix; Janaway, 2009, xxxvii). Or they hold that Schopenhauer *should* have made this identification (Janaway, 2012, 455). But this move is too fast, for unlike the metaphysical will, which is supposed to be 'one' in the sense of 'being independent of individuation,' the intelligible character is individuated and multiple. There are, for Schopenhauer, as many intelligible characters as there are individual persons. Accordingly, it is important to note in the above quotation that Schopenhauer refers to the foundation of a person's transcendental freedom in *individuated* form as "*his* intelligible character [*sein intelligibler Charakter*], i.e. *his* will as thing in itself [*sein Wille als Ding an sich*]" rather than as un-individuated thing in itself. Far from being identical to the metaphysical will, the intelligible character is best understood as what he elsewhere describes as a person's "own individual Idea" (WWR1 156) or as a "specific Idea corresponding to a distinctive act of the will's objectivation . . . This act itself would then be the person's intelligible character, and the empirical character would be its appearance" (WWR1 188). In sum, the intelligible character is not to be identified with the will qua thing in itself, but rather, is something metaphysically intermediate between the world of representation and the thing in itself: It is a special Idea, which is itself an objectivation of *a particular act* of the metaphysical will [*Willensakt*].

Schopenhauer's official position, however, does link the freedom of the intelligible character to the freedom of "the will as thing-in-itself," which is fundamentally a matter of independence of the forms of the principle of sufficient reason, and hence of the law of causality. Freedom in this context is not to be construed in terms of freedom of action or decision, but rather in terms of the fact that no deterministic account of how or why an individual's intelligible character is as it is—that is, about how or why "the will as thing-in-itself" is objectified in just this way in this individual—is available. Given, then, that an individual's empirical character is as it is inasmuch as it is the manifestation in the phenomenal world of her intelligible character, and that there is no deterministic story to be told about why or how her intelligible character is as it is, then there can be no deterministic story—or at least none that points beyond the individual—about why her empirical character is as it is. It follows then, that while her actions are the result of the presentation of motives to her empirical character, and hence wholly empirically determined, her intelligible character remains free. Thus, it makes sense to hold her responsible for her (voluntary) actions. And in this double-sidedness of the subject as having both an empirical and an intelligible character lies moral or transcendental freedom: the subject is indeed the doer of her deeds.

But Schopenhauer's unofficial position, which emerges in his discussion of the sublime and ascetic renunciation, goes further than this in assigning a role to the intellect in this account of transcendental freedom. "[S]omeone who overcomes the world," for instance, has "achieved the cognition that leads him to renounce and negate the will to life that fills all things" (WWR1 456). Here cognition is the key to the emergence of the "freedom of this will" (WWR1 456). Similarly, the intellect plays a key role in freeing the subject temporarily from the normal dictates of his empirical character in sublime experience:

> if the spectator pays no attention to this obtrusive, hostile relation [of the threatening object] to his will, but rather, although perceiving and acknowledging it, consciously turns away from it by violently wrenching himself free from his will, and its relations and surrendering himself to cognition alone . . . grasping only their Ideas . . . then he is filled with the feeling of the *sublime*.
>
> (WWR1 238)

In this description the spectator's intellect "pays no attention" to the individual threat posed by the object, and "consciously turns away" from it, "violently wrenching himself free" (WWR1 238). Thus we see an active intellect that has broken free of its servitude to the individual will, so that it is no longer restricted to knowledge governed by the forms of the principle of sufficient reason. These cases of intellectual freedom then, somehow, mysteriously allow the intelligible character to change, bringing a corresponding transformation of the empirical character and the behavior of that character in response to motives in the empirical world.

Although Schopenhauer's phenomenological descriptions of sublime and ascetic experience certainly involve an active, spontaneous role for the intellect, he remains theoretically silent on the role of the intellect or reason in this picture. One might expect him to say more on the role of the intellect in intelligible character change, as well as the responsibility we bear for our own characters, in the three-page Appendix to FW which deals centrally with intellectual freedom, but here he describes intellectual freedom in a negative fashion only, as freedom from intoxication, madness, or deception, rather than as an active enabler of transcendental freedom, which it seems to be in the above cases.

A rare place where Schopenhauer does cursorily address the active nature of the intellect is found in WWR2:

> [w]hat makes this state [aesthetic experience] difficult and therefore rare is that in it the accident (the intellect), so to speak, subdues [*bemeistert*] and eliminates [*aufhebt*] the substance (the will), although only for a short time. Here also are to be found the analogy and even relationship of this with the denial of the will.
>
> (WWR2 369)

In this passage, Schopenhauer claims that the intellect subdues and eliminates the will at least temporarily along the same lines as in the more permanent denial of the will, but exactly how this works remains a mystery.

Here we have arrived at the central tension in Schopenhauer's mature view of freedom. In the official position, he vouchsafes the possibility and actuality of moral freedom—the possibility of choosing what one wills between two diametrically opposed options—and its compatibility with determinism by virtue of Kant's distinction between the empirical and intelligible character, a doctrine which Schopenhauer holds to be "one of the most excellent things anyone has ever said" (WWR1 599). Yet, he repudiates the rational, spontaneous-causal story that Kant utilizes to fill in the details of how this compatibilism makes sense, for "a cause must essentially be an appearance, not something entirely different in kind that lies beyond all appearance" (WWR1 601). The unofficial position, however, invokes something very close to a rational, spontaneous causal story insofar as the intellect somehow comes to subdue the will either temporarily (in aesthetic experience) or permanently (in ascetic renunciation), and thus apparently initiates an unconditioned causality in the world of appearance.

Exactly *how* it is that the human being can achieve sublime experience (actively detaching herself from egoistic striving for a time) and deny the will to life altogether remain ineluctably mysterious on Schopenhauer's post-dissertation account. After writing the EF, he attempts to distance himself from the Kantian location of freedom in reason, but in doing so, the ultimate source of this felt power to turn away from the goods of life, to will differently, becomes, for better or worse, more obscure. In sum, he keeps the intelligible/empirical distinction in place, locating transcendental freedom in the intelligible character or 'special Idea' of each human person, while attempting to excise the rational-spontaneous causal story from his overall Kantian picture, but he sometimes lapses into the rational-spontaneity model since *he puts no alternative explication in in its place.*

Conclusion

Schopenhauer himself appears unembarrassed by what I have suggested here amounts to a significant lacuna in his account of transcendental freedom. We "understand what the most excellent Malebranche could mean in (correctly) saying: 'freedom is a mystery'" (WWR1 478). Ultimately, Schopenhauer seems content to leave unexplained and mysterious the relationship between the freedom of the will as grounded in the intelligible character, on the one hand, and the capacity in rational beings for aesthetic experience, denial of the will-to-life, and moral responsibility for our character.

With respect to the relationship between the intelligible character, the intellect, and transcendental freedom, then, Schopenhauer's system has it that there just are points at which explanation comes to an end, and that this is one of them. Far from being a hard determinist, however, I hope to have shown, through an exploration of the development of Schopenhauer's views on freedom, that Schopenhauer always held onto a compatibilism between the determinism of the natural world and human freedom along the lines of Kant, but this compatibilism undergoes a subtle but significant development from Schopenhauer's dissertation (1813) to his mature views on freedom as expounded in FW (1839/42). While the explication of this freedom *must* remain a mystery, for the nature of the intelligible character lies outside the bounds of legitimate application of the PSR and thus beyond the possibility of explanation, the possibility of freedom is vouchsafed by Schopenhauer's metaphysics and the actuality of freedom is attested to in aesthetic experience, in asceticism, and in the ineluctable feeling of responsibility for our characters.

Yet, despite the intentional excising of the rational spontaneity view from the later version of the FR and other post-dissertation writings, the ghost of Kantian freedom continues to haunt Schopenhauer's thought. The ghost appears whenever Schopenhauer offers some phenomenological detail on the degrees of will-suppression and will-denial that are possible for humans to achieve. In his descriptions of these phenomena, there seems indeed to be a causal role for reason or the intellect, insofar as it enables a change in a person's intelligible character that enters into the phenomenal world. But post-dissertation, Schopenhauer is content to leave this role of reason in transcendental freedom ineluctably mysterious.[10]

Notes

1 Arguably, it would still make sense to offer an *evaluative* theory of ethics, namely, one that delineates and defends a certain picture of the good and the right without prescribing that people conform to this picture. And Schopenhauer does claim sometimes that he merely describes rather than prescribes. Yet in BM he does prescribe insofar as he enjoins human beings to bring about better treatment of human beings and animals, in the form of the abolition of slavery and the formation of animal protection societies in particular (See BM 218, 229, 230n.)

2 For a defence of a prescriptive view of Schopenhauer's ethics of compassion see Shapshay & Ferrell (2015).

3 By 'mysterianism,' I mean the view that some philosophical problems, in this case, the nature of freedom, are completely intractable given the kinds of cognitive faculties human beings have. The most outspoken proponent of mysterianism with respect to the mind-body problem, free will and other philosophical problems is Colin McGinn (1999, esp. chapter 7). But before him Thomas Nagel argued for mysterianism with respect to the problem of consciousness (Nagel, 1974).

4 Quoted in Kant (1967, 22).

5 In principle, then, one could accurately predict a human being's actions, but in practice—given that one only comes to know a person's individual character, including one's own, through much experience, and that discerning the competing motives in a human being's consciousness is a complex business—this is likely to be difficult.

6 In addition, Schopenhauer offers a quasi-empirical reason for the inborn and unchangeable nature of the empirical character. By analogy with all other kinds of beings in nature, the empirical character of a human being must be like a force. Since forces of nature are original and unchangeable, so too must be the empirical character (FW 56–7). Finally, Schopenhauer offers some pretty weak empirical reasons to bolster his case, writing that "[w]e can obtain confirmation of this truth from daily experience; but the most striking is obtained when after twenty or thirty years we meet an acquaintance again and soon spot in him precisely the same old tricks as before" (FW 50). Also, we never trust anyone who has deceived us in the past and *mutatis mutandis* for those we have previously trusted.

7 I am indebted to Jonathan Head for pressing me on this point.

8 Here it sounds as though the only free choice would be to deny the will-to-life, and thus to act in a manner contrary to one's empirical character, but this is not the case. Schopenhauer does think that rational beings may freely *affirm* will-to-life as well. In such a case one wouldn't be acting "out of character" but rather, *choosing* to act in harmony with one's empirical character. What would be "out of character" in the affirmation case, would be *the free choice* to affirm the will-to-life. From an epistemic point of view, however, it would be very hard to tell if a person freely affirms the will-to-life and much easier to detect cases of denial of the will-to-life.

9 Schopenhauer attests to his full adherence to Kant's distinction between the empirical and intelligible characters, and believes that this distinction grounds the "doctrine of the coexistence of freedom with necessity." Kant's doctrine, he suggests, affords "a thorough knowledge of the compatibility of human freedom with necessity" (FW 73).

10 An earlier version of this paper was co-authored with Alex Neill and published as "Moral and Aesthetic Freedom in Schopenhauer's Metaphysics" (Neill & Shapshay, 2013). The current essay represents a development of my thinking since that time and differs from the previous one by foregrounding the developmental (non-static) nature of Schopenhauer's theory of freedom and highlighting the persistent Kantian influence on it from the early FR to his final writings on the subject. I would like to thank Allen Wood, Alex Neill, Fred Rush, Sarah Adams, Jonathan Head, and Dennis Vanden Auweele for helpful feedback in the development of this essay.

Bibliography

Guyer, P. 'Pleasure and Knowledge in Schopenhauer's Aesthetics,' in D. Jacquette (ed.), *Schopenhauer, Philosophy and the Arts*. Cambridge: Cambridge University Press, 1996, 109–132.

Jacquette, D. *The Philosophy of Schopenhauer*. Acumen, Chesham: Acumen Press, 2005.

Janaway, C. Introduction to Arthur Schopenhauer's *The Two Fundamental Problems of Ethics*, trans. and ed. Christopher Janaway. Cambridge: Cambridge University Press, 2009.

Janaway, C. 'Necessity, Responsibility and Character: Schopenhauer on Freedom of the Will', *Kantian Review* 17, 2012: 431–457.

Kant, I. *Philosophical Correspondence 1759–1799*, ed. Arnulf Zweig. Chicago: University of Chicago Press, 1967.

McGinn, C. *The Mysterious Flame: Conscious Minds in a Material World*. New York: Basic Books, 1999.

Nagel, T. 'What Is It like to Be a Bat?', *Philosophical Review* 83, 1974: 435–450.

Neill, A. & Shapshay, S. 'Moral and Aesthetic Freedom in Schopenhauer's Metaphysics', *International Yearbook of German Idealism/Internationales Jahrbuch des Deutschen Idealismus* 11, May 2013: 245–264.

Shapshay, S. & Ferrell, Z. 'Compassion or Renunciation? That Is the Question of Schopenhauer's Ethics', *Enrahonar: Quaderns de Filosofia* 55, 2015: 51–69. Available at http://revistes.uab.cat/enrahonar/article/view/v55-shapshay-ferrell

White, F.C. *Schopenhauer's Early Fourfold Root: Translation and Commentary*. Aldershot: Avebury Press, 1997.

Zöller, G. Introduction to Arthur Schopenhauer's *Prize Essay on the Freedom of the Will*. Cambridge: Cambridge University Press, 2004.

6 'A Most Beloved Piece of Nonsense'

The Ontological Argument and Metaphysics

Dennis Vanden Auweele[1]

Early in the second chapter of *The Fourfold Root of the Principle of Sufficient Reason* (hereafter, *Fourfold Root*), Schopenhauer concisely argues that the ontological argument for the existence of God is at best "a most beloved piece of nonsense" (FR 10). In his view, the ontological argument confuses the "two foremost meanings of the principle of sufficient reason" and is as such nothing but a "conjurer's trick" pulled on philosophy (FR 10). The ontological argument establishes that the logical definition of a certain concept at the same time includes the cause of its existence. In other words, the existence of the object is included in the predicates that analytically apply to this concept and so, according to Schopenhauer, begs the question by already including the predicate 'existence' in the definition of the subject of predication.

This contribution will mine Schopenhauer's rejection of the ontological argument for its implication for Schopenhauer's later on established metaphysics of will in *The World as Will and Representation*. It will be argued that Schopenhauer's critical reformulation of the relationship between the in-itself (will) and appearances (representation) as the will being the rational ground, but not the cause of representational reality, provides a better perspective so as to understand Schopenhauer's claiming knowledge of the in-itself of reality. Numerous scholars have traditionally pointed out, namely, that Schopenhauer's characterization of the in-itself of reality nervously conflicts with his general epistemological allegiance to Kant's critical limitation of knowledge to the reach of possible experience.[2] These critics have not queried, however, what Schopenhauer understood Kant's transcendental idealism to imply. By investigating *Fourfold Root*, Schopenhauer can be read as arguing that transcendental idealism holds to a strict separation between phenomenal and noumenal reality, and that the venture from the one to the other could not be made by means of way of reasoning in accordance with causality. Schopenhauer's sense of knowledge of the in-itself is then necessarily removed from traditional speculative knowledge of the in-itself and his identification of the in-itself with will is rehabilitated as a consistent argument.[3]

The traditional criticism levelled against Schopenhauer reads that he is some kind of post-Kantian dogmatic metaphysician, but this critique is indebted to a lack of engagement with Schopenhauer's doctoral dissertation where he clearly advocates a novel relationship between representational and noumenal reality. To make these claims, I will delineate Schopenhauer's discomfort with the ontological argument so as to clarify what kind of 'metaphysics' can remain after the destruction of this argument. This will provide the tools to understand how nevertheless knowledge of the will as the in-itself of reality remains possible and how Schopenhauer develops a metaphysics perfectly consistent with, and within the strictures placed upon knowledge by, Kant's transcendental idealism.

The Ontological Argument

The ontological argument might be the most widely discussed issue in the history of philosophy of religion.[4] One of the earliest formulations of the argument appears in St. Anselm of Canterbury's *Proslogion*. After writing his *Monologion* in 1076–1077 on the subject of various classical proofs for the existence of God, Anselm wanted to develop a single argument that could be invariably persuasive. In other words, he wanted to formulate an a priori argument of speculative or natural theology, not an a posteriori argument based upon revealed theology (e.g., the cosmological argument, the argument from revelation, the physico-teleological argument). To Anselm, the existence of God is never really into question, nor is it necessary to guarantee or justify this through logical argumentation; instead, the argument primarily serves so as to render comprehensible the hyperbolic nature of divinity.[5]

Anselm argues that even the fool who denies the existence of God will admit to having at least a concept of God. How could something of which we have no concept be denied? Anselm proposes to define concept of God as "something than which nothing greater is able to be thought" (Anselm, 2013, 23). By initially here separating the cognitive from the empirical reality of God, Anselm grants that anyone will be able to understand the notion of divine perfection without necessarily assuming its existence. A number of authors already take issue with the ontological argument at this initial stage. For instance, Blaise Pascal objects that this step assumes the concept of God to be comprehensible for human beings: "If there is a God, he is infinitely incomprehensible, since, having neither parts nor limits, he has no relation to us: we are, therefore, incapable to know either what he is, or if he is" (Pascal, 2013, 109). More recently, Patrick Masterson objects similarly that we cannot establish at the outset of our investigation that "the idea of God, as the necessarily existing greatest conceivable perfection, is in fact a coherent and positively possible idea rather than a contradictory one" (Masterson, 2013, 37).

Anselm assumes, however, that that which we denote by perfection is in fact a coherent thought. The above objection resonates with Schopenhauer's take on this issue, since he too refuses to ground reality on a rational principle of internal coherence (the principle of sufficient reason). Rational thought loses all legitimacy beyond the realm of representation since the principle of rational thought is a characteristic of the subjective, and not the objective, experience of reality. In Schopenhauer's words, the principle of sufficient reason "is not an eternal truth [. . .] and has merely a relative and conditional validity within appearances alone. As a result, the inner being of the world, the thing in itself, can never be discovered using this as our guide" (WWR1 38). Accordingly, Schopenhauer would agree that we cannot assume that the absolute or the in-itself is rationally comprehensible.

Anselm continues that perfection must necessarily include the predicate 'existence' since if "that than which a greater is not able to be thought is in understanding alone, then the very that than which a greater is not able to be thought is that than which a greater is able to be thought" (Anselm, 2013, 23). Namely, if absolute perfection was only found to be a thought-entity, then a greater perfection could be thought that also includes the predicate 'existence'. As such, a perfect being necessarily also is an existing being. Kant's famous objection to the ontological argument takes issue with this step of the argument by arguing that existence is not a real predicate. In his view, the ontological argument assigns a number of predicates to God provisionally, yet thought itself cannot analytically predicate existence. Accordingly, the ontological argument only establishes that God, if He exists, must exist necessarily. Whether or not such an entity exists does not add in any way to its intelligible content: "Being is obviously not a real predicate, i.e. a concept of something that could add to the concept of a thing. It is merely the positing of a thing or of certain determinations in themselves" (B626/A599). While Schopenhauer usually copies without reserve Kant's objections to transcendental realism and absolute idealism, he interestingly does not rehash Kant's objection to the ontological argument. Instead, he formulates his discomfort with the ontological argument as relating to two different ways of cognition (i.e., 'knowing' and 'becoming').

Schopenhauer on the Ontological Argument

Already in his doctoral dissertation, Schopenhauer expresses serious discomfort with regard to the ontological argument (FR 9–12) and repeats this in his *Critique of the Kantian Philosophy* in the first volume of *The World as Will and Representation* (e.g., WWR1 606) and in the first volume of *Parerga and Paralipomena* (PP1 113–118). In the latter, Schopenhauer notes that while philosophers experienced difficulty in trying to establish the existence of God on the basis of empirical evidence, they turned to a different kind of argument that would "establish God as a necessary being" (PP1 113). Schopenhauer points out, however, that 'necessity' is nothing but a relationship of an effect to a cause on the basis of one of the roots of the principle of sufficient reason. In the case of the ontological argument, it is argued that by taking "the principle of sufficient reason of knowing", one can "[make] the necessity of God's existence a logical one" (PP1 116). Accordingly, God's existence arises throughout this argument "as the result of merely analytical reasoning" (PP1 116).

Schopenhauer, somewhat snidely, takes issue with the mode of operation and remarks that if one includes 'existence' in another predicate such as 'perfection', one cannot fail to find 'existence' to be a necessary predicate of an object to which 'perfection' is predicated. This, however, "in no way demonstrates the justification for asserting the whole concept; rather, it either was completely arbitrarily invented or introduced by the cosmological proof" (PP1 116). In other words, what is being claimed here might be logically correct, but it cannot prove the empirical reality of the concept. In Schopenhauer's view, this is "a sleight of hand [*tour de passe-passe*] that tries to show the logically necessary as the actually necessary" (PP1 118) and the ontological argument is "nothing more than a sophistical and utterly unconvincing play of concepts" (WWR1 606). In his doctoral dissertation, Schopenhauer turns more extensively, and with a different emphasis, to the ontological argument. There, he discusses Descartes's formulation of the ontological argument in the fifth *Meditation*. He believes that this argument depends upon intently misunderstanding and confusing two of the different roots of the principle of sufficient reason, namely the principle of knowing and of becoming.[6]

Schopenhauer believes that philosophers assign to the concept of God the absolute *summum* of predicates (e.g., the 'greatest of greatest, or 'an immensity', or 'sum of perfection'). They do so because this would grant credibility to the argument that God "[would] require no cause in order to exist" (FR 9). In other words, the very conceptual, rational nature of the concept of God would excuse him from needing a cause of existence. A cause is generally understood as the empirical enabling condition of anything, but if something does not seem to belong to the domain of the empirical, then no empirical cause can ever be found to be appropriate. And as such, God becomes either nonexistent or uncaused—philosophers, because of their Christian 'pay-masters', have preferred the latter option. In turn, Schopenhauer emphasizes that the principle of knowing (the concept) and the principle of becoming (the cause) are two different things which may not be jumbled together: the conceptual content of something cannot have any repercussions on its causal determination. Put differently, to understand some concept's rational ground and logical identity does not provide any insight into its causal and empirical identity.

Interestingly, Schopenhauer will on fairly similar grounds (without recognizing this himself) object to Kant's introduction of a thing-in-itself. Schopenhauer, namely, notes that the Kantian doctrine of thing-in-itself is central to transcendental idealism—as erecting a radical difference between in-itself and appearance—but Kant introduced this notion illegitimately, that is, "through an inference from grounded to ground" (WWR1 200).

The operation by which Kant introduced the thing-in-itself thus rests on a similar confusion of 'ground' and 'cause'. He namely understood that intuitions have to be grounded in something in-itself, but forgot how this in-itself cannot be their cause since causal explanations do not apply to this interaction. Schopenhauer inherited this objection from his philosophical mentor, G. E. Schulze who, in his *Aenesidimus*, launched a skeptical attack on Kant's transcendental philosophy by, among others, arguing that Kant had no legitimate grounds to assume a thing-in-itself. Kant grounded the assumption of a thing-in-itself namely on the argument that intuitions need to be caused by something.

Scholars are to date still at odds what exactly is the source of affection in Kant's philosophy.[7] Causality is, according to Schopenhauer and Schulze, only valid with regard to the realm of appearances and can thus not be predicated upon the in-itself. Without espousing Schulze's further skeptical conclusions, Schopenhauer equally objects to using a causal argument to ground the reality of representations. As such, the in-itself is not the cause of reality, but rather its ground: it serves to make sense of representations, but is not the cause of representations. As I will similarly show, Schopenhauer's metaphysics implicates the in-itself (will) only as a grounding thought of reality, but not causally implicated in it. Representational reality is a manifestation of the will, not its consequent.

Schopenhauer's Metaphysics as Something of an Ontological Argument

To establish the necessary reality of God, Descartes commences the third *Meditation* by scanning the various ideas in his cogito to discover an idea of which the objective reality exceeds the potency of the cogito to be its originator. After establishing the absolute certainty of the self-legitimating activity of thinking, he wonders whether he will be able to build a bridge from thought to the external world by means of something unconditioned outside of himself. He does so by locating a second absolute certainty in the existence of God as the causal originator of the idea of perfection which is, according to Descartes at least, present in the I-think. As I will show in this section, Schopenhauer uses a similar methodology to positively determine the in-itself of reality—that is, to scan his consciousness for a kind of awareness that is not conditioned by representational logic (or, that is beyond the principle of sufficient reason).

Schopenhauer's methodology is obviously not completely novel. Johann Gottlieb Fichte similarly appealed to rational intuition to finalize Kant's system of reason, and Friedrich Heinrich Jacobi argued for the self-evident certainty that God exists. These philosophers searched for a way to obtain knowledge about reality beyond possible experience by means of the intimate experience of something that would be certain without the mediator of empirical verification. Where Jacobi found God and Fichte reason, however, Schopenhauer believed that which we are most intimately assured of, without requiring empirical verification, is that our inner essence is will. In *Fourfold Root*, Schopenhauer ridicules Fichte's and Jacobi's argument in a memorable passage:

> The name of reason, however, was assigned to a completely imaginary, or in plain language, a made-up faculty, in which one had something like a little window that opened upon the superlunary, or indeed the supernatural world, a window through which could be received, fully finished and prepared, all the truths that old-fashioned, honest, reflective, and deliberative reason had previously troubled itself with and struggled over in vain for centuries.
>
> (FR 123)

The critical difference between Schopenhauer and his contemporaries is that he does not seek recourse in reason or any special cognitive faculties, but rather looks to our bodily existence and conative awareness of ourselves so as to express a deep truth about reality. Some commentators have found Schopenhauer's own argument as fallacious as the ones he ridicules. For instance, Julian Young rhetorically ponders:

> How could a man who takes such relish in lampooning the idea of 'rational intuition' , of little 'windows' through which Hegelians peer at the Absolute, entertain seriously, even for a moment, the idea of 'subterranean passages' to the noumenal? Why should a tunnel be any better than a window?
>
> (Young, 1987, 29)

Nietzsche will mock the trajectory of idealistic philosophy after Kant on similar grounds, and even blamed Kant himself for putting this into motion: "How are synthetic judgments a priori possible? Kant asked himself,—and what really was his answer? By virtue of a faculty, which is to say: enabled by an ability [*Vermöge eines Vermögens*]" (Nietzsche, 2002, 12). Nietzsche belittles Kant's suggestion by comparing it to Molière's doctor's famous and rather uninformative statement in *Le Malade imaginaire*: "Because there is a dormative virtue in it / whose nature is to put the senses to sleep" (Nietzsche, 2002, 12). Basically, Kant (and his intellectual progeny) argued that humanity's specific abilities were enabled by an 'ability'. The regrettable aftereffect of Kant's argumentation was, according to Nietzsche, that German philosophy took this argumentative trend of Transcendental Philosophy to heart: "The honeymoon of German philosophy had arrived; all the young theologians of the Tübingen seminary ran off into the bushes—they were all looking for 'faculties'" (Nietzsche, 2002, p. 13). Is Schopenhauer then also one of these Tübingen theologians who was vexed by Kant's critical limitation of speculative reason and consequently searched for a different faculty that could provide knowledge of the in-itself? By taking seriously Schopenhauer's objection to the ontological argument, I will show how his identification of the in-itself with will, as a genuine metaphysics, is an argument not only perfectly in tune with transcendental idealism, but also a more legitimate consequence of transcendental idealism.

At the onset of the second book of WWR1, Schopenhauer quotes the German occult alchemist Agrippa von Nettesheim, who claimed the following about alchemy in a letter to his friend and protector Aurelius ab Aquapendente: "It dwells in us, not in the underworld, nor in the heavenly stars: All this is brought to pass by the living spirit in us" (WWR1 112). Agrippa made this statement with respect to the truth-claims and magical properties of alchemy, namely that it is to be understood as the workings of an inner spirit, not an exterior demon or angel. Similarly, Schopenhauer will advocate that the meaning of outer reality (the 'in-itself') is to be found within the human agent, not beyond or below it. In the first edition of WWR1, Schopenhauer used a line from Goethe's Faust as the epitaph to the second book of WWR1: "That I may discover what holds the world's innermost core together, see all its effective power and seeds, and no longer mess around with words" (WWR1 p. 573). What is of particular interest about these quotations is that both refer to a kind of heretical and forbidden knowledge, whether through alchemy (Agrippa) or through a deal with the devil (Faust). The forbidden nature of this knowledge derives from its violation of Kant's critical limitation of knowledge to the reach of possible experience. Schopenhauer believes that one can obtain such knowledge beyond sensory experience and the principle of sufficient reason, but that this bit of knowledge is not to be found outside of the human subject or in some rational faculty, but in the deepest a-rational core of that agent.

Schopenhauer seems to establish as a premise that the hidden essence of reality into which he inquires is of a totally different (*toto genere*) nature than the representational world. As such, he believes that the tools to inquire into this hidden essence of representations must also be very different from the appropriate tools to understand representational reality. In other words, our reasoning concerning noumenal reality may not utilize the principle of sufficient reason, but must seek refuge in a different form of awareness. Such awareness may be a type of cognition, but cannot be rational. Such cognition is available to us, since we are not "a pure subject of cognition (a winged cherub's head without a body)", but we are "rooted in this world" (WWR1 118). What Schopenhauer means by this is that human agents have a direct (his word is 'immediate') link to reality in-itself since we inhabit a body that is the immediate expression of the essence of reality—not just a projection of our subjective consciousness. Our awareness of our body is, namely, of a very different nature than our awareness of other extended objects.

In the first book of WWR1, Schopenhauer already assigned a specific function to the body as the necessary mediator of any representational knowledge since it is the body's receptivity to stimuli that allows for representations to be formed. Next to this mediating function for representational knowledge (where our body is just another body among bodies), the body is also given to us in an altogether different capacity, namely "as something immediately familiar to everyone, something designated by the word will" (WWR1 199). As such, Schopenhauer argues that our body is known to us in a non-rational capacity or, as he puts it, as an 'immediate object' of which we do not have to form a representation for it to be cognized. Schopenhauer's identification of the body with 'will' is prone to misunderstanding and many scholars suggest that Schopenhauer would have been better of using a term like 'energy'.[8] Nevertheless, Schopenhauer emphasizes that it is not a matter of indifference which name is used to designate the inner, immediate familiar essence of the body: "I will be misunderstood by anyone who thinks it is ultimately a matter of indifference whether the word will or some other word is used to designate the essence in itself of all appearance" (WWR1 132). This is so because Schopenhauer believes that we know our inner essence not as something inferred abstractly, but as something "of which we have immediate cognition" (WWR1 133). Since we are not merely assigning a name to an assumed reality, the word 'will' must denote—and in Schopenhauer's view does denote—the exact extension of what is felt as the inner essence of reality.

One way to understand Schopenhauer's argument here is to liken it to Descartes's a posteriori version of the ontological argument. Namely, after having found that a certain idea appears not a home in typical human consciousness as such, Descartes proceeded by assigning a broader reality to that idea beyond the scope of personal consciousness. Descartes established the absolutely necessary and transcendent existence of God as a result of the consideration that the idea of God could not be generated by the cogito, but must derive from a source at least as real as this idea. Similarly, Schopenhauer argues that our nonrational cognitive awareness of our body is not something mediated by representational cognition that is dependent upon the principle of sufficient reason. It would stand to reason, then, that subjective cognition is not the originator of, or even implicated at all, in this type of cognitive awareness. There is then a bit of knowledge about the human being's inner essence that is not dependent upon the principle of sufficient reason. But Schopenhauer does not stop at this conclusion! Like Descartes, Schopenhauer will proceed by taking his own familiarity with his own will and assign to it "a broader scope than it has had before" (WWR1 132)—much as Descartes assigned a non-subjective or non-idealist relevance to the notion of infinity. Like Descartes argued that something within self-consciousness pointed toward something outside that consciousness, Schopenhauer believes he can make a kind of 'naturalistic assumption' that "other objects are like the body" (WWR1 124) or that "the microcosm is equivalent to the macrocosm" (WWR2 676). In other words, Schopenhauer believes that he is justified in extending his own immediate familiarity to encompass all of reality. Is he then not at risk of turning an idiosyncratic self-awareness into a just as idiosyncratic metaphysics? Is this not a very unjustified and perhaps even pernicious form of psychologism to which Schopenhauer remained happily oblivious? In other words, is Schopenhauer merely using a fairly implausible form of analogical reasoning to establish that other entities are analogous to myself?[9]

To understand Schopenhauer's assumption here, it might be helpful to refer to the influence Goethe had on his philosophical formation. Already in his early notebook fragments, Schopenhauer regrets the speculative agnosticism of Kant and attributes to none other than Goethe, who briefly served as his mentor, the salvific function of redeeming him from that metaphysical ignorance:

> If Goethe had not been sent into the world simultaneously with Kant in order to counterbalance him, so to speak, in the spirit of the age, the latter would have haunted like a nightmare many an aspiring mind and would have oppressed it under great affliction . But now the two have an infinitely wholesome effect from opposite directions and will possibly raise the German spirit to a height surpassing even that of antiquity. (MR, I, 13)

Schopenhauer believes Kant's epistemological humility to be undeserved since the human agent has a unique gateway beyond experience, namely through the bodily awareness of ourselves as will. While Goethe was not a Romantic, he did share the Romantic passion for a nonrational approach to reality mainly built upon desire or *eros* (*Sturm und Drang*). Schopenhauer did take Goethe's hint seriously and tries to substantiate his mentor's conviction that all of reality is desire—much like he tried to consolidate Goethe's theory of colors in his essay *On Vision and Colors*. Does this change anything to the fact that Schopenhauer seems to make an idiosyncratic leap of judgment? How can he extend his own immediate familiarity with his own bodily essence as will to encompass the whole of reality?

What is unique about Schopenhauer's position is that he does not exactly 'argue' for this sense of naturalism but rather 'assumes' this to be the case. The paragraph in which he establishes this is so central that it merits to be quoted in full:

> The knowing individual must choose between two assumptions: on the one hand, he could assume that the distinctive feature of this one representation [i.e. the human body] is just that it is the only one he knows in this double way [i.e. as will and representation], that only this *one* object in intuition is simultaneously accessible via two avenues of insight, and that this is not due to any difference between this one object and all the others, but rather is due to a difference between the relationship his cognition has to this one object and the relation it has

to all other objects. Alternatively, the cognizing individual could assume that this one object is essentially different from all other objects, that it is unique among objects in being simultaneously will and representation, that all other representations are mere representations, i.e. mere phantoms, and therefore, that his body is the only real individual in the world, i.e. the only appearance of the will, and the only immediate object of the subject.

(WWR1 123–124)

To entertain the second possible assumption would lead to either skepticism or solipsism. To Schopenhauer, however, solipsism or 'theoretical egoism' is never a real philosophical position but is used "for show. As a genuine conviction it can only be found in a madhouse: accordingly, it should be treated with medication, not refutation" (WWR1 124). This position does on a theoretical level what egoism does on a practical or moral level (i.e., it elevates the world of the particular subject over the rest of reality). Where Schopenhauer argues that practical egoism bars the possibility of meta-physical insight on a practical level, theoretical egoism as an assumption impedes theoretical insight into the inner essence of reality. Accordingly, Schopenhauer does not overtly argue for his sense of naturalism but finds this the more plausible assumption to make given the two abovementioned options. To then provide some kind of argumentation for his position would mean that the assumption requires argumentation and would then ironically render it implausible or at least problematic. In this vein, Schopenhauer establishes well before Darwin the deep inner similarities between human and animal life, as well as the basic similar make-up of organic and inorganic matter. What buoys this assumption is the immediate familiarity the particular subject has to his or her inner essence.

Metaphysics and *Fourfold Root*

How have these considerations put to rest the traditional worry that Schopenhauer erects a dogmatic metaphysics after swearing fealty to transcendental idealism? Schopenhauer's criticism of what he calls 'dogmatic' philosophy revolves around a twofold misunderstanding this makes with regard to the principle of sufficient reason: on the one hand, philosophers have assumed this principle to be valid beyond representational reality, and on the other hand, they have made the move from representational reality toward noumenal reality by means of a conflation of different roots of the principle of sufficient reason (most often, they have confused the principle of 'becoming' and of 'being'). The necessary conclusion of Kant's transcendental idealism was, at least according to Schopenhauer, that the in-itself is totally different from representational reality and knowledge of the in-itself cannot be gained via representational logic. Ironically, Schopenhauer suggests that ultimately even Kant fell prey to the latter mistake. Schopenhauer's metaphysics avoids both pitfalls and because of that is in tune with transcendental idealism.

The former issue is the most well-known aspect of Schopenhauer's metaphysics: since the principle of sufficient reason is a subjective condition of representational experience, it cannot be postulated to belong to objective reality. Schopenhauer even considers the radical separation of the phenomenal from the noumenal the single most important event to have occurred in Modern philosophy. Schopenhauer's philosophy thus follows Kant's third way which he laid out between idealism and realism: there is an objective world independent from the subject (realism), but rational knowledge is always subjective and the objective world remains inaccessible (idealism). His understanding of the separation of the ideal from the real takes on very radical proportions: "The real side must be something *toto genere* different from the world as representation, namely, that which things are in themselves; and it is this complete diversity of the ideal and the real that Kant has most thoroughly demonstrated" (WWR2 216).

Schopenhauer's most pressing adversary on this account is any form of transcendental realism which holds that the principles of cognition (such as time, space, causality, and motivation) are determinations of the objective world. In the second volume of *The World as Will and Representation*, Schopenhauer suggests a number of arguments to disarm transcendental realism.[10] He does so by primarily showing how human agents naturally relate in a subjective manner to reality in that they are not interested in truth per se but in absorbing the kind of relevant information that would suit their designs. Whether this really establishes that the in-itself must be *toto genere* different from representational reality remains questionable: would a close correlation between a subjective and objective perspective on reality not be far more helpful to suit the need of the individuals? If our subjective information of the world was radically different from objective information, would this not dramatically impede our survival? To understand properly Schopenhauer's radical separation of the subjective from the objective perspective, we have to turn to the second issue involved in his analysis of the fourfold root of the principle of sufficient reason.

Not only is the principle of sufficient reason only valid from representational reality, this principle cannot be used uncritically as a 'springboard' to move from representational reality toward noumenal reality. Since there is no pure experience of the in-itself, it can never be the subject of the root of 'becoming' of the principle of sufficient reason. Only by means of the principle of 'knowing' (i.e., the principle that establishes the grounds of certain objects) can any kind of inference be made beyond representational reality. Ironically, the principle of knowing will then infer to a necessary ground of representational reality in something that is without any kind of rationality. What Schopenhauer has thus noticed is that rationality cannot have its ground in itself but must be a manifestation of something that is not just a-rational, but pre-rational.

Thinking through the consequences of Schopenhauer's conception of the metaphysical will as the ground of representational reality and not its cause can be helpful to clarify this further. Insofar as something is causally implicated in the genesis of an object, there arises a certain tendency to homogenize the qualitative nature of cause and object. For instance, if I have a general concept of a chair, the effective causal process I undertake to generate that chair will necessarily attempt to externalize that concept. The concept of the chair is in such a way causally implicated in the genesis of the chair I would produce. Therefore any metaphysical system that allows conceptual rationality to be causally implicated in objective reality does necessarily establish some sense of continuity between the concept (cause) and the object (effect). Schopenhauer has dismantled this way of thinking about the relationship between the in-itself and the representation which renders impossible any sort of continuity between these two. He has done this by strenuously insisting upon the difference between 'ground' and 'cause', the confusion of which he calls, anticipating Heidegger, the "onto-theological [*ontotheologischen*] principle" (FR 14). The in-itself then only is the necessary ground of and necessary other to representation as that which explains the occurrence of representation. Schopenhauer then turns out to be more Neo-Platonic than Platonic since for Plato the ideas were not only the logical ground of objects, but also their cause (objects are 'shadows' of the ideas). In Neo-Platonism, objects have their ground in the 'Nous' (intellect) and emanate from this, but do not entertain a direct causal link to the 'Nous'.

Conclusion

Schopenhauer refutes the ontological argument on the basis that, on the one hand, it begs the question in including the concluding predicate (existence) in the mediating predicate (perfection) and, on the other hand, it conflates two roots of the principle of sufficient reason ('becoming' and 'knowing'). He believes that there is no legitimate way to establish the causal reality of an entity simply by analyzing its concept. What is then interesting is that Schopenhauer walks a similar path in establishing his metaphysics of will. He is namely intimately aware of the will being his own inner essence and feels justified in assuming that this is similarly so for the rest of reality. Accordingly, Schopenhauer has a reverse ontological argument that establishes an absolute (the will) as the supreme principle of reality because the inner essence of my own self is identical to the inner essence of the rest of reality. His thought-pattern in establishing this metaphysics takes profoundly serious the implication that conceptual logic (the principle of sufficient reason) does not ground reality but has its ground in something other than conceptual logic. And since any causal connection between the ground and the representation is excluded, there cannot be any similarity between these. Schopenhauer's metaphysics is then perfectly in tune with the most important aspects of transcendental idealism.

Notes

1 I would like to express my gratitude toward the participants of the conference *Schopenhauer's Fourfold Root: 200 Years On* for their questions and comments to an earlier version of this paper. Special thanks go to Jonathan Head for the extensive discussion of the topic of this paper.
2 A few examples of this traditional assumption: Copleston (1947, 64–65), Gardiner (1963, 49–66), Hamlyn (1980, 83–94), Magee (1983, 125–136) and Janaway (1989, 192–193).
3 As such, this essay provides a new vantage point to augment the arguments of a number of recent Schopenhauer-scholars that make similar claims: Young (1987, 27–35), Neeley (2003, 1–52), Shapshay (2008, 211–229), and Gardner (2012, 375–401).
4 For a concise overview of the historical reception of the ontological argument: Nagasawa (2011, 1–45).
5 Many interpreters would claim that Anselm's argument is circular since his meditation on the existence of God comes in the form of a prayer in which Anselm begs insight from God. Alternatively, I would suggest that Anselm in fact does not 'prove' the existence of God as one would prove a mathematical proposition, but rather calls for reason to assist his faith in rendering comprehensible something of which he is intimately assured—*fides quarens intellectum*. Cf. Desmond (2008, 143–144).
6 Interestingly, Schopenhauer only included the reproach 'intently' in the second edition of the *Fourfold Root*. In the first edition, Schopenhauer remains rather appreciative of Descartes (FR 10: editor note 20).
7 For an overview: De Boer (2014, 221–260).
8 See: Magee (1983, 119 ff.), Atwell (1995, 26), Young (2005, 53 ff.) and Wicks (2008, 53 ff.).
9 For this objection: Atwell (1995, 94 ff.).
10 For a full overview of these arguments: McDermid (2012, 73–79).

Bibliography

Atwell, J. *Schopenhauer on the Character of the World: The Metaphysics of Will.* Berkeley: University of California Press, 1995.
Copleston, F. *Arthur Schopenhauer: Philosopher of Pessimism.* London: Oates and Washbourne, 1947.
De Boer, K. 'Kant's Multi-Layered Conception of Things in Themselves, Transcendental Objects, and Monads', *Kant-Studien* 105, 2014: 221–260.
Desmond, W. *God and the Between.* Oxford: Blackwell Publishing, 2008.
Gardiner, P. *Schopenhauer.* Harmondsworth: Penguin Publishing, 1963.
Gardner, S. 'Schopenhauer's Contraction of Reason: Clarifying Kant and Undoing German Idealism', *The Kantian Review* 17, 2012: 375–401.
Hamlyn, D. *Schopenhauer.* London: Routledge, 1980.
Janaway, C. *Self and World in Schopenhauer's Philosophy.* Oxford: Clarendon Press, 1989.
Magee, B. *The Philosophy of Arthur Schopenhauer.* Oxford: Clarendon Press, 1983.
Masterson, P. *Approaching God: Between Phenomenology and Theology.* London: Bloomsbury, 2013.
McDermid, D. 'Schopenhauer and Transcendental Idealism', in B. Vandenabeele (ed.), *A Companion to Schopenhauer.* Oxford: Wiley-Blackwell, 2012, 70–88.
Nagasawa, Y. *The Existence of God: A Philosophical Introduction.* London: Routledge, 2011.

Neeley, G.S. *Schopenhauer: A Consistent Reading*. New York: Edwin Mellen Press, 2003.

Nietzsche, F. *Beyond Good and Evil*, ed. and trans. R. Horstmann and J. Norman. Cambridge: Cambridge University Press, 2002.

Pascal, P. *Thoughts*. Cambridge: Cambridge University Press, 2013.

Shapshay, S. 'Poetic Intuition and the Bounds of Sense: Metaphor and Metonymy in Schopenhauer's Philosophy', *European Journal of Philosophy* 16, 2008: 211–229.

St. Anselm of Canterbury. *Proslogion*, trans. with Introduction and Notes by Matthew Walz. South Bend, IN: St. Augustine Press, 2013.

Wicks, R. *Schopenhauer*. Oxford: Blackwell Publishing, 2008.

Young, J. *Willing and Unwilling: A Study in the Philosophy of Arthur Schopenhauer*. Boston: Martinus Nijhoff Publishers, 1987.

Young, J. *Schopenhauer*. London: Routledge Publishing, 2005.

Part III

Consciousness and Sensation in *Fourfold Root*

7 Who Gets the Best of the Winged Cherub?

Reid and Schopenhauer Confront Early Modern Angelism

Graham McAleer

In *The World as Will and Representation*, Schopenhauer makes an astute observation. In 1818, he seeks a course correction. Revisiting the development of modern philosophy from Descartes to Berkeley and up to Kant, Schopenhauer identifies, and wants to block, the prevailing idea that the knowing subject is "a winged cherub's head without a body" (WWR1 118). Schopenhauer, is, I think, correct: angelism is a fair summation of the philosophical doctrine wrought by the introduction of Descartes's idealism.

Modern idealism has many medieval tributaries. Aquinas's account of angelic time consciousness is one, and another source is the scholastic debate about disembodied sensation. University authorities at Paris in the 1270s twice condemned the proposition: the disembodied souls of the damned do not feel physical fire.[1] Giles of Rome and Peter John Olivi, to name only two, agreed with the university leadership that sensations do not require movements of physical organs.[2] A sensation is a mental seizing of an object-content, they argued: the soul is a total cause of perception, with the sensed object having no more than an occasionalist standing.

Descartes, Malebranche, Berkeley, Hume, and Thomas Reid all think disembodied sensation possible, and some even think it normative. Reid found Berkeley's idealism not easily answerable. "Nor can any man shew, by any good argument" writes Reid, "that all our sensations might not have been as they are, though no body, nor quality of body, had ever existed."[3] In Berkeley, angelism is full-blown: the only things that exist are minds and mental events.[4] For him, flesh, objects, the world, are all interconnections amongst ideas. Berkeley's arguments are ingenious, but Descartes is in the background and the scholastic debate haunts his opening meditations:

> I will imagine that the sky, air, earth, colours, shapes, sounds and everything external to me are nothing more than the creatures of dreams by means of which an evil spirit entraps my credulity. I shall imagine myself as if I had no hands, no eyes, no flesh, no blood, no senses at all, but as if my belief in all these things were false.[5]

Modern idealism owes much to its medieval parent.

Though Schopenhauer rejects the idea of the knowing subject as a 'winged cherub's head without a body', his whole philosophy has an uncanny similarity to this scholastic debate. Consider: in Olivi's account, God surrounds the damned with flames. Unable to halt the experience of the flames, the emotion of hatred (*affectio detestativa*) floods the soul and triggers a forlorn effort on the part of the damned to be rid of the fire. The knowing subject is similarly afflicted in Schopenhauer. The will surges in consciousness, and its manifestations afflict the person who, lacerated by the torments of the will, seeks refuge in aesthetic experience and final escape in self-annihilation. The effort is futile, for though the self might slip away, its very dissolution is fodder for the will's ever-renewing mortification. The self will be rebuilt, albeit under different conditions of identity, and once more afflicted by the will it perversely fed in its own escape.

Reid and Schopenhauer are great admirers of Bishop Berkeley. Until about thirty years old, Reid was a convinced Berkeleyian. The first page of WWR1 draws to a close with Schopenhauer praising Berkeley's "immortal service to philosophy." Praise is due, thinks Schopenhauer, for Berkeley brings to utter clarity an idea in Descartes: "the world is my representation" (WWR1 3). Nonetheless, both Schopenhauer and Reid recoil from Berkeley's angelism. In a frame set by Berkeley, each offers a refined realism (WWR1 120 & 128; cf. WWR2 430) and a fresh account of our embodiment. Schopenhauer also admired Reid yet described his own account as the inverse of Reid's (WWR2 24).[6] Their differences will become clear, but against Berkeley, Schopenhauer argues that an attentive phenomenology of will shows that experience is always a modification of the body.[7] For his part, Reid argues that Berkeley has missed the crucial place of the body in language and thus experience. Adjudicating between these modified realisms, I will argue that on the substantive issue—how to counter angelism with an adequate account of the role of the body in experience—it is Reid who gets the better of the winged cherub.

The hint of trouble in Schopenhauer's own account comes with the very opening of WWR1:

> 'The world is my representation':—this holds true for every living, cognitive being, although only a human being can bring it to abstract, reflective consciousness: and if he actually does so he has become philosophically sound. It immediately becomes clear and certain to him that he is not acquainted with either the sun or the earth, but rather only with an eye that sees a sun, with a hand that feels an earth.
>
> (WWR1 3)

So begins the philosophy book I most enjoy reading, but it is an odd start. Can the third part be true? Is it true I do not know the sun but 'only an eye that sees the sun'? Schopenhauer thinks it is true because, for him, a sensation is the striving of will embodied and phenomenologically present

(WWR1 128 and 181). However, in his desire to overcome Berkeley's angelism, has he oddly overstated the role of the body and therewith misconstrued sensation? In the identification of body and experience,[8] has he in fact folded the body back into the mind?[9] Has he surreptitiously over-mentalized sensation and slipped back into an ironclad idealism?

A comparison of Schopenhauer with Reid nimbly helps us decide these questions. Conceptually, at least three things stand out in a Reidian challenge to Schopenhauer: the role of language in the constitution of sensation; whether sensations are impoverished or content-laden; and the rival motifs of achievement and obedience in their respective treatments of intuition. In discussing these three points, my hope is to reveal certain philosophical commitments implicit in Schopenhauer's account of sensation and to assess whether he escapes angelism.

The Role of Language in Sensation

In the *Meditations,* Descartes complains that whilst trying to think silently about sensation, his mind leaps to the customary use of language:

> For although I think about these things to myself, silently and without speaking, I am still restricted to these words and am almost deceived by ordinary language. For we say that we see the wax itself if it is present, not that we judge that it is there from its colour and shape. From this way of talking I might conclude immediately that the wax is therefore known by how the eye sees and not by an inspection of the mind alone.[10]

Descartes's worry that language obscures perception is Berkeley's point of attack. Developing the medieval British tradition of nominalism in a highly original way, Berkeley argues that experience and language are entwined. In particular, he argues that the identity of any object given to us in sensation is secured by a name. He writes:

> men combine together several ideas, apprehended by divers senses, or by the same sense at different times, or in different circumstances but observed however to have some connexion in Nature, either with respect to co-existence or succession; all which they refer to one name, and consider as one thing.[11]

Reid tells us that for a good while he was a convinced Berkeleyian. He credits Berkeley with an insight that structured all his subsequent thinking: "It is therefore a just and important observation of the Bishop of Cloyne, That the visible appearance of objects is a kind of language used by nature, to inform us of their distance, magnitude, and figure" (IE 64).

Berkeley thinks that objects, space, and time are structures of language, and though Reid is smitten with Berkeley's "language of nature" thesis, he deftly turns it away from idealism by defending the claim that perceptions are signs witnessing to extra-mental objects (IE 43–44). Schopenhauer hints at the Berkeleyian theme when speaking of science as only able to stand before nature as before "hieroglyphics we do not comprehend" (WWR1 115) but nonetheless lodges language firmly in rationality. He leaves this British strain of reflection on sensation and "the language of nature" fallow, and it hampers his effort to develop a robust but sober account of embodiment.

Reid argues that language is impossible without an intuitive grasp of the body: language is, foundationally, movement of the body.[12] The body, an organized, complex object moving in time and spread out in space, is inseparable from human experience and belief. National and technical languages build upon natural language. Reid: "The elements of this natural language, or the signs that are naturally expressive of our thoughts, may, I think, be reduced to these three kinds: modulations of the voice, gestures, and features" (IE 33). If, as Berkeley argues, language is necessary to stabilize sensations and thus constitutive of the perception of objects, then, adds Reid, perception also relies on a prior exposure to a complex object cohering in space and time, the body: for language ultimately sits atop a gestural body. This argument—that experience of the body is inherently linguistic—is also powerful against Schopenhauer.

Despite his high regard for Berkeley and Reid, Schopenhauer does not pursue this line of inquiry into language (WWR2 160). Does Schopenhauer's mentalized account of language damage his efforts against the winged cherub?

The heart of Schopenhauer's account of sensation is found in Section 21 of *Fourfold Root*. He refers to this section frequently in both volumes of WWR. He is far closer to Descartes, minimizing the role of language and emphasizing the mental contribution to perception. He does mention the body, of course: it is the immediate object of our empirical consciousness. A great passage from *Fourfold Root* captures wonderfully the grasping hand of the will spoken of in WWR1. He writes: "Ultimately the perceptions of sight refer to touch; indeed, vision is to be considered an imperfect, but extensive touch that makes use of light rays as long feelers" (FR 55). The body here is akin to a proboscis relaying data and not yet gestural.

This is confirmed both by Schopenhauer's repeated formulations of sensations as data and his firmly lodging language in the faculty of reason. Intuitive perception is a function of the understanding and is distinct from conceptual reason in Schopenhauer (WWR1 46–47): and crucially, language belongs squarely with the latter. Speech, "a highly perfected telegraph that communicates arbitrary signs" (WWR1 47), is the first product of reason, he says, and "reason accomplishes its greatest feats [the compacts of civilization] only by means of language" (WWR1 44). An exchange of concepts, language is "reason [speaking] to reason" (WWR1 47). Hearing is called "the sense of reason," he says, because it is the medium of language (FR

55). By contrast, Reid thinks "the compacts of civilization" expressive of original and inescapable prior unions and agreements (IE 32).

In Schopenhauer, the empirical body always appears under the principle of sufficient reason and therefore, as organized, but he does not think the body is intrinsically linguistic. Experience is not the language of nature made visible in the gestural body. The winged cherub bests Schopenhauer: well in the grip of Cartesian intellectualism, he leaves fallow Reid's bodily theory of signs.

Whether Sensations Are Impoverished or Content-Laden

Our own body is "the starting-point for each of us in the perception of the world" (WWR1 22) and Schopenhauer puts his point nicely, "it is true that space is only in my head; but empirically my head is in space" (WWR2 22). And then there is the following superb image:

> Therefore the 'outside us' to which we refer objects on the occasion of the sensation of sight, itself resides inside our head, for there is its whole scene of action; much the same as in the theatre we see mountains, forest, and sea, yet everything remains within the house.
>
> (WWR2 26)

Far from an idealist, Reid is a metaphysical realist, and instead of the theatre he relies on the image of the courtroom.[13] Reid believes sensations a *witness* to discrete bodies in space and time. Realism, says Schopenhauer, "overlooks the fact that the object no longer remains object apart from its reference to the subject, and that, if one takes this away or abstracts from it, all objective existence is also immediately nullified" (FR 37). Reid would think Schopenhauer has overlooked the possibility that just as the will is double in aspect so is representation: sensations give testimony of things we indeed never directly experience. He writes:

> In the testimony of nature given by the senses, as well as in human testimony given by language, things are signified to us by signs: and in one as well as the other, the mind, either by original principles or by custom, passes from the sign to the conception and belief of the things signified.
>
> (IE 90)

Just as in a court of law, the witness recounts events that the jury did not see, and never can see, so sensations recount events that consciousness has no direct relationship to, nor ever can. This does not stop experience being reportage.

Schopenhauer relies significantly on optics and physiology. There is, he tells us, a "wide gulf" between sensation and perception and "the law of causality alone [can bridge across] this gulf" (WWR2 208). Sensations, he believes, are "much too uniform and lacking in data" (FR 57) to account for our perception. We never have such a thing as a "mere sensation" so how does Schopenhauer know such raw, impoverished things exist? About a very eighteenth-century ailment, his gout, Reid says:

> I have not only a notion of pain, but a belief of its existence, and a belief of some disorder in my toe which occasions it; and this belief is not produced by comparing ideas, and perceiving their agreements and disagreements: it is included in the very nature of the sensation.
>
> (IE 118)

To make his point, Schopenhauer turns to certain puzzles in optics. Struck by the fact that in vision twin 'images' lodge one in each eye and yet we see but one object, he concludes: "That which is doubly felt through the sense is only singly perceived intuitively" (FR 59). Further, in vision the impression of the object is first on the retina reversed and upside down. The understanding uses its causal law to move backward from the sensation "whereby the cause presents itself upright, externally, as an object in space" (FR 59). Sensation, therefore, is intellectual and not simply sensuous.

Optics shows, therefore, sensation is "nothing more than a local, specific feeling," "a process within the organism itself . . . confined to the region beneath the skin," "heightened by the confluence of nerve-endings" (FR 53). Along similar lines, in the second volume of the WWR he gives us an anatomical argument:

> How small the share of the senses is in perception compared with that of the intellect is proved also by comparing the nerve-apparatus for receiving impressions with that for elaborating them. For the mass of the nerves of sensation of all the sense-organs is very small compared with the mass of the brain.
>
> (WWR2 23–24)

Employing the law of causality and the forms of space and time, "the understanding first creates and produces this objective world" (FR 52). This performative character of the understanding is not learnt. "Physiologically, it is a function of the brain, which learns this function from experience no more than the stomach to digest or the liver to secrete bile" (FR 57).

Reid would wonder, though, whether Schopenhauer does not in fact back into Berkeley's and his idea of an original and customary language of nature. He might probe Schopenhauer on whether he can adequately distinguish the principle of sufficient reason from belief. Beliefs are linguistic, and Schopenhauer's problem is that although he wants to minimize the content of sensation, he also acknowledges that sight, for example, "provides the understanding with great deal of finely determined data" (FR 55) and touch "provides the data for cognition of size, shape, hardness, softness, dryness, moisture, smoothness, temperature, and so on" (FR 56). Schopenhauer also grants that "muscular power" "aids" the understanding with data about the weight, solidity, toughness or brittleness of bodies.[14] It is hard to see why all this information is not best thought of as a set of beliefs. More importantly, Schopenhauer appears to concede something of Reid's position.[15] Though insisting on the work of the understanding for intuitive perception, he acknowledges the detailed data of touch as a consequence of "the shape and movement of the arms, hands, and fingers *from the position of which* the understanding takes away the data for spatial construction of bodies . . . all with minimal possibility for deception" (FR 56; emphasis added). Either this is a slip or Schopenhauer grants that, to a not insignificant degree, the body's organization prompts an already spatially organized, content-laden field of sensation.

How laden with belief is sensation? Reid points to his gout to answer 'heavily laden' but for the contrary claim, Schopenhauer points to the seventeenth-century Cambridge don, Saunderson: a man born blind who nonetheless came to have a magnificent understanding of space (FR 57). Even more startling is the case of Eva Lauk who, Schopenhauer tells us, born with no legs or arms, gained intuitive perception of the external world by means of sight alone, and as fast as other able-bodied child (FR 57). These cases prove, he thinks, that "sensation merely furnishes the opportunity" to have perception but "time, space, and causality do not come to us from the outside, neither through vision, nor through touch, but have an internal origin, and thus not an empirical, but an intellectual origin" (FR 57).

Again, it is not that Reid utterly disagrees with what Schopenhauer expresses here but whereas Schopenhauer downgrades sensation, Reid thinks of sensation as having a cognitive alacrity, so to say. A sensation "serves only as a sign to introduce to the mind something else [. . .] overlooking the appearance, we immediately conceive the real figure" (IE 63). Relatively little sensation is needed before triggering our 'immediate' conceptions of the world about us. Schopenhauer's example of Eva Lauk recalls Reid's wonderful image of a child staring at and manipulating an object, coming at the object from all different angels and vantages (IE 103). Poor Eva will have come at the world with a barrage of senses, including the sense of touch from other parts of her body.

What of those cases of blind people who later gain their sight? These are sad cases. Cases are rare, and seldom do the newly sighted prosper. These patients come to see, but what they see has no coherence. Even in the Bible, when Jesus heals the blind man, the man reports, 'I see men as trees, walking'. The late British Neurologist, Oliver Sacks, believed the profound difficulties encountered may be because the brain is being asked to reverse a lifetime of adapting and specializing to compensate.[16] Patients pick up visual details but struggle to form a complex perception. Can their brains simply not apply the law of causality to vision? A strange detail repeated in cases across the centuries: patients observed holding a cat, looking intently at an ear, and then at a paw, and touching each part gently. They know the cat, the cat coheres to touch, but not in vision.[17]

For Schopenhauer, one would expect the principle of sufficient reason to kick in and bring coherence to sight. Perhaps Schopenhauer would rely on Sack's observation. For Reid, if relatively little sensation is needed to trigger our conceptions of the world, one would again expect coherent experience. For an explanation, he might turn to some curious facts: patients newly sighted report finding people's bodies ugly, the stains and blemishes on skin, disgusting.[18] They avoid looking at faces and even a year after the operation cannot recognize individual faces or facial expressions.[19] Is natural language scrambled for these patients? Can they not see because there is a language deficit?

Howsoever these cases should be adjudicated, Reid contends that there is nothing waiting for the intellect works up or "recasts" (*umarbeitet*) as Schopenhauer claims (FR 54).[20] Reid would push Schopenhauer to either admit to his use of the bodily theory of signs or concede his intellectualism and angelism.

The Motif of Work

Celebrating Kant's greatness, Schopenhauer nonetheless declares meaningless Kant's claim that empirical reality "is given to us" (WWR1 509–511). Schopenhauer relies extensively on the motif of work in his account of sensation in *Fourfold Root* but does not thematize it there, or in WWR. His theory of sensation shows Cartesian pedigree. Prior to the work of the mind, sensations are rudimentary things: not as bleak as Descartes's *res extensa* perhaps but still not the content-rich perceptions that populate our experience. The mind must first mentalize the "raw material" of sensation: work, for Schopenhauer, is not the *artes mechanicae* that craft human objects from the integrity and resistance encountered in the world. Time and again, Schopenhauer's thought is drawn from the pole of the world to that of the mind, weakening his effort to develop a modified realism. Wanting to balance idealism with a metaphysics of the will, Schopenhauer seemingly needs a porous embodiment that responds to a textured nature. Yet there is something crystalline about the knowing subject in Schopenhauer, as though, despite his own efforts, the sovereign *cogito* has a grip on his thought.

The idea of work pervades Schopenhauer's account of sensation. "But now I will first more precisely demonstrate," says Schopenhauer, "the great gulf between sensation and intuition as I explain *how raw is the stuff* from which this beautiful work proceeds" (FR 54; emphasis added). Schopenhauer's distinction is quite classical. About the wax, Descartes tells us: "But what should be noticed is that perceiving it is not a case of seeing, touching or imagining, nor was it ever such although it seemed that way earlier, but it is an inspection of the mind alone"[21] The medievals made a distinction within a sensation between the *immutatio naturalis* and the *immutatio intentionalis*, that is, between the organic aspect of the sensation and the mental operation on the organic material, which is said to "make" (*facit*) the perception.[22]

For Schopenhauer, intuitional consciousness has a certain complexity: rudimentary sense data suffers "a powerful transformation" (FR 53) by the labour of the understanding, working up sense material by application of the principle of sufficient reason: "For, there is a very great disparity between mere sensation in the hand and a representation of causality, materiality, and movement in space mediated through time!" (FR 57) Why does he not favour Reid's simpler account (IE 118)? There, sensations are natural signs, akin to a language, immediately prompting beliefs about the properties of external objects (IE 41), including spatial location (IE 88). For brutes, idiots, children, as well as those of us of "common understanding," "the language of Nature is the universal study" (IE 102).

Reid is a challenge to Schopenhauer's claim that the perception of an object is an *achievement* of the mind organizing sensations lodged under the skin of the body. Schopenhauer thinks I do not know the sun but only an eye that sees the sun because he thinks it true that the human person is one who "as the condition of all objects, carries and supports just this entire world" (WWR1 242). The straining work of Atlas is not for Reid: for him, it is not too strong to say that perception is an obedient conduit of the world's manifestation.

According to Schopenhauer, the laws of understanding known *a priori* "work up," "combine," "elaborate," and "shift" a sensory manifold of "raw material" and "refer" it to the law of causality (WWR1 14; WWR2 7). Yet Schopenhauer's reliance on the idea of work is by no means obvious. The Cambridge Platonist Cudworth talks of outward objects inviting the mind to ruminate and revolve upon itself and thereby by some "strange parturiency" it births perception: the mind, he says, by "the display of its own innate vigour from within . . . doth conquer, master, and command its objects, and so begets a clear, serene, victorious, and satisfactory sense."[23] Here, the motif is not work but political command.

Reid's is an obediential view of how humans fit into the world. If, as I have argued, Schopenhauer struggles in his wrestle with the winged cherub, why did he eschew the line of inquiry inaugurated by Berkeley into language and perception? In his excellent book, Patrick Gardiner points out that Schopenhauer for years toyed with the idea of making a translation of David Hume's *Dialogues concerning Natural Religion*.[24] Schopenhauer knew that Reid was an admiring critic of Hume. He was also aware, no doubt, that Reid, like Berkeley, was a churchman.

On at least three occasions in *Fourfold Root*, Schopenhauer warns philosophers against their tendency to "theological flirting" (FR 40). Hume's basic argument in his *Dialogues* is that religions are intellectually unsound because they rely so heavily on testimony for which other means of verification are absent. Reid's clever response is to show that all perception relies on witness. Though Reid was quite critical of Hume and Smith's celebration of commercial societies, and the ethics of sympathy underwriting this celebration,[25] he nonetheless stayed close to the serenity implicit in their theories. Humans, for Schopenhauer, are not set serenely in the world, calmly responsive to its manifestation.

Purifying philosophy of theology, Schopenhauer concludes that human standing in the world is fraught, painful, and toilsome. For the human person is, at root, "the will [that] needs to keep striving" (WWR1 240). Is Schopenhauer right about our ontological condition? Contra Carl Schmitt, is it in fact possible to purge philosophy of theology? Reid does not think so, but nor does he need the winged cherub to serve his purpose. The body is a sign, a witness to extra-mental objects, events, and persons, and itself extra-mental. The body manifests itself in consciousness as signs. For Reid, it is enough that the sensuous and gestural body is rich, not bleak.

Notes

1 The propositions and their exact wording are listed in many places, but see Putallaz (2001, 889–901).
2 See: McAleer (2006) and McAleer (forthcoming).
3 Reid (1983, 40, 44); hereafter abbreviated as 'IE'.
4 For the medieval background to Berkeley's angelism, see Peirce's (1958, 9–38).
5 Descartes (2003, 22). There are, of course, a number of passages like this.
6 Contrasting with "a thoroughly contemptible fellow as Hegel" (FR 11), Schopenhauer compliments Reid for his "excellent book" *Inquiry into the Human Mind*, and cites the first edition of 1764 and the sixth edition of 1810. The book is "very instructive and well worth reading" because it offers a "thorough and acute demonstration that the collective sensations of the senses do not bear the least resemblance to the world known through perception." This position is "very clearly and beautifully described by Dr. Thomas Reid" (WWR2 24).
7 For a thorough and profound exploration of the Schopenhauerian thesis, see O'Shaughnessy (1980).
8 "The intellect is really like the reflecting surface of water, but the water itself is like the will, whose disturbance therefore at once destroys the clearness of that mirror and the distinctness of its images" (WWR2 148).
9 "Without this intellectual operation [application of the law of causality], for which the forms must lie ready in us, the perception of an *objective, external world* could never arise from a mere *sensation* inside our skin" (WWR2 43).
10 Descartes (2003, 28–29).
11 Berkeley (2003, 127; see also 113, 129–130).
12 Alex South touches upon the role of the body in meaning (South, 2011, 151–167).
13 "That those things do really exist which we distinctly perceive by our senses, and are what we perceive them to be" (IE 278).
14 Schopenhauer may get this point from the Scot, Thomas Brown, who otherwise is derided in FR. For Brown's idea that muscular sensations found our experience of space, see Ganson (1999, 49–62).
15 Cf. Henle (1992, 125–140).
16 Sacks (1995, 143).
17 Ibid., p. 123.
18 Idem.

19 Ibid., p. 117.
20 Patrick Gardiner raises some similar worries with Schopenhauer's account (Gardiner, 1962, 106–109).
21 Descartes (2003, 28).
22 See McAleer (2010, 115).
23 As cited in Mortera (2011, 128).
24 Gardiner (1963, 19).
25 McAleer (2011, 111–121).

Bibliography

Berkeley, G. *Three Dialogues between Hylas and Philonous*. Oxford: Oxford University Press, 2003.

Descartes, R. *Meditations and Other Metaphysical Writings*, trans. D. Clarke. London: Penguin, 2003.

Ganson, T. 'Berkeley, Reid and Thomas Brown on the Origins of Our Spatial Concepts', *Reid Studies: An International Review of Scottish Studies* 3(1), 1999: 49–62.

Gardiner, R. *Schopenhauer*. London: Penguin Books, 1963.

Henle, R. 'Schopenhauer and Direct Realism', *The Review of Metaphysics* 46(1), 1992: 125–140.

McAleer, G. '1277 and the Causality of Damnation in Giles of Rome', *Modern Schoolman* 83, 2006: 285–300.

McAleer, G. 'Duns Scotus and Giles of Rome on Whether Sensations are Intentional', in M. Ingham (ed.), *John Duns Sotus, Philosopher: Proceedings of "the Quadruple Congress" on John Duns Scotus, Part 1*. Archa Verbi Subsidia 3, Franciscan Institute, 2010.

McAleer, G. 'Vanity and Temptation: Was Thomas Reid a Critic of the Scottish Enlightenment?', *Journal of Scottish Thought* 4, 2011: 111–121.

McAleer, G. '1277 and the Sensations of the Damned: Peter John Olivi and the Augustinian Origins of Early Modern Angelism', *Studia Patristica* (forthcoming).

Mortera, E. 'Dugald Stewart in Innate Ideas and the Origin of Knowledge', *Journal of Scottish Thought* 4, 2011: 123–140.

O'Shaughnessy, B. *The Will: Dual Aspect Theory, Volumes 1 & 2*. Cambridge: Cambridge University Press, 1980.

Peirce, C.S. 'Fraser's Edition of the Works of George Berkeley', in C. Hartshorne and P. Weiss (eds.), *Collected Papers of Charles Sanders Peirce*, Vol. 8. Cambridge, MA: Harvard University Press, 1958, 9–38.

Putallaz, F. 'L'âme et le feu: Notes franciscaines sur le feu de l'enfer après 1277', in C. Janaway (ed.), *Nach der verurteilung von 1277: Philosophie und Theologie an der Universität von Paris im letzten Viertel des 13. Jahrhunderts: Studien und Texte*. Berlin: W. de Gruyter, 2001, 889–901.

Reid, T. *Inquiry and Essays*. Indianapolis: Hackett Publishing, 1983.

Sacks, O. *An Anthropologist on Mars*. New York: Knopf, 1995.

South, A. 'Two Worlds? Gesture and Speech in Thomas Reid and Maurice Merleau-Ponty', *Journal of Scottish Thought* 4, 2011: 151–167.

8 Idea and Concept in Schopenhauer

From the Early Manuscripts to the World as Will and Representation

Marco Casucci

This contribution aims to illustrate the evolution of the relationship between idea (*Idee*)[1] and concept (*Begriff*) from Schopenhauer's *Early Manuscripts* (1804–1818) to *The World as Will and Representation* (1818/19). The distinction between those two terms is very important in the evolution of Schopenhauer's thought, and in particular for what concerns the creation of his 'system' as it appears in his *magnum opus*, even if this problem is not clearly stated by Schopenhauer in his works. The main distinction between 'representation' and 'will', presented in WWR1, attracts the attention of the reader more than that of 'idea' and 'concept', which is normally subordinated to the former as its derivation. Idea and concept are in fact considered in WWR1 as forms of the manifestation of the will (for what concerns the idea) and that of representation (for what concerns the concept). In any case, neither seem to have a leading role in the philosophy of Schopenhauer, but appear to be mere functions of the more important opposition between 'will' and 'representation'.

By engaging this issue with regard to the relationship between idea and concept, this contribution suggests the possibility of reading Schopenhauer's system with a different interpretive key, which starts from the distinction between the two levels of consciousness made by Schopenhauer in the *Early Manuscripts*. This paper will begin by presenting the idea in the *Early Manuscripts* and its link with 'better consciousness' (section one), then engage the emergence of the concept of will, and the problematic relationship between idea and concept in the *Early Manuscripts* (section two), following this the development of the relationship between idea and concept in the two editions of *Fourfold Root* is explored (section three), and finally the development of the problematic relationship between concept and idea in the second and third book of WWR will be outlined (section four).

Idea and 'Better Consciousness' in the *Early Manuscripts*

Readers of Schopenhauer's *Early Manuscripts*, in which he formed his philosophy and prepared his masterpiece, will note a significant transformation in the development of many subjects that the German philosopher will go on to address later on. First of all, one remarkable fact is the absence of one of the most important contributions of Schopenhauer's philosophy: the 'will'. This concept, which in his later writings will be underlined by Schopenhauer himself as the most important element of his thought, is in fact subordinated to another distinction, which is central in his notes until at least 1816. This distinction is not between 'will' and 'representation', but rather between 'better consciousness' and 'empirical consciousness'. Those two 'levels of consciousness' represent a duality which involves the entire human being, and being in general, in its specific quality, implying that the consciousness consists of a 'better' and 'empirical' dimension.[2] Thus, consciousness cannot be distinguished into two parts, but can be understood on different levels of being itself. To recall a Heideggerian concept, it is possible to say that there is a type of 'ontological difference' between the better and the empirical consciousness, by virtue of which the world can be understood differently: as a product of a cognitive process of an individual and finite subject, or in its integral and original vision, as an idea.[3]

Therefore, we can introduce another central element in the distinction between these two levels of consciousness, which pertains to the fundamental distinction between knowledge and the contemplation of the idea itself. Knowledge, for the young Schopenhauer, generally concerns the level of the empirical consciousness, which is completely interwoven with time. Empirical consciousness is the temporal dimension of consciousness both on the side of the subject and on the side of the object, so that time can be considered as the main thread which connects all the finite and relative knowledge of the subject with the finitude of what is finite, of everything which passes by, as Plato said: "Always becoming, never being".[4] So time belongs to the empirical consciousness as a typical element, as the principle of every relativity, and thus of every illusion in which the subject, with his world, is involved. Or, as Schopenhauer, states in fragment 225:

> *Time* is that in which everything to be found in it becomes a complete nothing (the past), after it has deluded an indivisible moment (the present) with the semblance of an existence. And indeed, in order to delude us, it does not conceal this nothingness behind any artificial appearance. No; freely and openly it is for ever becoming nothing in our hands. For us nothing exists except an indivisible moment (the present) and before and after this moment simply nothing. And this state of ours is called living. Men are so pleased with it that they rest content in the hope that after this life a new one will begin again at once.
>
> (MR1 141)[5]

As can easily be understood from this brief analysis of the temporality of empirical consciousness, it is possible to argue that time plays a very important role in Schopenhauer's philosophy, probably much more so than Schopenhauer himself might have imagined when he transformed his radical criticism of the temporality of knowledge and existence into the 'ontol-ogy' of the will. Time is the basic element from which it becomes possible to criticize the world and the subject in its relative and finite dimension. Schopenhauer wants to underline the fluidity of everything that manifests itself in time, or in the derived forms of knowledge that belong to it. If past, present, and future are the three main dimensions in which every experience is articulated, it is clear that for the German philosopher everything becomes nothing, as much as every present is only an inconsistent line between the nothingness of the past (which is no longer), and the nothingness of the future (which has yet come to pass).

Therefore, Schopenhauer's critical stance with regard to the concept of time is one of the most important and long-lasting elements of his thought and becomes the means which permits him to overcome the empirical level of the consciousness. In turn, this allows to achieve the higher level of the better consciousness, obviously the only real dimension of consciousness itself for Schopenhauer. In his words, the experience of the inconsistency of time leads itself to the consciousness of what overcomes it: the conscious-ness of the nothingness of the past and of the future is the temporal express-ion of the super-temporal nature of being:

> The infinity of *time* and the vanity and unreality of all its contents fol-low, the one from the other. What is given without end and without measure from inexhaustibility cannot by itself be anything, can be only a deception, cannot have any value. That in which I do not have to economize, which I do not have to save and preserve (time and its con-tents) must be given in infinite measure and flow out of inexhaustibility.
> (MR1 96)

This means, through a sort of dialectic awareness, that the act of under-standing the critical dimension of time and its finitude by itself implies access to a higher dimension, from which it is possible for the consciousness to gain the criterion which makes the criticism possible, and this, Platonically speaking, is of course the 'idea': the super-temporal criterion of temporal nothingness: "Everything except the (Platonic) Ideas, except the objects of art, are absolutely nothing but relation, nothing but an empty and unsub-stantial existence. That which exists in any place and at any time is finite, and that which is finite does not really exists at all" (MR1 235–236).

Therefore, the better consciousness is structurally connected with the idea as its correlated, pure element. For Schopenhauer, the idea means the 'pure object' which offers itself for the 'pure subject', as it would be devel-oped in WWR1. The emphasis in this statement is not on the gnosiologically compromised terms 'subject' and 'object', but on the adjective 'pure', which implies the free dimension in which the 'better' consciousness meets its cor-relate. Free from the forms of knowledge, from the forms of the principle of sufficient reason, then free from time and from every form of empirical subjectivity, the idea manifests itself as concrete reality, as a pure object, in which reality itself is not merely known, but can be contemplated in a vision in which a form of interpenetration emerges, by virtue of which eternity can rise as the 'best', in which the 'better consciousness' and the 'idea' become linked.[6]

The idea is the concreteness of reality which reveals its integrity beyond the limits of the analytic intellect, which always represents only portions of reality, and is useful for the survival of finite agents. The idea, on the contrary, by admitting the eternal dimension of its being, overcomes the boundaries of death, and with this gesture establishes the basis for a non-fragmented, total vision of reality itself. For this reason it is important to underline a strong ascetical dimension in the thought of the young Schopenhauer, for which the better consciousness and its 'object'—the idea—are the terms in which it is possible to rediscover a pure and positive sense of the reality beyond the gnosiological illusion of the representation.

The connection between Schopenhauerian thought and Platonism is therefore evident. In his *Early Manuscripts*, Schopenhauer's philosophy is profoundly Platonic in advancing an ascetical dimension to the contemplation of the idea, which means a real detachment from the finite forms of living and access to a completely different level of thinking, feeling, and willing. In this sense, it also becomes clear how Kantian philosophy is read in line with Schopenhauer's discovery of Platonic thought. As Schopenhauer states in fragment 228 of the *Early Manuscripts*: "The Platonic doctrine by which not visible and palpable things, but only the Ideas, in their eternal forms, really exists, is only another expression of Kant's doctrine that *time* and *space* do not pertain to the thing-in-themselves, but are merely forms of my intuitive perception" (MR1 143).

What the above citation underlines is the identification between the idea and the Kantian thing in itself.[7] The idea is the true reality which is above the forms of knowledge, and its accessibility is given by an ascetic elevation of mind in all three of its forms: in an aesthetical, theoretical, or moral/religious way.[8] Those three forms can be determined in their finitude, and remain imprisoned in the empirical condition, or be elevated to a different status in the better consciousness, in which they are enhanced and made eternal. In any case, the will is strongly limited in its metaphysical sense, and appears only as the mark of the finitude of the empirical consciousness, as Schopenhauer recognizes in fragment 220 where he says that "as the *subject of willing* I am an exceedingly wretched being and all our suffering consists in willing. Willing, desiring, striving and aspiring are simply the state of being finite, simply death and distress" (MR1 137).

It is now clear why, for the young Schopenhauer, the idea could not be confused with the concept, because the latter is in fact a mere abstraction, a product of the intellect which is only a representation of the representation,[9] something which is far from the punctual vision of the real being, the idea. Simply put, the concept is an instrument for life, something which makes it possible to represent groups of interrelated phenomena in a general form, whose only sense is their usefulness in restraining the flow of the multiplicity in the unstoppable passage of time. The idea, by contrast, is something 'for which we can die' because it is something which transcends our finite life, opening the doors of eternity to us: "For an Idea (and not everyone is capable of one) men gladly die, and such a death is a supreme virtue, be the Idea so preposterous and absurd. For it represents the better consciousness and what is done for it has been done for the better consciousness, for the affirmation and maintenance of this" (MR1 83).

In other words, it is possible to say that the concept totally pertains to the empirical consciousness, as it is strictly related to the needs of life, and completely submitted to them. The concept in general is the highest instrument which life has to maintain itself in the perpetual struggle of the becoming of time; on the other hand, the idea is that which, exceeding time, exceeds life itself, transcending every need in the eternity of a completely detached vision of the whole. The idea is the core of the contemplation of the 'genius', a figure of the 'better consciousness', where the single lines of existence converge as in a "concave mirror" (MR1 92).

The Emergence of the Will in the *Early Manuscripts*: A First Change in the Distinction between Idea and Concept

This distinction explored above does not remain consistent in Schopenhauer's work. One can already detect a change in the *Early Manuscripts* themselves, which gives rise to some confusion between those two dimensions of thought. Idea and concept move progressively closer to each other, up to the point where it is difficult to distinguish between them. This is a process of conceptualization of the idea which intervenes as Schopenhauer's system starts to develop in the preparatory notes of WWR1. This conception will arise with a reinforcement of the will in Schopenhauer's philosophy, and as this section will attempt to demonstrate, will determine a marked change in the differentiation between concept and idea.

For that purpose, fragment 287 of 1814, in which Schopenhauer underlines a difficulty concerning the relationship between concept and idea, is of particular interest. Here, he brings to light the basic metaphysical question of the relationship between the one and multiplicity. He begins by considering that the principles of differentiation are time and space, through which all multiplicity emerges, while, on the contrary, only in the idea can the plural dimension of the world be unified in a single vision.[10] Up until this point there is no doubt that Schopenhauer is following his usual path of affirming the distinction between idea and phenomenon, but a change first occurs when he says that there is a connection between the idea and natural laws, more precisely when he admits that in a certain sense the 'natural laws' and the 'natural elements' are 'ideas' which consist in nothing more than a *reductio ad unum* of the perception's data—just as it happens in the abstraction process typical of conceptualization.[11] Therefore, while he has to admit that even when the process of unification occurs in the act of ideal-ization/conceptualization (as now there is a difficulty in distinguishing one from the other), there remain some questions.

After the elimination of empirical multiplicity, it is possible to find another kind of difference which Schopenhauer calls 'transcendental dif-ference'. That is the diversity of the species itself, and of the natural laws and elements—by virtue of which a dog is not a horse, the law of gravity is not a principle of thermodynamics, and metal is not water. In this sense, Schopenhauer has to face the problem of that kind of multiplicity, when exactly it arises and, alongside that, he has to admit that the only element that every species has in common is the matter which is differentiated only by the principle of sufficient reason (time, space, and causality).[12] At this point, Schopenhauer realizes that there is no difference between idea and concept, and therefore has to admit a concordance between them, which demonstrates a sort of correlation between nature and reason—something quite implausible if we consider how Schopenhauer emphasizes their radi-cal distinctness in his previous fragments.[13] Schopenhauer must recognize an incongruity between concept and idea that remains, so that the concept can lead the abstraction process to the maximal reduction of the being, oth-erwise to the wider concepts of subject and object;[14] thus he asks himself if it is possible to do the same with the idea, answering that this reduction is probably inadmissible—because the idea is what remains after the spatial/temporal multiplicity has been removed, or the essential that remains, the forms of nature.[15] By contrast, the concept, in this case, is a principle of unification, which permits the reunification not only of the spatial/temporal multiplicity, but also of the 'transcendental difference' emblematic of ideas. In this sense it would be possible to conclude that the concept is, in a cogni-tive sense, a more fundamental notion than the idea: a sort of radical U-turn in Schopenhauer's thought, which must be underlined, and which he himself understands when he asks poetically at the end of the fragment: "Out of this valley's depth's / Shall I the outlet find?" (MR1 194).

In general, the problem is to understand how to unify the two parts, idea and concept. But that kind of problem can arise only in the dimension of the cognitive subject for which the distinction from the object remains insuperable. Here Schopenhauer probably neglects to consider the authen-tic essence of the better consciousness: the fact that on this level all three dimensions of the human experience (aesthetical, theoretical, and moral) are enhanced to the point that the basic distinction between subject and object is not a problem, because the consciousness itself reaches purity, transcend-ing any and all dualism. Thus, it is clear how, for the 'aesthetical' subject, his sensibility is perfectly adapted to the beauty of what he is contemplat-ing, for the 'theoretical' subject the concept is perfectly commensurate to the idea he tries to express, and the same can be said for the 'moral' subject, whose action will perfectly express the idea he wants to realize. The better consciousness is therefore the non-problematic level on which every problem, every πρo-βλεµατα—in the etymological sense of the word, as what is 'thrown-forward'—is overcome and the consciousness itself manifests its attitude to be a horizon in which subject and object can be reunified, over every gnosiological distinction in which the true essence of being is lost in a sort of kaleidoscopic game of mirrors.[16]

When Schopenhauer called into question the relationship between idea and concept, in the note previously analysed, he is clearly attempting to understand this relationship on the level of the empirical consciousness, in which the distinction between 'subject' and 'object' is taken as something insuperable. In this sense we can immediately experience, in a qualitative dimension, how the idea is reduced to something very close to a scientific concept (a force of nature, a chemical element, and so on) and on the other hand, how the concept becomes the real principle of unification, once the idea has lost its original power as a pure correlate of the better consciousness. So either the idea remains linked to the better consciousness, or it becomes a concept with all the incongruities which this change implies.

Once Schopenhauer has lost the original belonging of idea and consciousness on the higher level, the problems are going to multiply, because it is now necessary to find another basis on which the unification can be supported. So, it is no coincidence that in fragment 278,[17] for the first time in Schopenhauer's texts, the 'will' is mentioned as the thing in itself. It becomes the principle of the unification of reality, which must resolve the radical distinction between subject and object, risen again from the ashes of the abandoned 'ontological difference' between the two levels of consciousness. Instead of that duality, another distinction appears, which will be completely affirmed in WWR1, between 'knowledge' and 'will'.[18] This dualism, which replaces the duality of the early manuscripts, is what generates many of the contradictions which are typical of Schopenhauer's philosophy.

Idea and Concept in *Fourfold Root*

The fragment analysed in the previous section was written by Schopenhauer in 1814, one year after the publication of the first edition of *Fourfold Root*. Thus it is possible to say that when Schopenhauer put the final touches on his dissertation, he also came to his mature view and the transformation of the relationship between idea and concept. In *Fourfold Root* we have traces of that change occurring in the interpretation of those two terms of thought, in particular for what concerns the prominence of the concept as a fundamental element in knowledge. On the other hand, however, *Fourfold Root* is focused almost uniquely on the characteristics of representational thought, and as such Schopenhauer's claims here are mostly useful for that type of knowledge. With regard to that purpose, it is important to highlight the title, "Uses of Concepts" (FR 100), of §27 (§28 in the first edition), where Schopenhauer underlines the usefulness of the concept for its capacity of abstraction. In particular he claims that they make possible dealing with a large number of object with a very simple concept (see also FR 100).

Therefore, in *Fourfold Root*, Schopenhauer believes that the concept remains, on the one hand, a mere 'representation of representation' (which is implied by its characteristic of abstraction), but on the other hand, conceptual abstraction is emphasized as highly useful for reasoning, which wants to unify a lot of data. But the most important element, already in the first edition of *Fourfold Root*, for the topic which concerns us, is in particular underlined in §29, where the concept is compared with the 'mental image' whose function was described by Schopenhauer in §22. Here, it is said that the concept should not be confused with the 'mental image', even if they are both elements of thought which appear in the absence of the immediate presence of a concrete perceivable object. The 'mental image', in fact, is defined by Schopenhauer as a complete representation which is not submitted to the principle of causality;[19] it is a product of the imagination by virtue of which it is possible to have a full representation without the immediate experience of the object in the forms of space and time. The 'mental image' in §29 is defined as the 'representative' of the concept, what we can we call into mind when we want to imagine what the concept represents in its abstract generality:

> As has already been said, a concept is not at all to be confused with a mental image, which is a complete and particular representation neither brought about through the immediate object nor belonging to the complex of experience. However, a mental image is then also to be distinguished from a concept when a mental image is used as a *representative of a concept*. This occurs when one wants to have the representation itself that the concept is a representation of, and that corresponds to the concept.
>
> (EF 177)[20]

The concept must be distinguished from the 'mental image', because the latter is only an imperfect exemplification of the former: it is a sort of intermediary between the immediate presence of the perceivable object and the abstractness of the concept. That is why its epistemic dimension is at the same time as imperfect as necessary, in order to connect the concept with the multiplicity of the empirical object, even if the 'mental image' itself is always inadequate as a representative of the concept, because it is full of arbitrary elements and never entirely fills the field of significance of the concept in its universality.

Consequently, it is very important that in this argumentation, which entirely concerns the cognitive relationship between two terms of knowledge such as 'concept' and 'mental image', Schopenhauer calls into question the idea in a very short parenthesis which refers to a note found in §40.[21] In that note, he underlines the original sense of the idea, as what makes possible a synthesis between the universality of the concept and the concreteness of the sensible intuition:

> Perhaps *Platonic* Ideas can be described as normal intuitions [*Normalanschauungen*], which, unlike mathematical intuitions, would not only be valid for the formal aspect of complete representations, but also for the material aspect; thus, they would be complete representations that as such would be thoroughly determinate, and at the same time, like concepts, would concern many things; i.e. according to the explanation given in §28, they would be representative of concepts, completely adequate as such.
>
> (FR 135)

The idea puts together the empty formal universality of the concept and the concrete materiality of the sensibility, so that it can be defined as a 'complete representation', by virtue of which the representative of the concept is perfectly adequate for them. Those statements are very important, because it is possible to note once again how Schopenhauer problematically swings between two dimensions of the idea: on the one hand, the idea is in fact a concrete unity, which brings together universality and plurality, unity and multiplicity; on the other hand, the idea is inappropriately compared with the concept as if it was a bigger mental image, a more perfect imagining which is able to fill all the emptiness of the concept itself. Saying that the idea is the 'adequate' representative of the concept puts that in a sort of subordination for which the idea becomes a sort of 'object', which loses its ontological difference from the gnosiological dimension, rather than remaining in its absoluteness on the level of the better consciousness. Now the idea can be grasped by the concept, it can be analysed, it can become an object of science, and it can be confused with it, thereby becoming a metaphysical object. Without the support of the 'ontological difference' between better and empirical consciousness, the Schopenhauerian analysis of the relationship between idea and concept shifts toward an abstract metaphysics, in which it is difficult to distinguish the real qualitative level on which the idea can be contemplated in its entirety and totality. Without the awareness of that ontological difference, the idea becomes a duplicate of the empirical world, an abstraction (much like the previous example of zinc and copper), and therefore an objecthood of the will, rather than a pure contemplation of the real being capable to free man from the will itself.

That is why, in the end, it is necessary to analyse the relationship between idea and concept in WWR1, in connection with the 'will'. We are set on this path by the conclusion of *Fourfold Root*, which ends with the analysis of the principle of motivation, the last and most inner root of the principle of sufficient reason, which gives the possibility of cognitive access to the metaphysical core of the Kantian subject: the will—nothing more than an inversion of the principle of sufficient reason itself, its 'dark side'.[22] As has already been highlighted, the will emerges as the 'thing in itself', as long as the distinction between idea and concept is removed. The reduction of the idea to a mere 'representative' of the concept is what allows its transformation into that 'objecthood' of the will, as it would be presented in WWR1, generating those contradictions typical of what is known as the 'metaphysics of the will'.

Idea and Concept in the World as Will and Representation

In order to conclude our investigation of the evolution of the idea and concept in Schopenhauer's early thoughts, it becomes essential to consider WWR1, because there the transformation of the idea is brought about, and at the same time it is also preserves in part the original ascetic view proposed by Schopenhauer in the *Early Manuscripts*. We may say that it was probably the desire to realize a system, radically alternative to those of the German idealists, which put Schopenhauer on the path to making the will into an absolute, as something of a negative response to idealistic reason. The will should become the opposite of absolute reason in the Hegelian system, in order to underline the unsolvable negativity of the world as a criticism of dialectical reason.[23]

Let us proceed in order and see how these considerations about idea and concept can lead to a different interpretation of Schopenhauer's philosophy, which starts with a 'duality' (between 'better' and 'empirical' consciousness) which must be radically distinguished from every 'dualism', but does end up in an apparent 'dualism' (between 'representation'/'knowledge' and 'will') in which the 'duality', never completely denied, saves the system from 'dualism' itself by a final negation in which everything must be reread and reinterpreted. The tension between 'duality' and 'dualism' is clearly presented in the problematic tension between 'idea' and 'concept' as it is expressed in the second and third books of WWR1, where the 'doctrine of the idea' is mentioned and analysed.

In the second book, in particular, the problematic assimilation of idea and concept can be considered as concluded when Schopenhauer, in §§ 24 to 29, links the idea as an objecthood of the will to 'natural forces' like magnetism, electricity, gravity, etc. The aim of Schopenhauer's analysis in these sections is to outline how, at the basis of the relationships represented in the horizon of the principle of sufficient reason, there lies something that exceeds ordinary knowledge, and which can be considered a sort of *qualitas occulta*.[24] What Schopenhauer wants to find is the clear metaphysical basis of nature, in order to introduce the will as the unique kernel of the world. In any case, what is accomplished with this process is the identification of the idea with the natural laws, which are mere products of conceptual knowledge. Even if Schopenhauer tries to remove the natural laws from the spatio-temporal determination of the principle of sufficient reason, by saying that the forces always remain outside the chain of cause and effect, we must recognize that the force itself can be scientifically considered as a concept, abstracted from the causal chain of the events as its universal condition and explanation. Hence, what Schopenhauer does not appear to admit is that all the ideas which he identifies as the basis of the world are no more than scientific concepts obtained by abstraction from empirical knowledge, and made absolute.[25] In this sense the ideas, as described in the second book of WWR1, are only abstractions whose aim is to prepare the introduction of the final and total abstraction: the will, which can be considered as the empty basis of the nothingness of the world. Therefore, it is possible to say that if it is true for Schopenhauer that the concept is a 'representation of a representation', at the same time it must be evident that the will is an 'abstraction of an abstraction'. In this sense the will is nothing more than the emptiness in which every representation, founded on the main gnosiological abstraction between subject and object, finds its finitude, imploding in on itself.

In any case, the objecthood of the idea, and its assimilation to the natural laws, drives many problems in WWR1. Even if Schopenhauer underlines that, with regard to the idea, both Plato and Kant formulated very similar doctrines, in the end he has to adjust his opinion when he has to explain the new collocation of the idea in his system. So the idea and the thing in itself are the same but are no longer identical, because here the idea is conceived as an objecthood of the will.[26] Thus the idea is clearly a medium between representation and will, whose knowledge must lead one to free oneself from the will itself. That median position of the idea creates a series of incongruities in the Schopenhauerian system, which in the end results in the previously highlighted dualism between will and knowledge. The most important among them is the presence of knowledge, generally submitted to the will, as its 'instrument' (as its 'μεχανη' as Schopenhauer says in § 27 of WWR1 175), which is suddenly able to free itself from its captivity, and in this way access the idea as an objecthood of the will. The question is: if the will is the omnipotent force of the world as its eternal basis, how is it possible to admit a failure in its system? And furthermore, how is it possible that knowledge can overcome the rules imposed on it from the principle of sufficient reason, which only gives knowledge its basis, and outside of which no knowledge is possible?[27] These two simple questions bring to light difficulties in the Schopenhauerian system, as he attempts to base it on the will as the 'thing in itself' by adapting the ontological dimension of the idea: from being a pure correlate of the consciousness freed by the limits of will and ordinary knowledge, into an intermediate abstraction between representation and will. As a medium between representation and will, the idea ceases to be the pure correlate of the better consciousness, and becomes a gnosilological instrument for the negation of the will.[28]

Indeed, it is clear that Schopenhauer struggles between two dimensions which are at the origin of the tension which is the soul of his philosophical

work: the intuitive dimension of pure contemplation, in which every dualism is overcome, and both subject and object are unified in a single and
concrete vision—the vision of the idea in its higher and original sense—and
the need to scientifically objectify the results of his meditations in a system,
attempting to indicate a process by which it becomes possible to 'know'
the will, and to overcome it. This element justifies the need for scientificity
which occurs in Schopenhauer's thought, even if its roots are completely different, because it is based in an experience which radically transcends every
conceptual universalization.

The problem is that the idea in its purity, as explained in his early notes,
is rare, and this basic element remains as a foundation of all Schopenhauer's
meditations. So, the occasions in which the idea can be contemplated are
rare, and only its rarity allows it to preserve its essence over the typical chat-
ter in which everyday life imprisons everything, preventing every elevation
to another level of consideration. It is no coincidence if, as Schopenhauer
explains in §34 of WWR1, the experience of the contemplation of the idea
as a complete abandonment of the ordinary way of considering the object
into a pure union with it, beyond every possible mediation—a description
which clearly recalls the mystical *Gelassenheit*[29]—he uses the adverb 'when'.
This temporal adverb highlights the rarity in which the event of the contemplation happens, a rarity which cannot be of every time, of every day, but
needs a sort of special atmosphere in which things can shine in a different
light, the light of the idea:

> When, elevated by strength of mind to stop viewing things in the ordi-
> nary way, no longer led by the forms of the principle of sufficient rea-
> son to pursue merely the relations between things (which in the end
> always aims at the relation to our own will), if we stop considering the
> Where, When, Why and Wherefore of things but simply and exclusively
> consider the *What*, if we do not allow our consciousness to become
> engrossed by abstract thinking, concept of reason; but if, instead of all
> this, we devote the entire power of our mind to intuition and immerse
> ourselves in this entirely, letting the whole of consciousness be filled
> with peaceful contemplation of the natural object [. . .], we *lose* our-
> selves in this object completely, i.e. we forget our individuality, our will,
> and continue to exist only as pure subject, the clear mirror of the object
> [. . .], then what we thus cognize is no longer the individual thing as
> such, but rather the *Idea*, the eternal form.
>
> (WWR1 201)

The aesthetic experience of the idea demonstrates that, even if concealed by
a pretension of a systematic organization of his masterpiece, Schopenhauer
remains tied to his original thought of a duality of consciousness. The
Gelassenheit in §34 of WWR1, the rarity typical of the genius's state of
mind, clearly shows that the contemplation of the idea is possible only under

determinate and singular conditions which lie outside every methodological approach. In this sense a genius is someone who passes a threshold which permits him to experience something which goes far beyond ordinary knowledge. With the contemplation of the idea an ontological difference is given, and with that it is given a quality which exceeds the finite approach to the world signed by the negativity of the will. A clear example of that is given by the beauty of the world which constitutes the corollary of the doctrine of the idea. It is truly remarkable that the severe master of the 'negation of the world' can't keep himself from asserting that everything is beautiful and everything has its specific beauty.[30] How is it possible that the world generated by the blind violence of the will can be contemplated in its beauty? How is it possible that the painful and sinful world of the will can produce beautiful things? That further contradiction in the texture of Schopenhauer's masterpiece shows the need to rethink the 'world' in another way, in a way which overcomes both representation and will—because it is clear that the beauty of the world which emerges in works of art is more than a mere appearance, more than a mere representation controlled by the blind will.

In this sense, the final negation, as presented in the §71 of WWR1, challenges the reader, who must prove his level of comprehension of the whole book: otherwise everything disappears for the consciousness still involved in the representation and in the will, and the 'nothing' remains as the last word of the book itself, or the thought has already crossed the threshold of the finitude, so that all the finite world "with all its suns and galaxies" (WWR1 487) is nothing, because everything has been overcome on another level of consciousness.[31] Hence it is possible to say that the 'better consciousness' remains as a trace for the 'epiphilosophy' which Schopenhauer drafts at the end of the WWR2. It is well known that for Schopenhauer this part must remain in a negative form, and cannot be explained by a systematic philosophy. However, it is possible to say, by a previous reading of the *Early Manuscripts*, that the idea—conceived as perfectly separated from the concept, and over every cognitive and voluntary dimension—is probably the basis of an aesthetic resurrection of the world over the limits of its finitude.

Conclusion

In closing, it is possible to say that the question concerning the relationship between idea and concept in its development from the *Early Manuscripts* to WWR1 shows how Schopenhauer's philosophy can be read as a philosophy of the 'levels of consciousness' more than a 'philosophy of the will'. The ambiguity of the idea as an objecthood of the will and the assertion of the will as the thing in itself in WWR is in fact what creates a diversion from the original distinction between '*bessere Bewusstsein*' and '*empirisches Bewusstsein*'. That duality is translated, and transformed, in WWR1 into the dualism between 'knowledge' and 'will'. In that transformation an important role is played by what this paper refers to as the 'conceptualization of the idea'. By the assimilation of the idea to the concepts derived from the natural sciences, Schopenhauer accomplishes the transformation of his philosophy into a great gnostic system, in which the 'world as will and representation' must be negated as the cause of the evil and every suffering in general. There is something, however, that Schopenhauer cannot completely eliminate with his gnostic asceticism: the beauty of the world which manifest itself in the contemplation of the idea, in rare moments, remains a contradiction in the system of the will and its negation.

That is why Schopenhauer asks the reader of his masterpiece to read it again after its conclusion: because the *noluntas* is not the end; because, probably, there is something to save in the process of the negation of the world, and this is the idea in its original sense as the pure correlate of the 'better consciousness'. In this sense the *noluntas* is nothing more than a threshold which separates the 'empirical' from the 'better' consciousness in which the idea can be reached again, beyond any confusion with the concept.

Notes

1 From this point the term 'idea' will represent the '*Idee*' as Schopenhauer conceived it in the Platonic meaning of the term, and I will translate the term '*Vorstellung*' with the more appropriate 'representation'.

2 Concerning the relationship between empirical and better consciousness, see: Mirri (1999, 2006a, 2006b), Janaway (2009) and Vandenabeele (2009).

3 In the *Early Manuscripts*, there are numerous fragments in which the difference between empirical and better consciousness is exposed. One striking one is the following: "If our temporal consciousness completely dominates us and we are in this way abandoned to desires and thus gravitate toward vice (i.e. negation of the better consciousness), our entire nature is *subjective*, that is to say we see in things nothing but their relation to our individuality and its needs. But on the other hand, as soon as we *objectively consider, i.e. contemplate* the things of the world, then for the moment *subjectivity* and thus the source of all misery has vanished, we are free, and the consciousness of the material world of the senses stands before us as something strange and foreign which no longer wears us down. Also we are no longer involved in considering the nexus of space, time and causality (useful for our individuality), but see the Platonic Idea of the object" (MR1 50). In particular, for the relationship between Heidegger and Schopenhauer see Young (2007, 169–177) and Moretti-Costanzi (2009(b)).

4 Plato, *Timaeus*, 27d—this is a Platonic line that Schopenhauer often cites.

5 Schopenhauer's critical stance toward time is a very original element in his thought. It is then no coincidence that the first fragment of the early writings is a translation of Milton's poem dedicated "To Time," in which the young Schopenhauer underlines its insatiable voracity (cfr. MR1 1). This aspect is also developed in fragment 22, where the German philosopher underlines the nothingness of the past and of the future, only divided by an unextended edge which is the present itself, so that our reality, the only place where our existence is possible, is something undefined which is in itself destined to pass into nothing as its most proper essence (cfr. MR1 15).

6 See in particular: Mirri (2006[a]), Atwell (2007, 84–92) and Janaway (2007, 43–51). What is important in the relationship between the subject and the object

in aesthetic contemplation is the purity of this relationship, which is beyond any relativity (i.e. beyond the individual subject of willing).

7 In this sense, Schopenhauer aligns with German idealism in his *Early Manuscripts*, even if he will make a strong break from it after the failure of his academic career in 1818, in Berlin. Concerning Schopenhauer's relationship with Fichte and Schelling in particular, see Gardner (2012).

8 The ascetical element in Schopenhauer's thought has been highlighted by Moretti-Costanzi (2009[a]), who notes that the asceticism in Schopenhauer is not limited to a mere negation of the world, but is concerned with the elevation of the soul to the higher regions of the spirit in which becomes possible to rediscover the true being of each self in its aesthetical, theoretical, and moral dimension, similar to Plato's philosophy (see also Janaway, 2007, 39–48).

9 See fragment 226: "Plato says: 'the ideas alone really *are*; everything else only appears to be'. And some (especially Herbart) have nevertheless given them out as mere *concepts*, that is to say as representations of representations! But they are the forms of things which are plastic and graphic and yet universal as well" (MR1 142).

10 "*The principle of diversity*, that whereby things are *different*, is *time* and *space*. On the other hand, that whereby things (of *one* species of course) are identical, is their (*Platonic*) *idea* or the *thing-in-itself*. To the extent that we are held captive in time and space, the latter always appears to us as a miracle and is the *inexplicable*, since all *explanation* is invariably nothing but showing the connexion of things in the separating medium (time and space) through the principle of sufficient reason or ground" (MR1 192).

11 "Such a miracle is pre-eminently the *infallibility of the laws of nature*, in other words that nature never once *forgets* her laws. Thus, for example, if there is once a law of nature that, when certain substances come together, there takes place some chemical process, a formation of gases, combustion, galvanic polarity, or something similar, then, whenever those substances come together, whether on purpose or by accident (where the strictest precision through the unexpected surprises us), whether today or a thousand years ago, the definite process occurs at once and without hesitation or reserve" (MR1 193).

12 "After the elimination of the diversity of individuals which is to be found solely in our perceiving them in time and space, there is still a diversity which is not to be found in them and which I would therefore like to call the transcendental diversity. This is the diversity of the species itself, we can also say the diversity of the (Platonic) Ideas" (MR1 193). The confusion Schopenhauer experiences between idea and concept, resulting from the improper assimilation of the idea to the natural species, is clear in this passage. He is therefore forced to move ambiguously in the orbit of the representation, even if he is desperately trying to overcome it.

13 "*The concept* embraces all the individuals of the species that are scattered and dispersed in time and space, and it therefore corresponds to the (*Platonic*) *Idea* of the species, to the *thing-in-itself*, although it is quite different from this. The Idea, the thing-in-itself, is that which manifests itself in all those individual things, scattered through time and space. The concept, on the other hand, is the representation of a representation, is abstracted from all those individuals; it is only for the faculty of reason. The (Platonic) Idea or the thing-in-itself must be regarded as a will of which bodies are the objectity; it is therefore not a representation at all, but just the thing-in-itself. But in spite of this great difference, in spite of this want of all relation and connexion, concept and (Platonic) Idea nevertheless do come together, and this is what I call the *agreement of nature with the faculty of reason* and find most inexplicable" (MR1 193–194).

14 "A third consideration arising out of the two foregoing is that concepts can become ever more universal right up to *ens*, or better to object and subject" (MR1 194).

15 Cfr. MR1 194.

16 In fragment 274 Schopenhauer writes: "The better consciousness (bliss in the real sense) is nevertheless not divided into subject and object and therefore being subject belongs to the empirical consciousness that is the state of wretchedness" (MR1 182).

17 Here Schopenhauer writes: "*The world as thing-in-itself* is a great will which knows not what it wills; for it does not *know* but merely *wills* just because it is a will and nothing else" (MR1 184–185). Then in fragment 305 he says: "The will is the Idea". And in a footnote Schopenhauer corrects himself by saying: "This is incorrect; the adequate objectity of the will is the Idea, but the phenomenon is the Idea that has entered in the *principium individuationis*. The will itself is Kant's thing in itself" (MR1 206). In these notes the passage to the will as the thing-in-itself is concluded and with this, the passage from the distinction between better and empirical consciousness to the distinction between will and knowledge is also completed: "But together with willing there is also knowing (and it is always only knowledge of willing), and this is the only good side of life; it is the true gospel of salvation and ensures to the will, bad as may be, final release" (MR1 206).

18 It is important to underline that the theme of the will as the thing in itself is anticipated by a series of notes in fragment 220 (MR1 136–138), 221 (MR1 138–140) and 274 (MR1 181–183) in which it is possible to trace the transformation from the difference between empirical and better consciousness into the distinction between knowledge and will.

19 "However, once representations have been immediately present to the subject through the mediation of the immediate object, without this mediation the subject is afterwards capable of voluntarily repeating representations, even with alterations of their order of connection. I call such repetitions *mental images* [*Phantasmata*] and the faculty of these, the *fantasy* [*Phantasie*] or *imagination* [*Einbildungskraft*]. Its representations are indeed *complete* (according to the explanation given in §18 [§17 in B]), but do not *belong to the totality of experience*" (EF 164).

20 For what concerns the epistemic status of the mental images in Schopenhauer's theory of knowledge, Frank White raises an important point: "Mental images are not poor substitutes for particulars; they are particulars themselves, and constitute the source of an extended kind of perception" (White, 1991, 68). White then underlines the importance of the mental images not only for the scientific knowledge but also for the production of artworks: "Schopenhauer holds that the understanding gives us an intuitive grasp of particulars and their causal interrelations; that the mind them thinks them over in words or in images; and that where images prevail original thought becomes possible" (White, 1991, 69). On the power of imagination in art see also Foster (1999).

21 "However, with the use of such a representative of a concept, one is always aware that the mental image does not adequately represent the concept, but is a wholly arbitrary determination. (See the note to §40 on Platonic ideas)" (EF 177). Here Schopenhauer refers to the §40 of the first edition which corresponds to §39 in the second edition, bearing the same title (cfr. EF 182, note 112).

22 Frank White similarly notes this problem, namely the tension in Schopenhauer's analysis of the principle of motivation, which should in turn lead us to the knowledge of the noumenon: "Schopenhauer's claim that in self-awareness we have knowledge of the noumenon seems *prima facie* decidedly implausible. It is

difficult to see how he thinks he can move justifiably from the assertion that we are aware of ourselves as subjects of willing to the assertion that in this awareness we confront the noumenon" (White, 1991, 126).

23 See Safranski (1989, 250–263).

24 See in particular what Schopenhauer says in §26: "The force itself lies entirely outside the chain of causes and effects that presupposes time, since the chain is meaningful only in relation to time: but the force lies outside of time as well. Individual alterations are always caused by alterations that are just as individual; they are not caused by the force whose expression they are. Because, however many times it may occur, a cause derives its efficacy from a force of nature which is groundless as such, i.e. lies completely outside the chain of causes and the province of principle of sufficient reason on general, and is known to philosophy as the immediate objecthood of the will, the in-itself of the whole of nature; but aetiology (physics in this case) establishes it as an original force, i.e. an occult quality" (WWR1 155). What is important to underline in this passage is that the force is "groundless", and therefore nothing more than the negativity of the principle of sufficient reason driven to its extreme consequences.

25 "Each universal, original force of nature is thus in its inner essence nothing other than the objecthood of the will at a low level: we call each of these levels an eternal *Idea* in Plato's sense. A *law of nature* however is the relation of the Idea to the form of its appearance" (WWR1 159). It is interesting to note that here there is a sort of graduation in which 'ideas' and 'natural laws' are in a strict relationship, so that it is possible to argue that the idea is no more than a further abstraction of the natural laws.

26 See in particular what Schopenhauer says in §32: "Despite the inner agreement between Kant and Plato, and despite the fact that both men have the same goal in mind and are compelled and inspired by the same world-view to do philosophy, we do not believe, given our discussion to this point, that Idea and thing in itself are simply one and the same: for us rather, the Idea is only the immediate and therefore adequate objecthood of the thing in itself, which is however itself the *will*, to the extent that it (the will) has not yet been objectified and become representation" (WWR1 205–206). He continues: "By contrast, the Platonic Idea is necessarily an object, something cognized, a representation and, for precisely this reason (but for only this reason), distinct from the thing in itself" (WWR1 206). It is clear here how Schopenhauer puts the idea as medium between representation and will, a sort of halfway step between the cognizable and the unknowable. In this sense we are very far from the former significance of the idea in the *Early Manuscripts*, where the idea, as the οντως ον, was completely identified with the thing in itself.

27 On these controversial aspects of the metaphysics of the will see Janaway (1989, 190–200), Hamlyn (1999, 55–61) and Neill (2009, 30–31).

28 §49 is very similar to fragment 287 of the *Early Manuscripts* and it is probable that Schopenhauer used his note to formulate that difference between Idea and concept. From a comparison between the two texts it is clear how Schopenhauer tries to resolve the question proposed in the early manuscript by submitting the idea to the concept by calling the former "adequate representative of the concept" (WWR1 276): "The *Idea* is unity shattered into multiplicity through the temporal and spatial form of our intuitive apprehension: the *concept*, on the other hand is unity reassembled from plurality by means of the abstraction of our reason: it can be designated as unity after the fact, and the Idea as unity before the fact" (WWR1 277).

29 Schopenhauer in §34 uses the verb "*lassen sein*" (letting be) to express the condition which makes possible the contemplation of the idea (cfr. *WWR1*, 210). This expression recalls the mystical dimension of the *Gelassenheit* which properly consists in 'letting the things be', a sort of abandonment in which the subject

ceases to apply his forms to the world, letting it manifest itself in its purity. It is well known that the *Gelassenheit* was introduced by the German mystic Meister Eckhart, who is referred to in the last pages of *WWR* (cfr. WWR1 450, 457).
30 See §41 (WWR1 247–248). That seems to show clearly the contrast which Schopenhauer expresses between a world condemned by its finitude to death and pain and another level of comprehension of the world itself which is contemplated in its pure beauty.
31 Cfr. WWR1 485–487.

Bibliography

Atwell, J.E. 'Art as Liberation: A Central Theme of Schopenhauer's Philosophy', in D. Jaquette (ed.), *Schopenhauer, Philosophy and the Arts*. Cambridge: Cambridge University Press, 2007, 81–103.

Foster, C. 'Ideas and Imagination: Schopenhauer on the Proper Foundation of Art', in C. Janaway (ed.), *The Cambridge Companion to Schopenhauer*. Cambridge: Cambridge University Press, 1999, 213–251.

Gardner, S. 'Schopenhauer's Contraction of Reason: Clarifying Kant and Undoing German Idealism', *Kantian Review* 17(3), 2012: 375–401.

Hamlyn, D. 'Schopenhauer and Knowledge', in C. Janaway (ed.), *The Cambridge Companion to Schopenhauer*. Cambridge: Cambridge University Press, 1999, 44–62.

Janaway, C. *Self and World in Schopenhauer's Philosophy*. Oxford: Clarendon Press, 1989.

Janaway, C. 'Knowledge and Tranquillity: Schopenhauer and the Value of Art', in D. Jacquette (ed.), *Schopenhauer, Philosophy and the Arts*. Cambridge: Cambridge University Press, 2007, 39–61.

Janaway, C. 'Schopenhauer's Philosophy of Value', in A. Neill and C. Janaway (eds.), *Better Consciousness: Schopenhauer's Philosophy of Value*. Oxford: Wiley-Blackwell, 2009, 1–10.

Mirri, E. 'Saggio introduttivo' to A. Schopenhauer *La dottrina dell'idea. Dai frammenti giovanili a Il mondo come volontà e rappresentazione*. Roma: Armando, 1999, 8–32.

Mirri, E. 'Un concetto perduto nella sistematica schopenhaueriana: la "migliore coscienza"', in E. Mirri (ed.), *Pensare il medesimo*, ed. F. Valori e M. Moschini. Napoli: ESI, 2006(a), 367–386.

Mirri, E. 'Volontà e idea nel giovane Schopenhauer', in E. Mirri (ed.), *Pensare il medesimo*, ed. F. Valori e M. Moschini, Napoli: ESI, 2006(b), 297–318.

Moretti-Costanzi, T. 'Schopenhauer', in T. Moretti-Costanzi (ed.), *Opere*, ed. E. Mirri e M. Moschini. Milano: Bompiani, 2009(a), 2221–2318.

Moretti-Costanzi, T. 'L'ascetica di Heidegger', in T. Moretti-Costanzi (ed.), *Opere*, ed. E. Mirri e M. Moschini. Milano: Bompiani, 2009(b), 2565–2600.

Neill, A. 'Aesthetics Experience in Schopenhauer's Metaphysics of Will', in A. Neill and C. Janaway (eds.), *Better Consciousness: Schopenhauer's Philosophy of Value*, Oxford: Wiley-Blackwell, 2009, 26–40.

Safranski, R. *Schopenhauer and the Wild Years of Philosophy*, trans. E. Osers. Cambridge, MA: Harvard University Press, 1989.

Vandenabeele, B. 'Schopenhauer on Aesthetic Understanding and the Values of Art', in A. Neill and Ch. Janaway (eds.), *Better Consciousness: Schopenhauer's Philosophy of Value*. Oxford: Wiley-Blackwell, 2009, 41–57.

White, F.C. *On Schopenhauer's "Fourfold Root of the Principle of Sufficient Reason"*. Leiden: Brill, 1991.

Young, J. 'Schopenhauer, Heidegger, Art and the Will', in D. Jacquette (ed.), *Schopenhauer, Philosophy and the Arts*. Cambridge: Cambridge University Press, 2007, 162–180.

9   Schopenhauer on Perception, Consciousness, and Self-Awareness

Luis de Sousa

This contribution will focus on the connection between Schopenhauer's conception of subjectivity and consciousness. We will be concerned, in particular, with that species of self-consciousness by means of which philosophers sought to identify and define the subject of cognition. This type of self-consciousness is what is ultimately at stake in Descartes's *cogito* and Kant's 'transcendental apperception', and it also plays a central role in German idealism, for instance in Fichte's or Hegel's thought.

According to the Cartesian tradition, one is fully a subject only when over and beyond being perceptively aware one is able to reflect and say, 'I think'. We will start by showing that Schopenhauer's theory of intuitive perception as presented in *The Fourfold Root of the Principle of Sufficient Reason* entails a view of consciousness that is opposed to the one that can be found in the Cartesian-rationalist tradition and appears then more akin to the tradition of British empiricism, in particular, to John Locke. According to the latter view, self-consciousness adds nothing new to what is already present in perceptive consciousness. In other words, perceptive awareness does not require a further act of reflection in order to be consciousness. Pre-conceptual perception is essentially already consciousness or, as we will see, perception is already pre-conceptual self-awareness. This view is buoyed by Schopenhauer's analysis of the nature of intuitive perception as an operation that does not require application of concepts and is, therefore, common to all animals. We will also show that this view underlies Schopenhauer's critique of Kant's principle of the transcendental apperception.

However, we will also show that already in *Fourfold Root* Schopenhauer's views in this respect were somewhat ambiguous. His explicit theory of subjectivity seems to indicate that he does hold separate views concerning the nature of animal and human consciousness. According to these passages, human consciousness is intrinsically characterized by some kind of reflexivity, even if pre-conceptual. Finally, we will show how this latter position is confirmed and developed in other texts. Thus, we will end by concluding that in this respect Schopenhauer has moved closer to Kant's stance than he was willing to admit, for he, too, just like Kant, ends up subscribing to the idea that full-blown subjectivity requires at least the ability to reflect on our perceptions.

Intuitive Perception in *Fourfold Root*

If we want to search for a theory of conscious awareness in Schopenhauer's philosophy, the place to start seems to be precisely his theory of intuitive perception (*Anschauung*),[1] which is in great measure presented in *The Fourfold Root*, in particular in its second, significantly enlarged edition from 1847.

For Schopenhauer, to be consciously aware of something is to have an intuitive perception of it. By this Schopenhauer means having a direct representation of a singular spatial and temporal object standing in causal relationship with other objects. Negatively this means that in order to have perception or conscious awareness of something, it is not necessary to be able to think about it. In other words, it is not necessary that we possess concepts (general or abstract representations) to turn sense-data into representation of an object. This latter view, to which Schopenhauer wishes to contrast his theory of intuitive perception, is roughly that of Kant. For Kant, intuition, at least for us humans, is merely a receptive faculty of the soul[2]— that is, sensuous representation, which, by itself, does not furnish us with any objective representation. In order to achieve an objective representation, a spontaneous operation of our cognitive faculty is required, in which the understanding thinks an object that corresponds to the data of intuition.

> Our cognition arises from two fundamental sources in the mind, the first of which is the reception of representations (the receptivity of impressions), the second the faculty for cognizing an object by means of these representations (spontaneity of concepts); through the former an object is given to us, through the latter it is thought in relation to that representation (as a mere determination of the mind). Intuition and concepts therefore constitute the elements of all our cognition, so that neither concepts without intuition corresponding to them in some way nor intuition without concepts can yield a cognition.
>
> (KrV A50/B74)

For Kant, the understanding represents objects in a mediate form by means of concepts (KrV A67–8/B92–3), and objective representation depends on the ability of applying concepts to what is intuitively given (KrV A92–3/B125, A103–5). In one of Kant's most famous statements: "Thoughts without content are empty, intuitions without concepts are blind" (KrV A51/B75), so that only the joint action of intuition and concept can provide us with objective cognition. This is, according to Schopenhauer, Kant's primordial error, his "*prôton pseudos*" (WWR1 419). According to Schopenhauer, Kant's theory of objectivity fails to distinguish adequately between intuitive-perceptive and abstract cognition (WWR1 514). First of all, Kant has refrained from presenting a theory of intuitive perception, having limited himself to the assertion "the empirical content of intuition is *given* to us" (WWR1 509). In the second place, he has not provided an adequate definition of the understanding. For Kant, the latter is a faculty of abstract knowledge, of knowledge by means of concepts, and at the same time a condition of objective perception:

> But this is how Kant imports thought into intuition and lays the ground for the fatal confusion of intuitive and abstract cognition that I am criticizing at present. He allows intuition, taken on its own, to be devoid of understanding, purely sensuous, and thus merely passive; and an *object* is grasped only through thought (category of the understanding): and this is how he brings *thought into intuition*. But then again the object of *thought* is an individual, real object; and this deprives thought of its essential character of universality and abstraction and entails that thought has individual things rather than universal concepts for its object; in doing this, Kant again brings *intuition into thought*.
>
> (WWR1 520–1)

According to Kant, empirical intuition of objects requires that we are able to apply to them certain a priori concepts, the categories, which do not have their origin in experience. It is well-known that for Kant there are twelve of these concepts, which he divides in four groups (KrV A80/B106). The categories define an object of possible experience, an object in general, irrespective of the way in which it is more concretely determined through experience. We know a priori that any object whatsoever must conform to at least some of the categories; otherwise it could not be an object of experience. For that reason, the categories are, as Kant says, concepts of an object in general.[3] To this formal or abstract object of experience Kant calls also 'the transcendental object'.[4] Schopenhauer points out that the way Kant introduces his 'transcendental object' reflects the same lack of clarity regarding the nature of both intuitive and abstract knowledge. The transcendental object is at the same time "an individual thing that is not in space and time, because it is not intuitive" and "the object of thought without being an abstract concept" (WWR1 526). As we will see in more detail, Schopenhauer is adamant about the fact that the outcome of the operation of the understanding is the object of perception and not an object, as it were, behind or beyond it.

Even though, as Schopenhauer points out, Kant's text is not without some ambiguity concerning this point, if we adopt the view that Kant argues that the application of a priori concepts to intuition is a necessary condition for any kind of relation to objects, including perception, we can see that Schopenhauer partakes with Kant the idea that passive reception of sense data is not sufficient to attain to an objective representation. Contrary to what I may have suggested thus far, Schopenhauer's revision of Kant's doctrine of the faculties does not entail going back to some version of sensualism (i.e., to the idea that cognition consists in the passive reception of sense-data). On the contrary, for Schopenhauer, the ability to be affected by objects other than ourselves (i.e. sensibility) amounts to a blind feeling of our own body as an immediate object for cognition and does not furnish us, by itself, with objective representations (WWR1 22–3). In order to achieve intuitive perception of objects, that is, *consciousness* of them, the understanding must play a part into action. It is for this reason that Schopenhauer says repeatedly that intuitive perception is *intellectual* (see, for instance, WWR1 13; FR 53).[5] The intellectual character of perception means that the affection of our sense-organs is not sufficient to produce an objective representation of objects external to our sensing body:

> For what a poor thing is mere sensation, after all! Even in the most refined of sense organs, sensation is nothing more than a local, specific feeling, capable in its own way of some variation, however, in itself always subjective, which as such can contain absolutely nothing objective, and so nothing similar to an intuitive perception.
>
> (FR 52; translation modified)

As already stated, the intellectual character of perception does not imply that intuitive perception is rational (i.e., mediated through concepts). Despite the 'intellectual' character of perception, the latter is "is not a conclusion drawn from abstract concepts; it does not take place in reflection and is not voluntary; rather it is immediate, necessary and certain" (WWR1 13). At this point, both meanings of *Anschauung*, both as intuition and perception, come into play: perception is, by its very nature, intuitive, that is, an immediate grasp of something at hand. For Schopenhauer, intuitive perception is enough to attain objective representation, and conceptual knowledge and all cognitive operations that hinge on concepts such as judging or reasoning are merely second-order cognition.

The understanding's function in perception consists in an immediate and intuitive application of cognition of causal relations to sense-data. The understanding traces the data furnished by the senses to their external cause and thereby generates consciousness, representation, or cognition—all these concepts are synonymous—of an object occupying space and time and in causal interaction with others, including, first of all, our own body (WWR1 23–4); "The changes that every animal body experiences are cognized immediately, that is, they are sensed; and in so far as this effect is referred back to its cause, the intuitive perception arises of this cause as an object" (WWR1 13; translation modified).

In *Fourfold Root* Schopenhauer goes into considerable detail concerning the transition from the sensation in the organism to the object as its cause both in the case of touch (FR 55ff.) as well as in that of sight (FR 57ff.). We will not here go into the intricacies of those descriptions, since they are more physiological than philosophical in nature.

It is easy to conclude that Schopenhauer is doubly opposed to Kant's account of cognition. In the first place, sensibility is for him no faculty of intuition. If we resort to Kant's terminology, we can say that through sensibility no object is given. Second, for cognition to take place an act of the understanding is required (as it is for Kant), but this is not an act of thinking, since there are no concepts involved in it. From Kant's twelve categories, only causality remains as a condition of cognition. However, knowledge of causality is here not conceptual, but rather intuitive, immediate.

Since intuitive perception does not require reason, which is exclusive of human beings, Schopenhauer claims that even animals possess consciousness in the form of cognition of spatial, temporal objects in causal interaction, even if they lack the ability to form concepts and engage in conceptual knowledge and reasoning:

> From what has been said it is clear that all animals, even the most imperfect, possess understanding: they all have cognition of objects, and this cognition serves as a motive that determines their movements.— Understanding is the same in all animals as well as in all human beings. It has the same unitary form in every case: cognition of causality, transition from effect to cause and from cause to effect and nothing else besides.
>
> (WWR1 24)

As is the case with humans, the understanding is present in animals, too, because they have the ability, however blunt, of perceiving an outside world. It is precisely on this ability of perceiving external objects that the essence of animals rest: "So *cognition*, together with the movement upon motives which it makes possible, is the fundamental *characteristic of animal life*" (WWR1 24). As we know, 'cognition' means in this quote the same as perception. These concepts are also equivalent to the ones of representing (*Vorstellen*) and consciousness (*Bewusstsein*). Schopenhauer argues, thus, as a consequence of his theory of intuitive perception that consciousness is essentially an animal feature:

> We do attribute consciousness to animals; so the concept of consciousness coincides with that of representation in general, of whatever kind, even though the word *Bewußtseyn*, consciousness, is derived from *Wissen*, knowledge. Consequently we do indeed attribute life to plants, but not consciousness.
>
> (WWR1 60)

Schopenhauer alludes here to the etymological affinity between the German words *Wissen*, which for Schopenhauer means always abstract knowledge, knowledge of reason, and *Bewusstsein*, consciousness. In spite of, and against this affinity, Schopenhauer is highlighting the fact that animals possess consciousness in the sense of intuitive perception, but not abstract knowledge, which would presuppose the ability to form concepts. As

Schopenhauer himself says, "consciousness is known to us positively only as a property of animal nature; consequently we may not, indeed we cannot, think of it otherwise than as *animal consciousness*, so that this expression is in fact tautological" (WWR2 227). And since possessing consciousness, being aware is equivalent to being a subject, we can say of animals that they, too, are in a way *subjects* of cognition.

Schopenhauer's Theory of Subjectivity and Reason

Up to this point, we have seen that Schopenhauer's theory of intuitive perception entails a theory of consciousness, according to which the latter does not involve any kind of rationality in Schopenhauer's sense. The question now is what Schopenhauer's explicit theory of subjectivity and self-consciousness tells us about the relation between consciousness and the ability to reflect on our representations (i.e. reason).

First of all, it should be remarked that when we speak here of self-consciousness we are employing the latter expression in a different sense from the one in which Schopenhauer usually uses to it. Schopenhauer uses 'Selbstbewusstsein' (i.e. 'self-consciousness') to refer to what Kant called 'inner sense'. The latter refers to the self-givenness of the subject, that is, to the fact that the subject is given to itself in temporal succession. This corresponds to a passive dimension of self-consciousness, one whereby, according to Kant, the subject is affected by itself. What will be of concern to us here is precisely the other sense of self-consciousness in Kant, the one he calls 'transcendental apperception'. In opposition to the former sense, 'transcendental apperception' points to an active dimension of self-consciousness, to the ability to say of any of my representations that it is I who think them, that I am consciously aware of them. It is Schopenhauer's version of this latter mode of self-consciousness that will be at stake here. In order to distinguish it from the former, we will sometimes refer to it also as 'cognitive self-consciousness'.

According to Schopenhauer, as to Kant before him, the subject of cognition cannot know itself directly as such, that is, as 'transcendental apperception'. On the contrary, the possibility of the subject knowing its own self depends precisely on the subject's temporal self-givenness. Self-knowledge is, thus, crucially dependent on inner sense. Without inner sense, there is no self-knowledge. As is well-known, Schopenhauer thinks we are, as it were, given to ourselves through our inner sense as 'will'. He puts much emphasis on this finding since, as it is well-known, it represents the cornerstone of his whole metaphysical edifice.

One of the reasons for Schopenhauer holding that the 'subject of cognition' or 'transcendental apperception' is incapable of self-knowledge is that the subject in this sense is the condition of all representation and for that reason it is always presupposed whenever it tries, as it were, to turn around in order to know itself: "Therefore there is no *cognition of the cognizing*

[*Erkennen des Erkennens*] because it would require that the subject separate itself from cognizing and yet cognize the cognizing, which is impossible" (FR 141).

As we saw above, intuitive knowledge is knowledge in its primary sense, whereas abstract knowledge is derivative in the sense of being always referred to and dependent on intuitive knowledge. Thus, when Schopenhauer says that there is no 'cognition of the cognizing' (*Erkennen des Erkennens*), he is claiming that intuitive cognition or perception cannot be self-referred (i.e., we are not able to cognize our own cognitive intuition in an *intuitive* manner).

Although Schopenhauer does not mention it explicitly, his thesis of the unknowable character of the subject is a way of recasting one of Kant's main contentions in the chapter 'Paralogisms of pure reason' from the *Critique of Pure Reason*. In that chapter, Kant engages in a refutation of what he calls 'Rational Psychology'. This refers to all attempts at establishing synthetic a priori knowledge of the subject or the soul as a simple, imperishable substance. Kant, too, holds that, since the 'transcendental apperception' is the presupposition of all cognition, it cannot know itself lest it should incur in circularity:

> Through this I, or He, or It (the thing), which thinks, nothing further is represented than a transcendental subject of thoughts=x, which is recognized only through the thoughts that are its predicates, and about which, in abstraction, we can never have even the least concept; because of which we therefore turn in a constant circle, since we must always already avail ourselves of the representation of it at all times in order to judge anything about it; we cannot separate ourselves from this inconvenience, because the consciousness in itself is not even a representation distinguishing a particular object, but rather a form of representation in general, insofar as it is to be called a cognition; for of it alone can I say that through it I think anything.
>
> (KrV A346/B404)

Kant expresses this idea in another way, namely by saying that knowledge of the 'transcendental subject' is merely analytic, whereas self-knowledge, insofar as it is to be substantial, must be of a synthetic nature. But it is precisely this synthetic self-knowledge that is not possible a priori. Self-knowledge is indeed possible, but only empirically, through awareness of my inner states succeeding one another in time. Thus, self-knowledge is possible only with recourse to inner sense. Starting from the pure 'I think' it is not possible to establish synthetic a priori judgments. Every proposition that one draws from the 'I think' is at bottom analytic, expressing merely the subjective conditions of objective cognition, that is, providing a nominal definition for the subject of knowledge. Conditions of subjectivity are, for instance, that we have to think ourselves as the ultimate subjects of thought, as a unity, as identical throughout time and as different from other things in space. These conditions define what it is to be a subject, that is, they are the conditions under which we may meaningfully refer to an instance of subjectivity. Every one of the four paralogisms Kant presents is based on a surreptitious transference of subjective conditions of thinking about ourselves and therewith of subjectivity into real proprieties of ourselves as beings·

Even though in a much more simple and abbreviated way, Schopenhauer makes precisely the same point as Kant when discussing the difference between knowledge of the 'I know' and knowledge of the 'I will'. According to him, in opposition to the proposition 'I will', which yields synthetic, albeit empirical, self-knowledge, 'I know' is merely an analytical proposition: "Beginning with cognition, one can say that 'I cognize' is an *analytic* proposition; in contrast, 'I will' is *synthetic* and, indeed, *a posteriori*; for it is given through experience, here through inner experience (i.e. only in time)" (FR 143).

It should be noted that the fact that we are unable to cognize ourselves as subjects of cognition does not mean that we are completely unaware of our cognitive dimension. Otherwise we would not be able to think of ourselves as the bearer of our representations, something that, according to Schopenhauer, represents the dawning of philosophical consciousness in human beings (WWR1 3). In this respect, it should be borne in mind that it is one thing to have a representation of the world as animals unquestionably do and another thing to be able to look at the world *as* representation. For the latter, one must be able to be conscious of oneself as the bearer of representations, that is, as the subject of cognition. Thus, it must always remain possible to reflect on cognition and say 'I cognize' or 'I know that I cognize'. In Kant's language, this means that it is necessarily possible to bring perceptions under the 'transcendental unity of apperception'. But whereas for Kant the necessity of this possibility has far-reaching consequences, especially in what concerns the deduction of the categories[6] (i.e., the proof of their objective validity) for Schopenhauer reflection in this sense, the ability each of us has of saying 'I know' does not convey any knowledge that is not already contained in an unreflective consciousness, that is, in perception. This is implied by the following passage:

> To the objection 'I not only cognize [*erkennen*], but I also know [weiss] that I cognize [*erkenne*]' I would answer: your knowing [wissen] of your cognizing [*Erkennen*] is different from your cognizing [*Erkennen*] only in its being expressed. 'I know [*weiss*] that I cognize [*erkenne*]', says nothing more than 'I cognize' [*Ich erkenne*], and then, without anything further, this says nothing more than 'I'.
>
> (FR 141)

Before we comment on this quote, it should be borne in mind that in Schopenhauer '*wissen*' means always abstract, rational, reflective knowledge.

On the other hand, '*erkennen*' and its derivatives are used by Schopenhauer in a more ambiguous manner. *Erkennen* is used in a broader sense meaning cognition or knowledge in general, be it intuitive or abstract. But it can also be used, as is the case here, in a stricter sense where it means intuitive knowledge, cognition, knowledge of the understanding (as opposed to knowledge of reason). Taking this conceptual clarification into account, we can see that Schopenhauer argues that the proposition 'I know that I cognize' (*ich weiss, daß ich erkenne*), which springs from reflection on ourselves as bearers of representations (mental states), is merely an abstract expression of our perceptive awareness, of our cognizing (*Erkennen*). This entails, first, that explicit reflection is not needed in order for us to become aware. It is perceptive cognition that originally constitutes awareness. This is confirmed by Schopenhauer's idea, stated right in the first page of *The World as Will and Representation*, that the world as representation begins with the appearance of any living, knowing being (WWR1 3).[7] Indeed, Schopenhauer criticizes Kant's principle of the 'transcendental unity of apperception' precisely because it contradicts the fact that animals are conscious beings. Kant's principle consists in the fact that the 'I think' must be able to accompany all my representations. Schopenhauer says that this principle has preposterous consequences:

> And what is the meaning of this claim that balances on such a fine point?—That all representing is thinking?—No it is not, and this would have been disastrous; there would then be nothing but abstract concepts (. . .) And then animals would have to think or they would not be able to represent.
>
> (WWR1 535)

It is true that Schopenhauer does not do full justice to Kant's principle since the latter does not establish that the 'I think' must, as a matter of fact, accompany all our representations, but only that it must *be able* to do so.[8] This notwithstanding, the passage shows that for Schopenhauer conscious awareness does not depend on reason precisely because we must be able to ascribe it to animals.

In this respect Schopenhauer's position on conscious awareness could be viewed as similar to that of John Locke. As is well known, Locke's starting-point in the first book of his *Essay* is the refutation of the thesis that there are innate ideas. It is in this context that he begins to put forward his view that there are no ideas in the mind without the mind being aware of them. For example, he argues, if there were innate ideas, we would have to be conscious of them since our earliest infancy.[9] One of the reasons Locke gives to account for this thesis is that perception intrinsically involves awareness. Locke does not distinguish between perceiving and thinking. Thinking just is to perceive that we have some idea—'idea' being Locke's jargon for whatever is the content of our mind. Perception and thinking could not be defined, not even made intelligible, if they were not intrinsically self-aware mental states, 'it being impossible for any one to perceive, without perceiving, that he does perceive' (Locke, 1975, 335). Thus, consciousness is, for Locke, intrinsically a 'knowing that one knows', no second-order act of reflection being required for us to be self-conscious.

We can take a glance at the type of rationalistic position which Schopenhauer's position implicitly targets if we consider Leibniz's critique of Locke presented in his *New Essays on Human Understanding*. This work is known precisely for being a critique of Locke's essays, in particular of Locke's contention that there are no innate ideas. In order to refute Locke's thesis, Leibniz introduces the distinction between perception and apperception. According to Leibniz, perception does not necessarily involve consciousness. He gives the famous example of the *petites perceptions*, minute perceptions, which are too feeble or tiny for us to be aware of them, that is, perceptions that are *unconscious*:

> Besides, there are hundreds of indications leading us to conclude that at every moment there is in us an infinity of perceptions, unaccompanied by awareness [*apperception*] or reflection; that is, of alterations in the soul itself, of which we are unaware because these impressions are either too minute [*petites*] and too numerous, or else too unvarying, so that they are not sufficiently distinctive on their own. But when they are combined with others they do nevertheless have their effect and make themselves felt, at least confusedly, within the whole.
>
> (Leibniz, 1996, 53)

According to Leibniz, evidence of unconscious perceptions can be found, for instance, when we are suddenly awoken by an increasingly loud noise. When we come to our senses, we realize that we must have been hearing the noise all along, but it is only when it reaches the appropriate intensity that it draws us out of sleep. Other example he gives concerns the acoustic perception of the sea's roar: for us to be explicitly aware of the roar as such it is necessary to be unconsciously aware of the sound of all its tiny drops (Leibniz, 1996, 54). The introduction of unconscious perception allows Leibniz to argue for the existence of ideas in the soul of which we are not aware and which therefore may be potentially innate.

For Leibniz, as opposed to Locke, perceptions may be either conscious or unconscious. To conscious perception he also attributes the term 'apperception'. Apperception means precisely awareness on the part of the soul of what is taking place inside of itself, of its unconscious ideas. In other words, for the soul to apperceive its ideas an act of reflection on its part must occur. As proof of this, Leibniz takes ideas to be inner objects that exist whether they are perceived (or better, apperceived) or not, and innate ideas could be said to be primarily those that spring from the soul's reflection on itself. They are 'reflective concepts' corresponding to the soul's awareness of its own operations. We can see that Schopenhauer's position seems to be almost diametrically opposed to that of Leibniz in that he does not think reflection is necessary to bring forth consciousness. Evidence of this is that animals are for him conscious beings notwithstanding the fact that they are not able to reflect on the contents of their minds.

After this detour let us return to the passage we were quoting from *Fourfold Root*. From what we have seen, Schopenhauer's criticism of Kant's transcendental apperception seems to confirm the hypothesis we have drawn from the former's theory of intuitive perception. In fact, if perception without concepts and judgments does not need to be submitted to the transcendental apperception and animal awareness is primordially perception then animals are fully conscious beings and the 'I think' is superfluous in this regard. However, Schopenhauer's position is much more ambiguous than what we have suggested until now. This can be best appreciated if we consider the statement that immediately follows the passage we were quoting above:

> If your cognizing [*erkennen*] and your knowing [*wissen*] of this cognizing [*erkennen*] are two different things, then try just once to have either by itself alone: first to cognize [*erkennen*] without knowing [*wissen*] about it, and then again, to know [wissen] simply of cognizing [*erkennen*] without this knowing [*wissen*] being at the same time cognizing [*erkennen*].
>
> (FR 141)

From this quote we can infer that intuitive knowledge is in a way intrinsically self-aware, for *erkennen* too implies *wissen*, that is, cognizing (*erkennen*) involves also knowing (*wissen*) that one cognizes. At the same time, this self-awareness, this 'knowledge of cognition' must be of a pre-conceptual nature, otherwise Schopenhauer would allow reflection to be a condition of cognition. If cognition were not intrinsically self-aware, Schopenhauer would have to admit a further operation in order for it to become full conscious awareness. Schopenhauer's position stems in part from an attempt to avoid the possibility of an 'infinite regress' of reflection. If intuitive perception were not pre-reflexively self-aware, self-awareness would only be achieved in an act of reflection. The fact that we can always reflect further and say 'I know that I know that I know, etc.' does not have any epistemic implication, for reflection does not generate any cognitive content that is not already contained in the first instance of 'I know'. Thus, one does not have to perform an explicit act of reflection in order to be self-aware. Self-awareness does not need to be conceptual, linguistic, or rational. One is a subject even if one does not perform explicit acts of self-reflection. Perception or cognition (*erkennen*) involves awareness that one is perceiving or cognizing so that explicit reflection is not only unnecessary for awareness, but also redundant, given that it does not increase our knowledge, merely making explicit what was already implicit in perceptive awareness.[10] In other words, perceptive cognition, that is, '*erkennen*' already involves pre-reflective consciousness of itself.[11] However, if this is so, if *erkennen* implies *wissen*, one can apply to Schopenhauer his own critique of Kant's transcendental apperception: either animals are able to think or we cannot say they are conscious beings at all. Does this mean that Schopenhauer ends up, even if implicitly, subscribing to Kant's principle of the transcendental apperception?

Human and Animal Self-Consciousness

From what have seen until now, Schopenhauer's theory of intuitive perception entails a view of consciousness as essentially pre-reflective. This view is partly confirmed by his thesis on cognitive self-consciousness inasmuch as according to this view reflection adds no new cognitive content to what is already included in consciousness *qua* intuitive perception. Reflection, the ability to say 'I' or 'I think' or even 'I am perceptively aware of something', is only an abstract way of expressing our awareness and it could be as well absent. This would have as consequence that animals are as conscious beings as humans. However, we also saw that Schopenhauer's stance on cognitive self-consciousness is more ambiguous. Now we will see precisely that in other relevant passages from his oeuvre, Schopenhauer seems, like Kant, to posit a difference between animal awareness and human awareness, however problematic this may be regarding his theory of perception and consciousness. It is to those passages that we will now turn.

First, Schopenhauer subscribes to Kant's idea that the subject as such must be unitary. In other words, consciousness is as such essentially unified. See, for instance, the following passage:

> If we summarize Kant's claims we will find that what he understands by the synthetic unity of apperception is something like the extensionless centre of the sphere of all our representations, whose radii converge on it. It is what I call the subject of cognition, the correlative of all representations.
>
> (WWR1 435–6)

Schopenhauer is here making reference to an aspect of the Kantian notion of subjectivity, which we have not discussed yet. The fact that the 'I think' must be able to accompany all my representations implies that it must be possible to unify them in one consciousness. Schopenhauer not only subscribes to this idea,[12] but goes even further than Kant, arguing that consciousness must be *in fact* unified, whether it is aware of that unity or not: "But a *consciousness* is essentially something uniform and united, and therefore always requires a central point of unity" (WWR2 284).

The claim that consciousness must form a unity may be partly seen as Kant's attempt at replying to David Hume's critique of the self.[13] In his famous analysis, Hume argues that when we observe the contents of our minds we do not find any subject of experience, a self (Hume, 2000, 164–171). Against this, Kant claims that there is only experience and a subject thereof, if the subject is not as diverse as its mental contents. The subject can only represent a multiplicity as multiplicity (i.e., for instance an A, a B, and a C) if it is able to unify them in a single consciousness. Otherwise there could exist a consciousness of A that would have nothing in common with a consciousness of B and therefore they would not be able to be unified in a single consciousness. There would be consciousness of A, consciousness of B, consciousness of C, etc., but not a consciousness of A *and* B *and* C.[14] In other words, there can only be awareness of a manifold as such (of the 'manifold of intuition' as Kant calls it) if the subject qua consciousness is able to represent itself as identical throughout that manifold. The awareness the subject has of itself as identical throughout its manifold representations is, therefore, the condition of possibility of representing the manifold as manifold.

Schopenhauer presents a version of Kant's argument for the unity of consciousness in the *Parerga* in the context of a commentary to Kant's critique of rational psychology (PP1 105ff.). There Schopenhauer claims that it is possible to be aware of the mind's successive contents only by contrast with the representation of something permanent. In the case of outer perception, it is the representation of matter as the substance of material phenomena that performs this function. In inner perception (i.e., in the flux of inner consciousness), it is precisely the representation of the subject of knowledge that, according to Schopenhauer, appears as the element of permanence that allows the representation of succession as such. Otherwise its various states would be scattered without being apprehended as moments of one and the same succession:

> For that reason I have said that if our consciousness, with its entire content, moved uniformly within the stream of time, we would not be able to notice this movement. Therefore, there must be something immovable in consciousness itself. However, this cannot be anything but the cognizing subject itself, which, unmoved and unchanged, watches the course of time and the change of its content. Before its gaze life runs its course to the end, like a drama.
>
> (PP1 106)

If this requirement of unity of the subject is to be taken seriously, animals cannot be said to be fully subjects of cognition. For, according to Schopenhauer, animal consciousness "is a mere succession of present events, none of which, however, exists as future before its appearance, or as past after its disappearance, this being the distinctive characteristic of human consciousness" (WWR2 64). The life of animals is, therefore, "a continual present. It lives on without reflection (*Besinnung*) and is deeply engrossed in the present" (WWR2 64). According to Schopenhauer, only human beings are able to represent past, present, and future as such (i.e., time as a whole) and therefore, also their own death. This ability is due precisely to the presence of reason in humans. The ability humans have of representing past and future and thus, the present as a *continuum* stems, according to Schopenhauer, from conceptual representation. The image of a sensible impression "preserved by the imagination is already weaker than the impression itself; day by day it grows weaker still, and in time becomes completely extinct" (WWR2 67). Even though words as signs for concepts are sensible, only the concept has a kind of objective existence not subject to time, that is, to succession. "There is only one thing, *the concept*, which is not subject either to that instantaneous vanishing of the impression, or to the gradual disappearance of its image, and consequently is free from the power of time" (WWR2 67).

Given the ability reason has of representing the past and the future in connection with the present and therefore of representing life as a whole, Schopenhauer says reason provides human consciousness with *Besonnenheit*[15] (i.e., circumspection) (FR 101; WWR1 43; WWR2 62–3). The human being is said to be circumspect (*besonnen*) because his or her action does not hang solely from present motives and circumstances. Most of the time, humans determine their actions in accordance with the future, that is, with possible states of affairs and events. Contrary to the animal, which is tied to those motives that are each time intuitively presented to it, the human being is able to consider different possible courses of action, to ponder them, deliberate, and decide accordingly. That is, the human being has the ability of making a truly *conscious* choice among motives. Besides this practical sense, *Besonnenheit* has also a more theoretical-cognitive connotation. According to the latter, it consists in the ability to look around, not in a spatial, but rather in a temporal sense, of representing past and future. Both senses of the word are connected by the fact that it is only because we possess this ability to 'look around' in temporal terms that we are able to deliberate among various possibilities of acting.

The possibility of putting life into perspective, of not being subject to the moment's fleeting impression, as animals are, gives human beings the possibility of being more than just 'actors' on the stage of reality, of placing themselves as 'spectators' and especially of spectators of their own life:

> The panoramic view of life as a whole, which gives human beings our advantage over the animals, can also be compared to a colour-less, abstract, geometrical miniature of life's course. Armed with this sketch, we have the same relation to the animals that a ship's pilot (. . .) has to the unskilled crew who see only waves and sky. So it

is noteworthy, indeed marvellous, that we human beings always lead a second, abstract life alongside our concrete life. In the first we are subject to all the storms of reality and are prey to the influence of the present: we must strive, suffer and die, just as animals do. But our abstract life, as it appears before us in rational contemplation, is the calm reflection of the first life and the world it is lived in; it is that miniature sketch just mentioned. In this realm of peaceful deliberation what had previously possessed us completely and moved us deeply, now appears cold, colourless and strange to the eye: here we are simply onlookers and spectators.

(WWR1 101–2)

Only humans, because they are rational beings, are able to survey their life as a whole and represent the absent past and the possible future as such. This feature is enough to establish a difference between animal and human consciousness, which Schopenhauer otherwise denies. Animals perceive consciously, but are not aware of their successive perceptions as moments of a single life. Furthermore, in *On the Will in Nature*, Schopenhauer goes as far as claiming that full cognitive self-consciousness requires reason:

The process of representation cannot itself be perceived, but can only be brought to consciousness afterwards in rational reflection, this second power of representing, that is, in abstract. Therefore simple represent-ing (intuiting) is related to actual thinking (i.e. to cognition in abstract concepts) as willing itself is related to inner awareness of willing (i.e. to consciousness). For this reason, completely clear and distinct conscious-ness of one's existence, like that of another's existence, first appears with reason (with the faculty of concepts), which as greatly elevates humans over animals as the mere faculty of intuitive representation elevates animals over plants.

(WN 68)

Here Schopenhauer argues for a clear distinction between mere plant life, animal perception, and rational consciousness. In particu-lar, whereas animal perception is not able to become explicitly aware of itself as such, humans as rational are fully self-aware. We see, thus, that Schopenhauer's position moves closer to the one laid out by Kant in his principle of the synthetic unity of apperception. If full subjectivity requires the ability to reflect on one's own perceptive awareness and is thereby essentially unified, it is the case that it must be at least possible for the subject to add an 'I think' to each one of her or his thoughts and perceptions. It goes without saying that this sits uncomfortably along-side Schopenhauer's doctrine that simple animal perception is enough to generate subjectivity.

Conclusion

Is Schopenhauer's position on cognitive self-awareness in the end consistent? We would like to conclude by arguing that it can be made so if we distinguish between animal and human awareness and limit Schopenhauer's thesis about the tautological character of reflection to the latter.

Pure animal perception, which even though can be said to be an instance of consciousness, is devoid of the possibility of reflection, and we would say is not aware of itself as such. In the light of this, Schopenhauer's theory of perception should be seen, thus, as applying primarily to animal consciousness and as laying the necessary requirements for a *minimum* of consciousness to take place. Human cognition, on the other hand, is characterized by the possibility of reflection and is for that reason intrinsically self-aware of itself as a moment of a continuous unified life. Thus, according to this interpretation, the proposition 'I know that I know' is only equivalent to or already implied in 'I know' (*ich erkenne*) if we construe the latter as an instance of human perceptive cognition. It is only superfluous or tautological to say 'I know' or 'I know that I know' if we presuppose a given rational human consciousness, which by definition is implicitly characterized by the possibility of saying 'I'. On the contrary, when compared with pure animal consciousness, the possibility of saying 'I' or 'I know' is anything but innocuous, for it makes possible a whole new level of awareness.

In sum, we can say that Schopenhauer was always faithful to the idea that animal perception—that is, pure perceptive awareness—is fully conscious. Proof of this is the fact that Schopenhauer has never given up on his theory of intuitive perception, which received, in fact, a thorough treatment in the second edition of *The Fourfold Root*. On the other hand, although he never mentioned it explicitly, his conception of human awareness implies that cognitive self-awareness requires the use of concepts, language and reason, for it is these that constitute full subjectivity.[16]

Notes

1 The new Cambridge translation of Schopenhauer's works translates *Anschauung* as 'intuition'. Although this is consistent with the standard translations of *Anschauung* in Kant, something feels lost by not making mention of the specific character of intuition in Schopenhauer as opposed to the way it is understood by Kant. Since, as we will see, Schopenhauer's thesis is that Kant's intuition is equivalent to perception, I opted for the expression 'intuitive perception' to translate Schopenhauer's *Anschauung*. Though, I will maintain the use of 'intuition' whenever the term is being used in its Kantian sense.

2 This is one of the central ideas of the 'transcendental aesthetic' and is presented right on its first page (KrV A19/B33).

3 This idea is frequently repeated by Kant. See, for instance, KrV A50/B74, A93–4/B125–6, B128, A245–6, A251, A254/B309.

4 On Kant's notion of the transcendental object see KrV A50/B74, A93/B126, B128, A104–6, A250–1.

5 There is, of course, an element of provocation to the fact that Schopenhauer calls intuitive perception *intellectual*. His philosophical rivals Fichte and Schelling also talked of an intellectual intuition. But whereas for the German idealists intellectual intuition is connected with intuition of the absolute, for Schopenhauer it is such a matter of course that it is, as we will see below, common to all animals.

6 See, for instance, KrV B135 where Kant says that the principle of the synthetic unity of apperception is in itself analytical but necessarily implies a synthesis.

7 For the idea that the world as representation arises with the appearance of animals see also WWR1 179. This does not contradict the idea presented above that only humans are able to look at the world as representation, for the world can be representation even if it is not recognized as such, as is the case with animals. Representation, *Vorstellung* in German, can take on a neutral sense, away from any idealistic connotations, meaning simply 'something we are aware of'.

8 That in this respect Schopenhauer misreads Kant's transcendental apperception was pointed out by Welsen (1995, 139ff).

9 "For to imprint any thing on the Mind without the Mind's perceiving it, seems to me hardly intelligible" (Locke, 1975, 49–50).

10 Janaway (1989, 122) claims that Schopenhauer should have allowed for subjects to have knowledge of their cognition since, according to him, 'I know c' and 'I know that I have a cognition of c' have different propositional contents. Without wanting to dispute this last claim, I think Janaway misses Schopenhauer's Kantian point here: knowledge of cognition is merely analytic, it does not extend our knowledge in what concerns the subject of knowledge.

11 I took the idea of a 'pre-reflective consciousness' from Dan Zahavi's analysis of subjectivity in Husserl (Zahavi, 2005). This expression was first introduced in philosophical jargon by Sartre.

12 This point is also made by Janaway (1989, 124–125).

13 See Hume (2000, 164–171). For an interpretation of Kant's apperception as a reply to Hume see, for example, Kitcher (1990, 97ff.)

14 Kant makes this point in a very clear manner, at least according to his standards, in KrV B 133–4. For analysis of this idea see also Allison (1983, 138–139).

15 On Schopenhauer's notion of *Besonnenheit* see Koßler (2002).

16 Welsen (1995, 139) claims that Schopenhauer subscribes to Kant's principle of the unity of apperception, in that the unity of consciousness presupposes the ability to employ concepts and judgements.

Bibliography

Allison, H. *Kant's Transcendental Idealism: An Interpretation and Defense*. New Haven: Yale University Press, 1983.

Hume, D. *Treatise of Human Nature*, ed. David Fate Norton and Mary J. Norton. Oxford: Oxford University Press, 2000.

Janaway, C. *Self and World in Schopenhauer's Philosophy*. Oxford: Oxford University Press, 1989.

Kitcher, P. *Kant's Transcendental Psychology*. Oxford: Oxford University Press, 1990.

Koßler, M. 'Zur Rolle der Besonnenheit in Schopenhauers Ästhetik', *Schopenhauer-Jahrbuch* 83, 2002: 119–133.

Leibniz, G.W.F. *New Essays on Human Understanding*, trans. Peter Remnant and Jonathan Bennett. Cambridge: Cambridge University Press, 1996.

Locke, J. *An Essay Concerning Human Understanding*, ed. Peter H. Nidditch. Oxford: Clarendon Press, 1975.

Welsen, P. *Schopenhauers Theorie des Subjekts. Ihre transzendentalphilosophischen, anthropologischen und naturmetaphysischen Grundlagen*. Würzburg: Königshausen & Neumann, 1995.

Zahavi, D. *Subjectivity and Selfhood: Investigating the First-Person Perspective*. Cambridge, MA: MIT Press, 2005.

10 Beyond the Principle of Sufficient Reason?

Schopenhauer's Aesthetic Phenomenology

Bart Vandenabeele

Schopenhauer's claims about the principle of sufficient reason face several significant problems, not in the least because he is adamant that his theory of knowledge is compatible with a metaphysical view that distinguishes sharply between the phenomenal world (the world as representation) and the world as it is in itself (the world as will). His intriguing analysis of the peculiar type of perception he qualifies as *aesthetic* further complicates matters, as it is also intricately linked up with his dyadic conception of will and representation. Since Schopenhauer insists that perceiving an object aesthetically requires an exceptional attitude which enables us to pierce the veil of Maya and capture a glimpse of how the will manifests itself most adequately in (or as) Ideas, the question arises not only what are the specific features of such a kind of knowledge beyond the principle of sufficient reason, but also whether qualifying aesthetic cognition in this way may lead to a coherent phenomenology of aesthetic experience which safeguards the life-affirming nature of the aesthetic. Those two questions, which will guide us in what follows, are of the utmost importance in the broader context not only of Schopenhauer's epistemology and philosophy of mind but also of his philosophy as a whole, for (or so I shall argue) answering them in a satisfactory way will enable us to give the lie to those who, like Nietzsche, unjustly repudiate his view of aesthetic experience as misguided and ultimately hostile to life.

First, then, I will briefly discuss the tenets of Schopenhauer's theory of sensory perception. I then contrast this with his account of aesthetic perception and cognition (*ästhetische Anschauung und Erkenntnis*), which arguably transcends the principle of sufficient reason. Further, I aim to show that the consensus view of Schopenhauer's theory of the aesthetic attitude, which reduces it to spiritual detachment and disembodied cognition is wholly inadequate. Even focussing on Schopenhauer's account of the beautiful (and disregarding his theory of the sublime) should suffice to show that, in Schopenhauer's view, aesthetic perception can really be active, imaginative, and genuinely life-affirming.[1]

I shall thus argue that Schopenhauer offers a rich phenomenological account of aesthetic experience, which shows that appreciating beautiful objects requires suspending our individual needs, desires, and appetites. This experience of *depersonalisation*, by which a willing individual feels himself to be transformed into a 'pure subject of knowledge', does not imply a glorification of dispassionate spectatorship, as Nietzsche and many other commentators have maintained, but rightly emphasises that aesthetic contemplation is imaginative as well as enthusiastic, and—as we shall see—requires a genuine interest in the intrinsic value of an object.

Sensory Perception and Aesthetic Experience

One of Schopenhauer's explicit goals is to naturalise Kant's theory of knowledge and to defend the value of embodied perception against idealising tendencies in Kant's epistemology and that of his followers. Schopenhauer criticises Kant's *Critique of Pure Reason* for being too much concerned with *pure* intuition and *abstract* judgment and reasoning, and he therefore develops a detailed account of the role of the body and, more specifically, of the senses in intuitive perception and knowledge of the world (see FR, § 17–25). Anticipating Nietzsche's views on embodied cognition but also phenomenologists such as Husserl and (especially) Merleau-Ponty, Schopenhauer contends that gaining adequate insight into knowledge and perception cannot proceed wholly along the lines of Kant and his idealistic followers Fichte, Schelling, and Hegel. For whilst Fichte held that the non-ego could be derived from the ego, "like a web from a spider" (WWR1 40), which turns the object into the effect of the subject, Schopenhauer insists not merely on the embodied nature of the subject, but also argues that the subject and the object of perception are *correlative*, for the principle of sufficient reason presupposes the object but is not valid before and outside it (see WWR1 § 7). The subject of knowledge and the object are not related to each other as cause and effect, but presuppose one another *a priori*. They are ultimately two sides of a single indivisible act of consciousness, of what Husserl calls an 'intentional act'.

Since the law of causality applies only within the world of representation, it cannot be applied properly to explain the correlation between subject and object. Representation is fundamentally 'bipolar'. It is of the utmost importance to note that Schopenhauer argues that this subject-object correlation is presupposed in *all* forms of cognition, hence including *aesthetic* cognition. Schopenhauer is faithful to Kant in defending the 'transcendental ideality' of the whole world of objects (WWR1 § 7 and *passim*; see also FR § 18–19 and *passim*), but he supplements this transcendental perspective with a naturalised account of how complete causal knowledge of objects of perception is possible (see FR, § 21). For Schopenhauer's insight that subject and object are correlative does not imply that the objects of perception do not causally interact with us. Schopenhauer is not a sceptic, and he thus urges that causal action exhausts the objects' (empirical) being. The perceived world in space and time, which includes perception of ourselves as embodied individuals, is perfectly real.

Yet how perceptual objects can be both a construct of the understanding (for they are transcendentally ideal) and yield the causal ground for perception remains unclear. As I argued elsewhere in more detail, this creates a number of complex paradoxes, which could only be disentangled if either Schopenhauer abandoned the naturalisation of his theory of knowledge, or he accepted that the physical objects that provide the 'raw material' for objective intuitions are radically different from the intuitions constructed on the basis of sensory perception, or he were prepared to reject the *a priori* nature of cognition and subject-object correlation altogether.[2]

These problems and paradoxes should not, however, blind us to the subtlety of Schopenhauer's account of cognition, which offers a rich panorama of the mechanisms of sensory perception. Developing and criticising some of Kant's anthropological views, and anticipating 20th-century phenomenological theories, he explores the richness and value of the senses. This is not the place to offer a detailed survey of Schopenhauer's hierarchy of the senses.[3] One of its more intriguing aspects should be taken into account, however, for it is directly related to the topic of this essay, since it connects, in a somewhat unexpected way, ordinary and aesthetic perception. In Schopenhauer's discussion of sensory perception the sense of sight possesses a privileged status. This is not surprising, for this privilege has dominated Western philosophy at least since Plato. Yet according to Schopenhauer, the sense of sight is to be distinguished qualitatively from the other senses for several rather surprising reasons.

First of all, the sense of sight is distinguished from the other senses, because it is the *aesthetic* sense par excellence. The reason for this is directly relevant to the issue of how and why aesthetic cognition could be cognition 'beyond' the principle of sufficient reason. For, unlike the other senses, the sense of sight can be affected without being immediately experienced as pleasurable or unpleasant. From this point of view it is more 'objective' than the other senses. Whereas the clearly 'subjective' senses, smell and taste, are emitted by things and can linger in the places from which their causes have departed, the sense of sight (and up to a certain point, also the sense of hearing) is related in a different way to its causal object. The visual appearance of my kitchen does not linger in a place after the kitchen has left it, and the kitchen is not represented in its smell in the way that it is in its visual image. In Schopenhauer's idiom, smells exist *for our will*. And if they are aesthetically interesting at all, it is through association and not through what I experience *in* the object—that is, it is through how it immediately affects me, through *what it brings to mind*, rather than through the meaning that we capture *in* the object.

Schopenhauer thus characterises seeing as 'objective', but he uses the latter term in at least two distinct senses: not immediately connected to an affective stirring of our will, on the one hand, and being capable of realising an objective intuition (*Anschauung*), on the other hand (see also FR § 21). This rather confusing usage may not be as innocent as we might suppose, for it ought to direct our attention to the important problem of the intelligibility of what Schopenhauer calls 'will-less perception' i.e., a way of perceiving objects that is not dominated by the interests of our will). This is a kind of perception that is 'pure' and somehow 'uprooted', i.e., *disconnected from the roots of the principle of sufficient reason that determine ordinary sensory perception*.

Common perception is not disinterested, Schopenhauer argues, but directs its "attention to things that stand in some sort of relation to his will", and "only ever affords cognition of relations" (WWR1 220–221). But does that imply that all will-less perception is necessarily disconnected from cognition which is determined by the principle of sufficient reason? To be able to answer this question, we should focus first on what Schopenhauer considers to be the proper target of aesthetic cognition, namely the Platonic Idea. Only after that will we be able to grasp the richness of Schopenhauer's analysis of the subjective component of aesthetic contemplation and obtain a more adequate understanding of why objective cognition that is not subservient to the principle of sufficient reason does not necessarily imply dispassionate, disembodied contemplation.

The Objects of Aesthetic Perception: Platonic Ideas

In emphasising that universals and not particulars are the proper object of aesthetic perception, Schopenhauer engages in a long tradition of idealist philosophers, including Plotinus, Schelling, and Hegel. This metaphysical tradition has always stressed the thought that aesthetic perception distinguishes itself from ordinary perception by focussing on an Idea that is embodied in a particular work of art. Much later, in the same vein, Arthur Danto will defend the view that works of art are to be distinguished from ordinary objects by being characterised by *aboutness* (i.e., by the fact that the former are external shapes that embody ideas—that are the content of the work of art, that which the work is *about*).

Despite *prima facie* similarities with this idealist tradition, which culminates in Hegel's and Danto's focus on ideas as the content of works of art, Schopenhauer's aesthetic theory is manifestly different from it in a number of significant ways. The hugely important differences between Schopenhauer's theory and his idealist colleagues are deeply connected with the problem of the principle of sufficient reason. Discussing all the discrepancies between Schopenhauer's views and the Hegelian strand of thought obviously falls beyond the scope of this essay. Here I shall focus on Schopenhauer's arguments with regard to aesthetic cognition and its objective correlates.

According to Schopenhauer, the target of aesthetic appreciation is neither the relation of the object to our personal interests, nor the relation of the object with other objects. Ordinary cognition is not merely guided by but determined by personal needs, appetites, and emotions. Aesthetic consciousness, by contrast, is a superior form of cognition which is "*a way of regarding things independently from the principle of sufficient reason*", and is based upon "the capacity . . . to lose oneself in intuition and to withdraw cognition that originally only existed in its service to the will from this service", and yields insight into *what* the object truly is (WWR1 218–219). Aesthetic, will-less perception yields 'objective' insight from the standpoint of eternity[4] (i.e., into the timeless kernel of things)—that is, the universal essences of the perceived objects, beyond mere appearance. This neo-Platonic approach identifies the objects of aesthetic consciousness with the timeless forms behind the mere appearances of common ordinary cognition, that is to say, Platonic Ideas.

Now, whilst common perception is always necessarily related to the individual's will and always demands only knowledge of the relations (i.e., knowledge determined by the principle of sufficient reason for which the abstract concept of the thing is sufficient), aesthetic consciousness offers a type of insight which surpasses merely conceptual knowledge and strives to grasp the Idea *in and through* the particular aesthetic object. The core of the object is thus known by a peculiar type of *imaginative perception*. (I will come back to this in the final part of this essay.)

Yet Schopenhauer's Platonic jargon should not deceive us, for Schopenhauer's aesthetic Ideas differ in a number of important ways from their counterparts in Platonic philosophy. Whereas for Plato the Ideas are the ontological essences of the whole world (i.e., the eternal universals that form the ultimate components of reality as a whole), for Schopenhauer they are the correlates of aesthetic imaginative perception and adequately manifest the abysmal core of the world, the one ultimate kernel of things, namely will. With the exception of music,[5] which is a direct copy of the will, Schopenhauer insists that all other art forms and aesthetic experiences cannot gain direct insight into the metaphysical core of the world, but merely indirectly, that is through its endless plurality of timeless Ideas, which in turn are embodied in concrete particulars, be it natural beauties or works of art.

Furthermore, and this is very important in the context of the problem of the relation between aesthetic cognition and the scope of the principle of sufficient reason, Schopenhauer refers to the categories of the understanding (or intellect) to construct a complex argument for the peculiar epistemological and metaphysical status of the Ideas in aesthetic perception.

We can summarise Schopenhauer's reasoning as follows:

i   the categories of space and time and the categories of the understanding (the principle of sufficient reason) construct the world as representation;

ii the world as representation therefore consists of multiple representations or different objects;

iii the principle of sufficient reason is limited to the world as representation;
iv the principle of sufficient reason does not apply to the thing-in-itself (the noumenon);
v the thing-in-itself beyond all phenomena cannot be characterised by multiplicity;
vi the Ideas are characterised by multiplicity;
vii the Ideas cannot be the noumenal thing-in-itself.

It is needless to point out that there are several problems with Schopenhauer's reasoning, especially concerning the awkward place occupied by the Platonic Ideas in the metaphysical realm, for the Platonic Ideas are not merely the most adequate objectifications of will; they clearly belong to the domain of representation, for (unlike the thing-in-itself) they are characterised by plurality, whereas they cannot be grasped by the kind of cognition that is determined by the ordinarily applying categories of understanding. The Ideas seem to be both within *and* beyond the world as representation. They seem to belong to the world as will, for they offer the most adequate access to the thing-in-itself, but they also seem to belong to the world as representation, for they are not only characterised by multiplicity (as *all* particular objects are) but are also grasped by a superior kind of cognition, which pierces through the veil of Maya. However, aesthetic perception offers merely another *veiled* access, which deceives us into believing that the plurality of Ideas are the ultimate components of reality, since for Schopenhauer the Platonic Ideas are neither concepts (as seems the case in Platonic philosophy), nor merely the products of the power of imagination (as the aesthetic ideas are in Kant's theory of art), nor the ideal revelation of the Absolute (as in Schelling and Hegel).

Although the ambivalent and complicated status of Schopenhauer's 'semi-Platonic' idealism cannot be ignored, understanding the specific characteristics of aesthetic perception and cognition does not presuppose the belief that the Platonic Ideas are the adequate objectifications of the will. For despite its differences with ordinary cognition, aesthetic cognition necessarily remains tied to empirical perception. A proper characterisation of the value of Schopenhauer's aesthetic theory should take into account his (anti-Hegelian) rehabilitation of sensory perception and its relevance to aesthetic contemplation and artistic creativity. Schopenhauer's aesthetic theory does not merely attempt to answer Plato's repudiation of the arts by offering a Platonic reply to it, as Christopher Janaway suggests,[6] he also aims to develop *an explanation of aesthetic appraisal which avoids the Platonic-Hegelian trap of demoting the senses in favour of spiritual contemplation.* Although Schopenhauer (rightly) departs from Kant's transcendental approach, which is entirely preoccupied with a critique of aesthetic *judgement*, and defends an aesthetic attitude theory which centres on aesthetic *contemplation*, he justly emphasises that aesthetic cognition involves sensory perception, and is thus necessarily a form of *embodied cognition*, and that its significance is intimately connected with the rich variety of the senses.

Schopenhauer's admiration for Plato's idealism should not be confused with a defence of some version of intellectualist aesthetics. On the contrary, Schopenhauer repeatedly warns against identifying Ideas with concepts, and insists that the latter are useless and even deleterious to aesthetic experience and the creation of art. Concepts are useful in ordinary life and necessary and productive in science, Schopenhauer holds, but they "will always be barren for art" (WWR1 277). Yet, artistic Ideas "develop representations that are novel with respect to concepts sharing the same name: the Idea is like a living and developing organism endowed with generative powers, an organism that can produce things that were not already packaged up inside it" (WWR1 277).

Contrary to Hegel and other idealists, Schopenhauer also holds that concepts are merely mental constructs that aid in grasping reality in general terms, whereas *Ideas* cannot be discovered by conceptual thinking, but solely by intuition or perception (*Anschauung*) and imagination (*Phantasie*). Aesthetic contemplation transports me out of myself and suspends my merely personal concerns and ambitions, but I do not therefore become a 'pure intellect' or 'pure spirit' (neither in a Platonic nor in a Hegelian sense). Moreover, Schopenhauer vehemently opposes merely conceptual and allegorical works of art, "in which we see the distinct, limited, cold dispassionate concept glimmer and finally appear": such works deserve nothing but our "disgust and indignation, for we see ourselves deceived and cheated of our interest and attention" (WWR2 465). And he also praises the creativity of lyrical poetry precisely for being "a free impulse of genius, without any admixture of deliberation or reflection" (WWR2 466).

As it is possible to view empirical objects in a way that somehow transcends their merely sensuous characteristics, this involves ultimately overcoming *not* sensory perception as such—which seems to be Hegel's and perhaps also Plato's ideal—but the dominance of our *personal* appetites, urges, worries, and needs, in order to value the purposefulness of the thing and appreciate it *for the thing that it is*. Schopenhauer's analysis of the senses and of perceptual cognition is integral to his approach of aesthetic perception. For in aesthetic perception, sensory perception is not discarded, because it is driven by what cannot be discarded *in principle*, namely will. One should not forget that, in Schopenhauer's view, the brain is a tool of the will: it assists the will in appearing in the phenomenal world. Yet in aesthetic cognition the cerebral system is no longer subservient to the *individual* will and operates, as it were, *detached from it*. This does not imply that we are merely passive mirrors, as Schopenhauer nevertheless oftentimes suggests, and that our mind is "temporarily cleared of the will, of all desire, emotion and felt need."[7] On the contrary, perceiving an object aesthetically requires a heightened state of awareness in which the character and content of aesthetic consciousness is fully determined by the aesthetic correlate. The ordinary ways of locating myself temporally, spatially, and causally abate, since sensory, imaginative perception of the aesthetic object suspends taking into account the ways in which the aesthetic correlate is causally or conceptually related to other things—that is to say, I transcend the kind of perception and cognition that is subservient to the principle of sufficient reason. This is hugely important. Instead of accepting what seems to have become a consensus opinion in Schopenhauer research, namely that Schopenhauer argues that aesthetic contemplation requires us to transcend sensory perception by 'spiritualising' it and becoming an unemotional and passive receptacle, I would like to emphasise that Schopenhauer does not defend such a view. On the contrary, he vindicates that aesthetic consciousness requires us to "devote the entire power of our mind to intuition . . . letting the whole of consciousness be filled with peaceful contemplation" of the aesthetic object (WWR1 210). Hence, relinquishing the ordinary way of considering things and "ceasing to follow under the guidance of the forms of the principle of sufficient reason" does *not* imply discarding perceptual and imaginative engagement with the world. Contrary to what most commentators suggest, Schopenhauer's characterisation of aesthetic perception (or intuition) does not involve "a condition of pure passivity" in which, as Julian Young unjustly argues, "the mind becomes a reflecting *tabula rasa*".[8] On the contrary, active imaginative engagement with the aesthetic aspects of the world is a necessary requirement of aesthetic attention. Schopenhauer avers that "everyone who reads a poem or contemplates a work of art must of course contribute from his own resources", and every beholder must *cooperate* with the work of art. Furthermore, his aesthetic pleasure results at least partly from "the fact that every work of art can only work through the medium of the imagination. It must therefore *excite the imagination, which can never be left out of the question and remain inactive.*" And Schopenhauer significantly adds: "This is a condition of aesthetic effect, and therefore a fundamental law of all the fine arts" (WWR2 463; italics added).

Thus, that aesthetic perception requires disinterestedness, idealization, and self-transcendence does not imply that we must become passive, estranged spectators of the world in aesthetic contemplation.[9] On the contrary, as we will see, on Schopenhauer's account, *homo aestheticus* is concerned with creating a place in which he feels at home, with expanding his emotional horizons, by inducing imaginative sympathy with what surrounds him.

Aesthetic Perception as Disinterested Self-Transcendence

According to Nietzsche, Schopenhauer's aesthetics centres exclusively on the spectator and neglects the perspective of the artist and would therefore identify aesthetic appreciation with disembodied, dispassionate contemplation, which is ultimately 'hostile to life'.[10] Many commentators have followed Nietzsche's (unjust) condemnation of Schopenhauer's aesthetic theory. Although Schopenhauer is clearly more interested in the ecstasy of genius than in his deliberate artistic activity, Schopenhauer's analysis of aesthetic subjectivity is not primarily concerned with passive spectatorship, as Nietzsche and numerous commentators hold. Schopenhauer does not develop two radically distinct accounts of aesthetic perception—one focusing on the artist and the other on the spectator. Although aesthetic contemplation is a fundamental part of artistic creativity, it does not follow that Schopenhauer dismisses the perspective of the artist, as Nietzsche nevertheless suggests. On the contrary, Schopenhauer's account of genius offers a privileged way to discover the richness and subtlety of his aesthetic attitude theory. Ultimately, the art lover and the artist are not radically different. Their aesthetic attitude differs only gradually and represents two sides of the same phenomenon: aesthetic consciousness, which is a superior state of mind, surpassing ordinary self-oriented consciousness, by being engaging, uplifting, and absorbing. It basically requires transcending our personal, instrumental interests and valuations, and becoming actively engaged with a beautiful object for its own sake (i.e., a process of what one might call disinterested self-transcendence).

One of Schopenhauer's key thoughts is that perceiving something aesthetically requires *suspending our merely personal interests in it and focusing exclusively on the way in which the object presents itself to us.* Whilst we spend the larger part of our lives looking restlessly for objects that can satisfy our needs and desires, the beauty of a string quartet, a landscape, a flower, or a painting urges us to admire the singular way in which things appear to us. On such occasions, we take a disinterested interest in things and "we stop considering the Where, When, Why, and Wherefore of things, but simply and exclusively consider the *What*", and

> we do not allow our consciousness to become engrossed by abstract thinking, concepts of reason; but if, instead of all this, we devote the entire power of our mind to intuition and immerse ourselves in this entirely . . . we forget individuality, our will . . . and we can no longer separate the intuited from the intuition as the two have become one, and the whole of consciousness is completely filled and engrossed by a single intuitive image.
>
> (WWR1 210)

What Schopenhauer implies here is that, when enjoying the beauty of a Beethoven string quartet, for instance, my attention is not focussed on some external interest, profit, or use the music may have *for me*, but on the unique performance of the string quartet itself here and now. I am wholly devoted to the unique, irreplaceable performance of this very string quartet. No other piece of music would 'do just as well'. Disinterested aesthetic perception is thus not passive or indifferent, but presupposes *engaging with* a singular object and appreciating it in and because of its unique significance. Schopenhauer thus rightly characterises aesthetic engagement as an attitude which is not determined by self-interest and is entirely *devoted to the present object*. He overstates his case here, since not every aesthetic engagement demands the kind of complete self-loss he evokes. Nonetheless, Schopenhauer's insistence that pure aesthetic contemplation cannot be reduced to conceptually understanding an object or immediately satisfying personal desires is plausible. Even though aesthetic contemplation ultimately fulfils our need for security and harmony and may therefore ultimately never be wholly unconditional, there is still an important distinction between the way in which we consider objects in daily life with a view of fulfilling our personal needs, appetites, and wants, and the way in which we engage aesthetically with things, that is, when we no longer consider them as mere means to an end but as ends in themselves, to be admired for their own sake (see WWR2 § 31).

However, admiring something aesthetically does not imply that we no longer perceive the particular, unique features of it. Although Schopenhauer may be right that, from a purely aesthetic point of view, "it is then all the same whether we see the setting sun from a prison or from a palace", enjoying this particular sunset in Venice will not guarantee that I will equally enjoy another Venetian sunset (WWR1 232). As Schopenhauer justly contends, my attentiveness is directed toward *the way this particular object presents itself to me*, and not toward any personal advantage, profit, or therapeutic reward it may offer. My attention is wholly devoted to the way in which this irreplaceable object appears to me.

This immensely important requirement of aesthetic experience might further explain why Schopenhauer's so-called Platonic idealism should not be taken at face value. Insisting that aesthetic contemplation is concerned merely with the universal category or 'paradigm' of concrete particulars is plainly wrong. Let us take Dutch still life painting, which Schopenhauer admires immensely, as a case in point. Whatever else it is that such paintings offer, they are clearly not devoted solely to timeless universals. Their often extremely moving effect follows from their exquisite eye for seemingly futile, contingent details, fleeting events, and transient, ethereal phenomena. They are not about flowers or food in general, nor about the timeless essence of carnations or tulips. By insisting that the proper object of aesthetic contemplation is a Platonic Idea, that is to say, a representation which has laid aside merely the subordinate forms of the phenomenon, all of which we include under the principle of sufficient reason, he unjustly downplays one of the most fundamental features of aesthetic contemplation, namely its focus upon the *singularity* of aesthetic objects.

However, as I have already indicated, what Schopenhauer refers to as (Platonic) Ideas in the context of art is not to be confused with concepts or universal categories, for Ideas "develop representations that are novel with respect to concepts sharing the same name" (WWR1 277). This is clearly reminiscent of Kant's definition of the *aesthetic* idea in the *Critique of Judgment* as "a presentation of the imagination which prompts much thought, but to which . . . no determinate concept can be adequate" (Kant, 2001, p. 314; translation modified). Yet, *contra* Kant, Schopenhauer sets up a contrast between ordinary cognition, which is imperfect for being subordinate to the will and the forms of the principle of sufficient reason, and aesthetic cognition, which is pure and unclouded—that is to say, yields clear insight into the grades of objectification of the will, of the true thing-in-itself, thus into Platonic Forms or Ideas.

On Schopenhauer's account, perceiving an object aesthetically implies apprehending Platonic Ideas, which are definitely not concepts, "which can be communicated coldly and dispassionately by words", but "inexhaustible" perceptual objects, "which leave behind something that, in spite of all our reflection on it, we cannot bring down to the distinctness of a concept" (WWR2 465). The works of art that express such Ideas are the product of genius that is, not of a passive onlooker, but "a kind of superfluity, that of the power of knowledge beyond the measure for the service of the will" and can only be apprehended through *imaginative perception* (i.e., the ability to go beyond the bounds of merely conceptual cognition) (WWR2 466).

The individual object will not therefore disappear from my consciousness, but it is *in* and *through* my intense attentiveness to it that a universal meaning may be discovered. Inspired by Plato and Kant, Schopenhauer rightly suggests that aesthetic values, and especially beauty, do not express merely personal preferences but invest objects with a peculiar significance. Beauty challenges us to capture and assess the exceptional meaning an object has. Beauty possesses existential value. We do not have to agree with Schopenhauer that we perceive Platonic Ideas in aesthetic contemplation to understand that aesthetic values are inextricably entwined with the peculiar meaning of things—things that challenge us to explore and deepen our lives in their light.

As I have already indicated, Schopenhauer exaggerates, when he advances that we lose ourselves completely in the object that we perceive (see WWR1 210–212 and 218–219). It would be sufficient to point out that aesthetic contemplation requires us to suspend our consideration of the causal and conceptual connections the object has with other objects and our self-centred interests. The so-called complete 'self-loss', which Schopenhauer nevertheless heavily emphasises, cannot be a sufficient condition for having an aesthetic experience. Aesthetic experience does require that we temporarily cast aside our self-interest and as it were, *surrender* our attention to the present object for its own sake. *Contra* Schopenhauer, I would suggest that temporarily suspending our egocentric interests, needs, and desires does not, however, preclude us from *returning to* our individual interests, experiences, and emotions in aesthetic contemplation. The 'self-loss' of aesthetic contemplation is not orgiastic or mystical: a link with our personal concerns is suspended but does not disappear altogether. In aesthetic contemplation a link remains with that which is suspended. Our personal aspirations are merely temporarily set aside but are not completely abolished. Aesthetic perception is still contemplative: we become, as it were, the impartial spectator of our personal desires, interests, and emotions. Claiming that in aesthetic contemplation our perception is completely detached from our will and "that the consciousness of our own selves vanishes" (WWR2 418) is definitely an overstatement. Indeed, aesthetic consciousness requires an "abnormal excess of intellect", especially of its imaginative capacity, and being immersed in the object, but cannot be identified with Dionysian rapture by which the self becomes an insignificant plaything of overwhelming forces. Aesthetic contemplation remains what the term suggests, namely contemplative, which implies that a passive individual is transformed into an *imaginatively engaged* subject that becomes disassociated from its *personal* concerns, needs, and urges (see WWR1 221).[11]

Now, Schopenhauer's attempt to undermine Plato's critique of the illusory nature of art, by pointing out that art does offer insight into eternal timeless universals, is—as said—hardly plausible as a general characterisation of the value of art and beauty. Nonetheless, Schopenhauer's emphasis on the cognitive import of art (i.e., the knowledge and insights works of art may yield) is very important. The insights works of art yield are usually tied up with specific experiences that cannot be reduced to discursive knowledge. And even though some artworks express experiences that can be formulated as propositions, artworks still connect with, for instance, the peculiar, non-propositional way in which someone experiences certain emotions or ideas. The existential fear that paintings by Edvard Munch or Francis Bacon depict has been conveyed by philosophers such as Kierkegaard and Heidegger, but Munch and Bacon *show* us nonetheless in a unique, non-propositional way what it is like to be overwhelmed by such an emotion. Schopenhauer thus rightly insists that art can have cognitive value. Yet the disturbing knowledge we acquire through, for instance, the psychotic main character in Alfred Hitchcock's *Psycho* (1960) does not (merely) reveal eternal Ideas but crucial aspects of certain pathologies, on the basis of which we gain insight into the darker aspects of the human mind and the suffocating atmosphere that characterises some parent-child relationships. Instead of offering immediate access to timeless essences, many works of art yield experiential knowledge of historically situated events, characters, views and emotions. This does not preclude valuing works of art because of the universal truths about man and world which they convey. An aesthetic experience is, however, not *merely* cognitive (and Schopenhauer fortunately never claims this).

According to Schopenhauer, aesthetic experience is characterised by the contemplating subject's awareness of an allegedly pleasurable state of will-lessness. Schopenhauer describes our will-lessness as a state of bliss, in which we seem to become an eye of the world (*Weltauge*) that loses itself completely in the object under contemplation. We cease to be aware of ourselves as distinct from the object. The aesthetic pleasure that I thus experience originates from two sources. First of all, I realise that my will no longer dominates me: I feel liberated from the burden of willing—this is the 'negative' aspect of aesthetic pleasure. Furthermore, I take pleasure *in* becoming immersed into the core of the perceived object—this is a form of 'positive' pleasure, which is not reducible to the feeling of liberation from the pain or suffering the will causes. This latter form of pleasure indeed originates from the objective intuition of the timeless Idea that the object instantiates:

> Cognition of the beautiful always posits the pure cognizing subject at the same time as, and inseparably from, the cognition of the Idea as object. And yet the source of aesthetic pleasure will sometimes be located more in the apprehension of the Ideas . . ., and sometimes more in the happiness and peace of mind of pure cognition that has been liberated from all willing and thus from all individuality and the pain that comes from it.
>
> (WWR 1 250)

Several commentators discover remnants from Kant's aesthetics in "the happiness and peace of mind . . . liberated from all willing", for this clearly reminds of the disinterested nature of Kantian aesthetic judgement. Nietzsche and Heidegger, amongst others, have linked Schopenhauer's aesthetics of will-lessness with Kant's emphasis upon the disinterested nature of aesthetic pleasure and judgment, and have judged Schopenhauer's analysis inferior to its predecessor's. The relation between Kant's and Schopenhauer's aesthetics is, however, much more complicated than has often been assumed and Schopenhauer's theory certainly moves beyond Kant's in many significant ways.[12]

Artistic Creativity and Imaginative Engagement

Schopenhauer's characterisation of aesthetic pleasure does not apply merely to the aesthetic spectator but (*pace* Nietzsche) also to the artist, which Schopenhauer refers to as 'genius'. The genius is not someone who has merely personal relations, but "a pure intellect that as such belongs to the whole of mankind", and that "has become unfaithful to its destiny", which is the service of his will (WWR2 445 and 440). For, unlike ordinary people, artists are able to *maintain* a state of pure will-less contemplation for a long time and to leave entirely out of sight their own interests, willing, and aims, and hence "to remain as the *pure cognitive subject*, the clear eye of the world: and this not just momentarily, but for as long and with as much clarity of mind [*Besonnenheit*] as is necessary to repeat what has been grasped in the form of well-considered art" (WWR1 219). Artists have an unnatural capacity for heightened perception: they see with more detail, intensity, and accuracy, which allows them to create imaginative artworks that offer cognition beyond the principle of sufficient reason. The genius has the capacity to distract from the immediate connections between things and 'express clearly what nature only stutters' (WWR1 262).

As Matthias Kossler has emphasised, the genius's power to tear away cognition from the service of the will—his 'clarity of mind' or 'thoughtful awareness' (*Besonnenheit*)—has a paradoxical role to fulfil in both the apprehension of the timeless essence of things and the execution of the artwork (see WWR2 437–443).[13] For it is hard to understand how the artist's *Besonnenheit* might offer both an escape from (individual) willing, which allows for pure aesthetic contemplation, and the purposeful, hence *will-driven* activity of conveying the perception of timeless Ideas through a work of art.

But Schopenhauer does not reduce the artistic creativity and genius merely to thoughtful awareness, and it would have been odd if had done so. He also rightly stresses the artist's vehemence and passionateness of willing and perhaps even more importantly, his *imaginative* capacities (*Phantasie*) to account for the activity of *expressing*—instead of merely conveying—the perceived Ideas in a work of art. Schopenhauer is surely right to refrain from reducing artworks to mere replicas of universal essences, and to put great emphasis on the expressive function of *imagination*, which allows artists to see in things not "what nature actually created, but rather what it was trying unsuccessfully to create" and "to complete, arrange, amplify, fix, retain, and repeat at pleasure all the significant pictures of life . . . On this rests the high value of imagination as an indispensable instrument of genius" (WWR1 220; WWR2 431).

The paradoxical foundations of Schopenhauer's view of aesthetic contemplation nonetheless remain intact: whilst the imaginative execution of a work of art, which strives to embody Ideas in particular representations, cannot take place without the activity of will, and is hence subordinate to the forms of the principle of sufficient reason, genius still consists in a decided predominance of pure knowing over willing—that is, the capacity *to suspend knowledge according to the principle of sufficient reason*, in order to grasp the inner essences of things. And this ability, in its turn, presupposes a purely objective frame of mind, so that it is as though the object alone existed without anyone to perceive it, and the entire consciousness is filled and absorbed by the perceived aesthetic correlate (see WWR1 § 34).

This is hugely significant. The basic characteristics of aesthetic engagement, namely self-transcendence and imaginative perception are not to be located exclusively in artists but also hold for art lovers and all people that spend time admiring the world aesthetically. Contrary to what most commentators suggest,[14] Schopenhauer's view of aesthetic perception cannot be reduced to passively mirroring the aesthetic qualities of a work of art: aesthetic contemplation requires an energetically active consciousness and 'lively', enthusiastic engagement. Thus Schopenhauer insists that "everyone . . . must of course contribute from his own resources" (WWR1 221; WWR2 462). Not merely the artist but the aesthetic beholder too actively engages with the work of art, for

> every work of art can act only through the medium of the imagination. It must therefore *excite the imagination, which can never be left out of the question and remain inactive.* This is a condition of aesthetic effect, and therefore a fundamental law of all the fine arts . . . *It must be born in the beholder's imagination.*
>
> (WWR2 463; italics added)

Hence, both the artist and the lover of natural beauty and art are ultimately actively engaged, enthusiastic spectators that are capable of momentarily transcending their limited individual point of view and obtaining fundamental insights and passionate attunement to the true essences of things. They transcend their egocentric concerns and remain "lively and steadfast" and "linger for very long with mere intuition" (WWR1 221).[15] Aesthetic consciousness is affectively heightened and cognitively enriched. Succinctly put, transcending cognition according to the principle of sufficient reason implies that awareness of the object is intensified and vividly transfigured by the power of imagination, so that consciousness of our practical, egocentric goals and concerns disappears.

Conclusion

Contrary to the standard view of Schopenhauer's aesthetic theory, I have argued that transcending subservience to the principle of sufficient reason does not turn aesthetic consciousness into a passive, disengaged receptacle of aesthetic properties and eternal forms. Schopenhauer's emphasis on, what Nietzsche calls, the *Selbststeigerung* typical of aesthetic delight does not imply a dispassionate, distant, intellectual, let alone a purely spiritual attitude toward the world. Schopenhauer's obsessive usage of terms such as 'objective', 'mirror', and especially 'will-less' to describe the phenomenological characteristics of aesthetic consciousness, and Nietzsche's spiteful criticism of the purportedly life-denying views of his 'noblest enemy' may well have obfuscated not only the accuracy and subtlety of Schopenhauer's analysis of aesthetic perception, but also the perhaps unsuspected *affirmative* potential of Schopenhauer's aesthetic theory and its just vindication of the imaginative engagement, exaltation, and delightful self-transcendence which fundamentally characterise our most valuable (aesthetic) experiences.

Notes

1 For a thorough critical examination of Schopenhauer's account of the sublime, see my book *The Sublime in Schopenhauer's Philosophy* (2015).
2 See my *The Sublime in Schopenhauer's Philosophy*, 2015, Ch. 2.
3 See my *The Sublime in Schopenhauer's Philosophy*, 2015, pp. 41–46.
4 More details on the objective character of aesthetic cognition can be found in my essay on 'Schopenhauer and the Objectivity of Art (2012)'.
5 See: Goehr (1996).
6 See: Janaway (1996).
7 Chris Janaway, 'Responses to Commentators', p. 133.
8 Young (1992, 122).
9 Here I take issue with Reginster (2009).
10 See Friedrich Nietzsche, *On the Genealogy of Morality* (1998).
11 Schopenhauer uses the terms 'Beschaulichkeit' and 'Kontemplation' to characterise aesthetic perception. Payne as well as Norman, Welchman and Janaway translate 'Beschaulichkeit' as 'thoughtfulness'. 'Meditativeness' might have been a better option, since cognition of the Ideas does not follow the principle of sufficient reason and is non-conceptual.
12 See *The Sublime in Schopenhauer's Philosophy*, 2015—especially Chs. 3 and 4.
13 See Matthias Kossler (2012, 201–202).
14 See, for instance, Janaway (1996, 58) and *passim*; Reginster (2009), *passim*; Young (1992, 122).
15 In a very illuminating passage Schopenhauer makes an important distinction between aesthetic contemplation and daydreaming. A daydreamer (*Phantast*) is chiefly concerned with manipulating reality to fit his own wishes and desires. He deceives himself "so that all he really comes to know are the relations between the figments of his imagination", and "will easily blend the images of his solitary self-amusement together with reality, for which he will then be unfit" (WWR 1, 220). Daydreaming is self-deceptive, since it denies the 'transcendence' of external reality. A strong imagination is thus not a sufficient condition for aesthetic contemplation and creativity. Aesthetic consciousness also requires 'objective perception', which is not self-indulging, manipulative, or merely looking for entertainment or excitement, but requires disinterested engagement with the world (WWR 1, 220).

Bibliography

Goehr, L. 'Schopenhauer and the Musicians: An Inquiry into the Sounds of Silence and the Limits of Philosophizing about Music', in D. Jacquette (ed.), *Schopenhauer, Philosophy, and the Arts*. Cambridge: Cambridge University Press, 1996, 200–228.

Janaway, C. 'Knowledge and Tranquillity: Schopenhauer on the Value of Art', in D. Jacquette (ed.), *Schopenhauer, Philosophy, and the Arts*. Cambridge: Cambridge University Press, 1996, 39–61.

Janaway, C. 'Responses to Commentators', *The European Journal of Philosophy* 17, 2009: 132–151.

Kant, I. *Critique of the Power of Judgment*, ed. Paul Guyer, trans. Paul Guyer and Eric Matthews. Cambridge: Cambridge University Press, 2001.

Kossler, M. 'The Artist as Subject of Pure Cognition', in B. Vandenabeele (ed.), *A Companion to Schopenhauer*. Oxford: Wiley-Blackwell, 2012, 193–205.

Nietzsche, F. *On the Genealogy of Morality*, trans. M. Clark and A. Swensen. Indianapolis: Hackett, 1998.

Reginster, B. 'Knowledge and Selflessness: Schopenhauer and the Paradox of Reflection', in A. Neill and C. Janaway (eds.), *Better Consciousness: Schopenhauer's Philosophy of Value*. Oxford: Wiley-Blackwell, 2009, 99–119.

Vandenabeele, B. 'Schopenhauer and the Objectivity of Art', in B. Vandenabeele (ed.), *A Companion to Schopenhauer*. Oxford: Wiley-Blackwell, 2012, 219–233.

Vandenabeele, B. *The Sublime in Schopenhauer's Philosophy*. Basingstoke; New York: Palgrave Macmillan, 2015.

Young, J. *Nietzsche's Philosophy of Art*. Cambridge: Cambridge University Press, 1992.

Part IV

Ethics, Motivation, and Action

11 The Fourth Root and 'the Miracle par Excellence'[1]

Gudrun von Tevenar and Christine Lopes

For Schopenhauer the principle of sufficient reason is a transcendental principle of human cognition. It cannot be proved but is rather the principle of proof. Moreover, since the requirement of proof is a requirement of rationality, the principle of sufficient reason is the general expression of any rational law of human cognition.

> Since through this treatise I hope to point out the different laws of our cognitive faculty, the common expression of which is the principle of sufficient reason, it will follow as a matter of course that the general principle is not to be proved.
>
> (FR 23)

According to Schopenhauer, there are four grounds or roots of the principle of sufficient reason, each expressing a specific form of necessity with which the subject cognizes objects and their causal relation. There are, correspondingly, four classes of objects for the subject of cognition. Each class of objects for the cognizing subject, its underlying principle of cognition, the kind of necessity that rules the connection among its objects, and corresponding subjective faculty of cognition, constitutes one of four roots or grounds of the principle of sufficient reason.

The first root, the principle of becoming, explains physical necessity among empirical objects (FR §§ 17–25). The second root, the principle of knowing, explains logical necessity among concepts (FR §§ 26–34). The third root, the principle of being, explains mathematical necessity among spatial-temporal objects (FR §§ 35–39). The fourth root, the principle of motivation, explains moral necessity in action (§§ 40–45). Schopenhauer does not follow accepted traditions of philosophical enquiry when positing these and just these four classes of objects. For example, we cannot group the latter into physical and mental objects, as Schopenhauer remains a strict non-dualist throughout his philosophy. Nor can we group them, tempting as it may be, into objects of epistemology or ethics, as Schopenhauer clearly states that his account of the relation between subject and objects in FR does not follow this division of philosophical enquiry (FR § 49, § 51, § 58).

So, the sole criterion for his division of all objects for a subject is that they are objects of cognition. The principle of division is thus cognitive: the four roots of the principle of sufficient reason are the four grounds on which alone a subject can cognize objects.

In this contribution, we focus on the difference between the first three and the fourth classes of objects of cognition. Schopenhauer himself draws attention to the fact that the fourth class is "quite unique, but very important (*eine gar eigene, aber sehr wichtige*)" (FR 140; translation amended). Its uniqueness lies in that the principle of motivation or action is based on moral necessity, but such a type of necessity operates with the same causal necessity found in the other three classes of objects. So, moral causation determines as necessarily as the physical, logical, and mathematical necessity of the first three roots of the principle of sufficient reason respectively. We examine whether this claim holds, and we conclude that Schopenhauer was not successful in showing this in FR, but that his 1840 prize essay, *On the Freedom of the Will,* did rather better. We also examine in detail the pivotal role of self-consciousness in the fourth root, which Schopenhauer famously calls "the miracle *par excellence*" (FR 143).

The Fourth Root

The text of the fourth root on the principle of motivation and its moral causal necessity constitutes Chapter 7 of FR, §§ 40–45. It is relatively short with just 9 pages compared with 64 pages for the first root. Equally noteworthy is the fact that it underwent substantial revision in the second edition with four of the original nine paragraphs deleted. Such extensive revision suggests dissatisfaction with the original text due to crucial developments in Schopenhauer's thought and his effort to bring the views of his younger self of 1813 in line with his mature philosophy of some thirty-four years later. It also helps to explain the somewhat sketchy and disjointed style of this chapter. Below we give an overview of the text of the fourth root paragraph by paragraph, followed by a critical examination of the theme of self-consciousness in §§41 and 42.

Schopenhauer opens § 40 with the statement that the fourth root has just one object, "namely the immediate object of the inner sense, *the subject of willing*" (FR 140).[2] But because this object is only given in our inner sense, it can appear only in time, and even there only "with a significant qualification" (FR 140). Schopenhauer does not say what this qualification is but we believe that he attempts to clarify its nature and significance in §42.

In line with his theory of subject–object correlation, Schopenhauer proposes in § 41 that, just like consciousness of other things, self-consciousness too "divides into that which is cognized and that which cognizes". However, "the subject cognizes itself only as *something that wills (ein Wollendes),* but not as *something that cognizes (ein Erkennendes)*" (FR 140). It follows that the subject of cognition can never become an object to itself. In other words, a cognizing subject can never cognize itself as a subject of cognition. To illustrate his point, Schopenhauer cites from the Upanishads: "that which sees all is not to be seen; that which hears all is not to be heard; (and so on)" (FR 141).

In § 42 Schopenhauer describes the process of inner self-cognition: aspects of this description are pivotal to all his subsequent works on the nature of willing.

> [W]hat is cognized in us as such is not something that cognizes, but something that wills, the subject of willing, will . . . If we introspect, we find ourselves always as *willing*. However, willing has many degrees, from the mildest wish up to passion . . . not only all affects, but also all of the inner movements subsumed under the broad concept of feeling, are states of will.
>
> (FR 143)

The function that Schopenhauer assigns to willing extends well beyond the one presumed by our everyday understanding of willing. It is also in some tension with his repeated statements throughout his work that willing is a blind and sheer striving force. Indeed, Schopenhauer goes further and claims that the cognizing subject and its object, the subject of willing, are identical in a somewhat mysterious way.

> The identity of the subject of willing with the cognizing subject, by means of which . . . the word 'I' includes and indicates both, is the knot of the world and therefore inexplicable . . . whoever truly realises the inexplicability of this identity will with me call it the miracle *par excellence*.
>
> (FR 143)

The claims in this passage are utterly remarkable, since it is fair to say that, for the ordinary person, the immediately perceived identity of herself as cognizer of her volitions and desires, as the one who wills and desires, is rather *unremarkable*! But unmoved by ordinariness, Schopenhauer claims in § 43: "Precisely because the subject of willing is immediately given in self-consciousness, what willing is cannot be further defined or described" (FR 144). Why not? Schopenhauer offers no explanation but proceeds instead with his views on motivation and remarks that whenever we observe decisions or actions of others or our own, we may ask 'Why?' This simple question reveals the assumption of a reason or ground, namely a motive, which is prior to decisions or actions. "It is as inconceivable", Schopenhauer tells us, "that there can be an action without a motive as that there can be a movement of an inanimate body without a push or pull" (FR 144). Hence motives are usually considered causes. However, while the interaction of cause and effect in the physical world often eludes us—"the interior of such events remains a secret to us" , we are aware of the influence of motives not just from without but immediately also from within. Hence Schopenhauer's famous statement: "*motivation is causality seen from within*" (FR 145). For further discussion on this topic, he refers the readers of the second edition to his later essay, *On the Freedom of the Will.*

The indication of a key development in his philosophical views about will is found in the title of § 44 of the second edition. § 44 of the first edition was deleted for the second edition, with a new § 44 replacing § 47 of the first edition. Compare the title of § 47: "*Causality of Will on Cognition—The will not only causally affects the immediate object and, thus, the external world, but also the cognizing subject*" (EF 185), with the title of the new § 44: "*Influence of Will on Cognition—The influence that will exercises on cognition is not based on causality strictly speaking, but on the identity of the cognising with the willing subject . . . since the will compels cognition*" (FR 145). Schopenhauer held in § 44 of the first edition that "*Acting* is not willing, but the effect of willing when it becomes causal" (EF 185). His mature position, however, is that volitions do not cause actions; rather, acts of the body are simply identical with acts of will with no causal link between them (WWR1 18). Of course, it is easy to dispense with causality if, as Schopenhauer claims, the cognizing and willing subject are indeed identical. Yet he nonetheless frequently uses language suggestive of causal aims, as in the title of FR § 44 where he writes that "will compels cognition".

In § 44 we also find an interesting theory of association of ideas as part of a description of the dependency of motivation on cognition, though Schopenhauer does not offer any details. Instead, he refers his readers to volume 2 of *The World as Will and Representation*, Chapter 14. But while we do find there much information on how association of ideas is linked to one's environment, memory, and intellectual capacity, and how associations arise from the unconscious, there is only this rather general statement regarding its function in motivation:

> What puts into activity the association of ideas itself . . . is the *will*. This drives its servant, the intellect, according to its powers to link one idea on to another, to recall the similar and the simultaneous, and to recognise grounds and consequents . . . Therefore the form of the principle of sufficient reason which governs the association of ideas and keeps it active is ultimately the law of motivation. For that which rules the sensorium, and determines it to follow analogy or another association of ideas in this or that direction, is the will of the thinking subject.
>
> (WWR2 149)

Note the emphasis here: the individual's will is *driving* the individual's intellect to produce ideas and associate them according to the will's direction, clearly pointing to the dominant part of the will in motivation. However, it seems fair to say that as an explanation of how motivation functions it is nonetheless insufficient to warrant the theory that actions follow upon motives with necessity.

In § 45, the final paragraph exclusively of the fourth root, we find a lengthy discussion of memory. Yet unfortunately, Schopenhauer does not, either in §45 of FR nor in chapter 14 of WWR2, explain in any helpful detail how memories can lead to motivations. On attempting, as readers, this task ourselves, we arrive at two possibilities. First, the motivations we identify for ourselves have emerged indirectly, through the association of ideas process. Of course, the intentional retrieval of memories is quite distinct from the almost arbitrary way representations arise during association of ideas. Nonetheless, a number of these associated representations will be representations of memories. Second, memories can directly produce motivations: we may be motivated to either actions or omissions because of the particular quality of memories in given contexts.

Although Schopenhauer does not discuss nonhuman animals in the text of the fourth root, he does so in FR §20, where he discusses causality generally as well as motivation as a variety of causality. He claims that the behaviour of higher species of nonhuman animals also falls under the law of motivation and thus not only under the law of stimulation. Schopenhauer holds that higher animals have understanding and hence the basic kind of cognition necessary for a process of motivation to unfold according to will and character. Obviously, in the case of nonhuman animals the character is species-specific and has not, as is the case with human animals, a high degree of individuality. For example, given their species-specific character of timidity and fear, a rabbit on hearing, say, a rustle in the undergrowth, will take flight, while a bold and curious fox will go and investigate in the hope of some prey. The role of human individual empirical character in motivation will be examined in our discussion of FW below.

Chapter 8 of FR has the title 'General remarks and results' and concludes the whole dissertation. It has an interesting discussion on the nature of necessity assigned to each of the four roots in §49,[3] and in §51 Schopenhauer links the four roots to various sciences. Regarding the fourth root he writes:

> If one considers all motives and maxims–whatever they be–to be data by which action is to be explained, the law of motivation is the principal guiding thread of history, politics, pragmatic psychology, etc. If, however, one makes motives and maxims themselves, according to their value and origin, into the subject of investigation, the law of motivation is the guiding thread of ethics.
>
> (FR 157)

This passage shows the great importance Schopenhauer attributes to his findings, not just for philosophy, but also for the foundation of sciences.

Yet, speaking solely for the fourth root, we must hold on to our initial objection that Schopenhauer's somewhat sketchy account of motivation in FR is unsatisfactory. What we find is a confusing account of self-consciousness and a conspicuous lack of arguments and explanations of why and how motives are causes leading to actions with necessity. For a better understanding, we must follow Schopenhauer's own advice and consult his wider metaphysics and 1840 prize essay FW.

We observed that Schopenhauer made major alterations to his account of will and motivation for the second edition of FR. One lengthy paragraph, previously § 46, was deleted in its entirety. Much of its content is indeed found in FW, such as, for instance, the relation between empirical and intelligible character. The following citation from the deleted § 46 is, we believe, of particular interest for us here, as it seems to express an uncertainty whether actions do indeed follow upon motivations, that is, whether moral causation proceeds with the same kind of necessity as does physical causation:

> [W]e are able to know motives, but we do not thereby know how the subject will subsequently act. For each subject has a particular empirical character, and perfect knowledge of the empirical character of an individual is impossible. Here the rule-governed quality that applies to the other forms of the principle of sufficient reason ceases because in that case we remain in the world governed by laws, but here we encounter a completely different world, bordering on the realm of freedom. If I compare my presentation of the first three forms of our principle with moving images I had cast on the wall with a magic lantern, then now with the fourth form, a trap door has opened, one through which there enters a light before which some of my images disappear, and some become fragmented, unclear, and confused.
>
> (EF 189–90)

Note that the deep uncertainty whether motivation works with the same causal effectiveness as in the other three roots of the principle of sufficient reason is not due to our cognitive limitations (i.e., because we cannot have perfect knowledge of an individual's empirical character). Rather, the uncertainty rests on the implication that with motivation we have somehow left the rule-governed world of natural laws and are now encountering a "completely different world bordering on the realm of freedom." In other words, Schopenhauer implies that we find ourselves now in a world where there is at least the possibility of freedom and where, therefore, the strict causal laws of nature no longer apply. This is, of course, in conflict with his mature views, and the deletion of this paragraph is thus a reliable indicator of how his views had developed in the intervening decades.

On the Freedom of the Human Will

We have objected that Schopenhauer's account of the causality of motivation in the text of the fourth root is unsatisfactory due to its sketchy and incomplete character. What we find there are hints and fragments, rather than a coherent narrative connecting the three elements of motivation, namely, will, motive, and character. This may be due in part to Schopenhauer's attempt to fuse the views of his younger self of 1813 with his mature philosophy. Yet the result of this attempted fusion is unfortunate, as it is unlikely that anyone can grasp the full content and philosophical relevance of the fourth root without some extensive knowledge of the main features of Schopenhauer's later philosophy. To be fair, as noted above, Schopenhauer himself was aware of this problem, and refers his readers several times to his later works, including FW. Indeed, FW contains a lucid and highly persuasive discussion of the central problems of the fourth root, and can thus be seen as having successfully completed the somewhat sketchy account given of them in FR. We will in the following provide a brief summary of the points relevant to the fourth root as discussed in FW, namely: the will, the function of cognition in motive formation, and the interaction of both with the individual empirical character of agents. These three points are discussed predominately in chapter III of FW. (Please note, we restrict ourselves solely to these three points and do not discuss FW as a whole.)

Schopenhauer states that, in contrast to the explication of will itself in chapter II of FW, now, in chapter III, we are concerned with "willing *beings moved by the will*" (FW 26, Schopenhauer's italics). This, he claims, is important in two ways: first, beings moved by will can also be objects for the external senses. Second, there is the advantage that "we can now avail ourselves in our investigation a much more perfect organ than that obscure, dull, one-sided, direct self-consciousness, or so-called inner sense, was—namely of the *understanding,* which is equipped with all its outer senses and all its powers of *objective* apprehension" (FW 26–7; Schopenhauer's italics). Note the low estimation of inner sense and self-consciousness in FW, while both are praised and elevated in FR as *'the miracle par excellence'*! It is unsurprising that the employment of the understanding, or intellect, should be of crucial importance for Schopenhauer as he now introduces, next to the familiar description of motivation as causality seen from within, another aspect of motivation, namely, as "causality that goes through *cognition*" (FW 31; Schopenhauer's italics). Cognition obviously requires a "faculty of representation, an intellect . . . presenting itself materially as nervous system and brain, and . . . consciousness" (FW 31–2). Hence motives are, Schopenhauer contends, certain representations, objects of cognition, presented to consciousness:

> The object which has effect as a motive (*das als Motiv wirkende Objekt*) needs nothing whatsoever apart from *being perceived, cognized;* while

it is quite indifferent for how long it came into apperception, whether far off or nearby, and how clearly it did so. Here all these differences do not alter the degree of the effect at all: once the motive has simply been perceived, it has effect in just the same way—assuming that it is anyway a determining ground of the will that is to be roused here.

(FW 32–3)

In order to function as a motive, the perceived object must of course be of a kind that excites the will of the particular perceiver so as to become fully determinate. In other words, the will has to *respond* to the cognized object and thus be activated in the appropriate way of willing, striving, desiring, and so on. Only then can the cognized object be a motive. And the required responsiveness of the will depends, in turn, on the particular empirical character of the perceiver of the object—to be discussed below.

Schopenhauer holds that, as human beings have in addition to understanding, which they share with animals, also reason and its faculty of concept formation, the objects that can become possible motives for humans are vast. Besides what is perceived intuitively in the here and now of space and time (which are the only objects available to animals), they also include thoughts, concepts, abstract ideas, images of the imagination, and distant or near memories. These kinds of objects can, moreover, remain motives over long periods of time. It seems plausible, therefore, to locate here, at this point, the main domain and function of the association of ideas process discussed by Schopenhauer in § 44 of FR. Recall that Schopenhauer there implies that through association of ideas, which is for him a process that is imposed on the intellect by the will, motives are kept alive and active by various representations associated with their original object of cognition.

Turning now to the role of character in motivation, Schopenhauer describes its role thus:

This specially and individually determined constitution of the will, because of which the reaction to the same motives is a different one in each human being, makes up what we call his *character*, and indeed, since it is known not *a priori* but through experience, his *empirical character*. It is through this, first of all, that the way in which the various kinds of motive affect a given human being is determined. For it lies at the basis of all the effects that motives call forth, just as the general natural forces do with the effects called forth by causes in the narrowest sense, and as the life force does with the effects of stimuli. And like the natural forces, it too is original, unalterable, inexplicable. In animals it is different in each species, in human beings in each individual.

(FW 48)

On what does Schopenhauer base his rather surprising claim that the empirical character of human and non-human animals is analogous to natural forces, like gravity in the case of physical causation, or the life forces in the case of stimulus causation? Schopenhauer asserts that, in addition to a basic species-specific character common to all humans, each individual human being also has an individual character that is innate, fixed, and unalterable. Behind this assertion lies the more relevant and weighty metaphysical claim that individual empirical characters are but manifestations or objectifications of their intelligible characters. More importantly, the intelligible character is simply the will as uniquely manifest in each individual. Hence Schopenhauer asserts that character functions in relevantly similar ways to natural forces. For the will is the one underlying fact of all there is and is, thus, equally manifest in organic and inorganic nature.

In the deleted § 46 of EF, entitled 'Motive, Decisions, Empirical and Intelligible Character', Schopenhauer expounds on this topic at length. There is no doubt that Schopenhauer's distinction between intelligible and empirical character owes much to Kant (though Kant would surely object to Schopenhauer's distinctive metaphysical interpretation). Indeed, in his *On the Basis of Morality* Schopenhauer gives lavish praise to Kant for this important insight (BM § 10). Yet, already in the first edition of FR Schopenhauer indicates his departure from Kant.

> Since these [empirical] expressions of the individual character are fragmentary, but indicate unity and unalterability of character, it must be thought of as the appearance of a permanent state, as it were, of the subject of will, lying outside time, which absolutely cannot be cognized . . . Kant has called this the *intelligible character* (perhaps it would more correctly be called *unintelligible*).
>
> (EF 188)

How do Schopenhauer's claims of the effects character has on motives manifest themselves in practice? As an example, consider a conflict situation which threatens to become violent. According to Schopenhauer, the representation of the situation, together with relevant beliefs, provides the motive, and any resulting action reflects the effect this motive has on the will and character of individuals. Different characters will act differently in the same situation For instance, when faced with a possibly violent conflict between others, a basically egoistic agent will leave immediately as she does not want to get involved. A basically compassionate agent will aim for reconciliation, while a basically malicious character will take the opportunity to wreak further havoc. It is the agent's character which determines her will. All things being equal, agents will always act according to character. A malicious character simply has such a weak motive to act for the well-being of others that she rarely if ever acts that way.

Because multiple motives can be present to human agents at any one time, conflict between motives is, as we all know, an ever-present possibility. Schopenhauer holds that, because of our capacity to reflect upon, and make a choice between, competing motives, agents have what one might call 'a relative freedom'. And he states that this relative freedom has been mistaken by "people who are educated, but who do not think deeply" as freedom of the will (FW 35). Rather, what happens is that an agent

> repeatedly allows the motives to test their force upon his will in competition with one another, whereby the will gets into the same state that a body is in when different forces work in different directions—until finally the decidedly strongest motive beats the others off the field and determines the will, an outcome that is called a resolve, and that occurs with full *necessity* as the result of the conflict.
>
> (FW 36)

The above brief exposition of key claims of FW shows clearly that Schopenhauer does indeed provide in FW the kind of insightful, coherent, and lucid account of the process of motivation as causation we claimed is lacking in FR.

Self-Consciousness and the *Miracle par Excellence*

As noted, the core proposition found in the text of the fourth root of the principle of sufficient reason is that the subject of cognition and the subject of willing is one and the same. The *locus* of this subjective identity is self-consciousness: the object of cognition here is not the subject of cognition *qua* cognizer but *qua* subject of willing. Schopenhauer calls this subjective dissonance 'the miracle *par excellence*': the object that I cognize in self-consciousness is myself as a willing subject only, never as a cognizing subject. Yet this proposed identity remains something of a mysterious metaphysical formula on which nonetheless much depends for Schopenhauer's key claims on will and morality. What *problem* does it posit, if any at all?

It seems a trivial truth that, in every decision and action we make, we are the ones who will what we will. Why should this not suffice as identity cognition? The traditional philosophical approach to this question is driven by concerns with morality and considers questions such as what makes an individual responsible for her decisions and actions. Questions about the morality of agency concern not just the determination of responsibility for a particular decision or action, but also and mainly, of the motives involved. In this way the identity of cognizing and willing subject is presupposed by the concept of moral agency. However, by concentrating solely on the nature of motivation, and challenging Schopenhauer's theory of it, commentators analytically sidestep Schopenhauer's emphatic proposition of the identity of cognizing and willing subject—'the miracle *par excellence*'.

One basic claim of Schopenhauer's metaphysics is that we are able to cognize the Kantian thing-in-itself. This is, for him, the will. Such cognition rests on our direct cognitive access to the will's manifestations in our own bodies in the form of sensations, desires, wants, urges, instincts, actions. Schopenhauer claims that "the body is the condition of cognition of my will. Consequently, I cannot truly imagine (*vorstellen*) my will without my body" (WWR1 121). In line with his adoption of Kant's transcendental idealism and its key terminology, Schopenhauer also attributes an intelligible and empirical character to agents. For Schopenhauer, the intelligible character is a non-spatial, non-temporal, constitutive presence of the will in individual agents capable of self-consciousness. This intelligible character is manifest empirically as an individual's empirical character which determines an individual's willing through decisions and actions.

F. C. White questions Schopenhauer's claim that in cognizing ourselves as willing subjects we also cognize the ultimate cause of our agency, that is, the will in general and our intelligible character in particular (White, 1992). White argues that, while it is possible to make sense of Schopenhauer's claim that in self-consciousness the subject of cognition cognizes itself as willing, as a willing self, there is little or no evidence that this subject simultaneously cognizes a transcendent reality behind her empirical willing.

> Schopenhauer's claim that in self-awareness we have knowledge of the noumenon seems *prima facie* decidedly implausible. It is difficult to see how he thinks he can move justifiably from the assertion that we are aware of ourselves as subjects of willing to the assertion that in this awareness we confront the noumenon . . . [I]f we have direct access to the noumenon through inner awareness, why should it be thought necessary to argue for it?[4]

One answer to White's question is that Schopenhauer nowhere explains his proposition that the cognizing and willing subject is one and the same—he simply states it. As a result, all of his subsequent metaphysical claims concerning the will, from FR onward, require arguments. An understanding of Schopenhauer's founding philosophical claims is needed before his metaphysical theory of motivation can be accepted.

Schopenhauer explicitly states in *The World as Will and Representation* that the identity of cognizing and willing is at the basis of his metaphysics of will. As willing subject, I cognise myself always as the subject of this or that particular decision, this or that particular action, this or that particular sensation. However, for every agent an individual character that responds to some motives and stimuli rather than others must be presupposed. And it is the intelligible character which drives the individual empirical response.

> [I]t is not essential whether a man plays for nuts or crowns; but whether in play a man cheats or goes about it honestly, this is what is essential. The latter is determined by the intelligible character, the former by external influences.
>
> (WWR1 189)

While it is clear that ordinary physical bodies are subject to natural, physical laws, how does Schopenhauer justify the claim of morality, that is, in one word, *freedom,* for a will that, in his view, fully and necessarily coincides with one's own, individual body? He needs to give a convincing answer to this question, lest the basic clause of moral meaning for actions is made redundant, namely, the clause that we are capable of free choice and can thus be held accountable, responsible as agents. White's worry concerning the explanatory inanity of Schopenhauer's claim that we have in self-consciousness the capacity for a direct cognition of our agency as transcendent, as the will as thing-in-itself, is inseparable from concerns with Schopenhauer's all-encompassing conception of will in the first place. So White's localized concern with the grounds for Schopenhauer holding that it is possible to have inner cognition of our agency as something that transcends our bodily existence indicates a more global concern with Schopenhauer's concept of will. For the will is at once a natural and an ethical-metaphysical force that causally determines the very being of agents and all things and beings that comprise the physical world. How so?

Matthias Koßler answered this question with rare subtlety, albeit, as White, in a manner which simply presupposes Schopenhauer's founding claim of subjective identity. Koßler is concerned with Schopenhauer's derivation of a theory of ethics from a metaphysics of will that extends the concept of will "to all affections of the body—sensations, passions, drives, even the arbitrary processes of a vegetative system"[5] (2008, 230). Koßler's starting point of presumed validity of Schopenhauer's claim of a subjective identity of willing and cognizing can be seen in his acknowledgment that the source of the derivation of ethics from such a global metaphysics of will is found in FR:[6]

> If therefore the essence of the world is will in that broader sense, and taking into account that Schopenhauer emphasizes that human action is fundamentally determined by the Principle of Sufficient Ground, the question is posed as to how a metaphysics of this sort can lead to a theory of ethics.[7]

One might argue that the bridge from this all-encompassing metaphysics of will to a theory of ethics is Schopenhauer's law of motivation, which rests, in turn, on his doctrine of character. While the individual, intelligible character varies from person to person, the law of motivation is naturalised so radically as to become analogous to the physical law of causality, and to the law of optics in particular.

> The law of causality can be compared to . . . the law of optics, which states that . . . the emitted light will either pass through the surface without any kind of change or will be reflected back to where it came from; where the light was before, it will be afterwards, and from the

constitutions at the onset the outcome can be foreseen. The law of motivation however is comparable to the effect of light on coloured bodies,
in which the same ray reflects red light from the one body, green from
the second, and if the third is black does not reflect at all. In fact the
way in which each different body reflects the light cannot be predicted
by knowledge of the constitution of the particular body, or of light.
Instead, the result can only be described by the actual appearance of
the light on the body, yet how the body reflects the light once, it will do
again, since there is only type of light.

(EF 57)[8]

However, in the second edition of FR, this account of motivation as a form
of causality turns into a full-on metaphysical statement.

Thus we cognize the influence of the motive, like all other causes, not
only from the outside, and hence only mediately, but we simultaneously
recognize it from the inside, quite immediately, and therefore in accordance with its entire way of acting. Here we stand behind the scenes,
as it were, and experience the secret of how, in accordance with its
innermost nature, the cause produces the effect, for here we cognize by
a completely different means, and thus in a complete different manner.
The result of this is the important proposition: *motivation is causality
seen from within.*

(FR 145)

The more general question thus arises, for both the young Schopenhauer of
EF and the mature Schopenhauer of WWR and the second edition of FR:
how does the intelligible character relate to empirical character? If motivation is 'causality seen from within', the subject has then reached a point of
self-awareness beyond which it just cannot go by asking 'What causes my
motivation in this way?' So the proposition that motivation is causality seen
from within is perhaps the ultimate proposition of self-consciousness, from
which the philosophical conclusion could indeed follow: the subject of cognition cannot cognize itself as cognizer but only as willing. Note that, seen
from this perspective, the intelligible character does not relate causally to
the empirical character, and so to decisions and actions. One may hypoth-
esise that Schopenhauer uses the expression 'causality seen from within'
negatively only, namely, to *signal* the point beyond which an empirical psychological reflection on the inner works of motivation simply cannot go.
The positive meaning Schopenhauer attributes to the expression is perhaps
clearer. If we are manifestations of will in the world and find our existence
empirically determined by natural laws just like any other object, then we
may indeed presume that not only our cognitions, decisions, behavior, and
actions are but manifestations of will and not effects and, similarly, our
motives and reasons too. The world, life itself, is but a mirror of will.

Koßler discusses in greater detail Schopenhauer's claim that the physical order *mirrors* the metaphysical order understood as ethics. This comparison between the physical and ethical order of the world has a key function in Schopenhauer's philosophy. Here is not the place to appraise Koßler's reading, but only to see how it deals with Schopenhauer's key proposition in FR of an identity of cognizing and willing.

What Schopenhauer seems to propose is that this identity is not only, or mainly, subjective, but also objective. The law of motivation is thus not only, or mainly, a rational scientific response to the question of sufficient reasons for action, but rather a lawful manifestation of will that applies with equal necessity to all sentient beings. So it looks as though the founding claim of identity of willing and cognizing plays a major role in the development of Schopenhauer's metaphysics of will and ethics. Yet Koßler appears to favour a narrower reading of this development, one in which the relation of *mirroring* between the physical order and the metaphysical or ethical order of the world is conceived as a philosophical negation rather than, effectively, an expansion of Schopenhauer's founding identity claim. For Koßler, the mature Schopenhauer becomes exclusively preoccupied with the nature of the subject of willing. Koßler seems to presume that Schopenhauer no longer considers the will, in general, and motivation, in particular, in connection with the nature of the subject of cognition and self-consciousness.

> Tracking back the metaphysics of will to its roots it becomes obvious that the point of departure is not the question as to how to found a metaphysical system, or how to uncover the thing in itself. The point of departure is the problem of responsibility. This led Schopenhauer to assume an intelligible character as the necessary condition for asking the question why a human action takes place. This is by no means a weighty metaphysical assumption, since it does not include more than the claim that the subject of my acts of willing is one and the same.[9]

Both White and Koßler seem to recognize the important role the 'miracle *par excellence*', the identity of willing and cognizing, plays in the economy of Schopenhauer's metaphysics of will. They seem, however, to hold this textual fact at face value. Yet it is crucial to examine the proposition of that identity in light of its metaphysical implications. For, according to Schopenhauer, from an empirical viewpoint I cognize myself as a free agent who chooses between motives and makes autonomous decisions, and, from a transcendental viewpoint I must see that my self-ascribed freedom of will is at best a justified presupposition of morality, and, at worst, an illusion. How to make sense of this complex claim? Below, we attempt to make sense of Schopenhauer's position by shedding an alternative light on his claim that human actions are necessitated in a manner analogous to the causal relation among physical objects.

The claim of an identity of cognizing and willing plays a major role in the whole of Schopenhauer's philosophy, from FR onward. It is present in the opening sentences of § 2 of WWR1 and also, crucially, in FW, in the distinction between naïve or natural (philosophically untrained) self-consciousness and philosophical self-consciousness. The former is characterised by the belief that "I can do what I will" or "If I will this, I can do it", while the latter is sceptical about inferring freedom of the will from the cognitive identity expressed in the proposition 'I am the one whose desires I desire'. While willing is contained in self-consciousness, the determining factors for its translation into my decision for one motive over another and so, possibly, for one action over another, are not.

We can find a contradiction in the way Schopenhauer uses the concept of self-consciousness in FR and in FW. It seems as though in FW he gives this concept the mere function of a theoretical platform on which inferences can be made concerning the nature of the relation between cognition, motivation, and will. But in FR, Schopenhauer seems to attribute to self-consciousness a crucial metaphysical function, namely, as the seat of a subjective identity of cognizing and willing. In FW he describes self-consciousness in considerably less enthusiastic tones, as that which 'merely contains willing', and must become consciousness of things other than its own inner presentation to enable action. It is also the case, as noted above, that Schopenhauer qualifies the concept of self-consciousness in FW in the context of a critical assessment of a naïve, non-philosophical use of the concept. Yet it is worth noting that, despite the variance in use of the concept of self-consciousness, FR and FW preserve the basic claim that this is the concept of a subjective identity of cognizing and willing.

How to explain this variance in his use of the concept of self-consciousness? We need a further distinction in order to answer this question. This time we need to distinguish not between naïve and philosophically trained self-consciousness, but rather focus on the very nature of the cognitive function of self-consciousness. The distinction would go as follows. Presented in FR as the epistemic *locus* of a subjective identity of cognizing and willing, self-consciousness is irrelevant to the question of how willing is determined. Presented in FW as the cognitive function of this identity, its epistemic value is rather enhanced. Indeed, it is only under the presupposition that self-consciousness is itself a cognitive function of the identity of cognizing and willing that questions about what determines willing into action can arise. What, if not self-consciousness, ensures that willing does not remain undetermined indefinitely—so that, for example, akrasia is not a permanent state? What, if not self-consciousness, ensures that a resolution is found for the cognitive self-appraisal that any one of opposing wishes with their motives could become a deed if they become acts of will? If this reading of the variance in Schopenhauer's accounts of self-consciousness in FR and FW is correct, then the identity of cognizing and willing precedes metaphysically the event of self-consciousness, in that the latter is regarded as a mere function of the former. If this interpretive claim is correct, then it is that identity, rather than its functional by-product in the form of a subjective capacity for being conscious of presentations as one's own, that actually remains unexplained by Schopenhauer. An explanation of this identity is offered next on Schopenhauer's behalf.

In spite of its centrality to his whole philosophy, nowhere in his works does Schopenhauer attempt a clarification of his claim of the subjective identity of cognizing and willing—of his 'miracle *par excellence*'. One could interpret this fact as evidence that he regarded this identity as a basic phenomenological given that withstands analysis. However, it is hard to see how this phenomenological status differs from what Schopenhauer himself would have seen as a naïve *self*-appraisal of it.

In his publication of the first edition of FR, Arthur Hübscher inserted a loose note by Schopenhauer to the official text in the reasonable belief of the note's usefulness for scholars. The note is formed of three entries. The second entry, quoted below in its entirety, may lead to a possible account of the claim that cognizing and willing are one and the same act in self-consciousness.

> Certainly things appear to us only as we *represent* them. But that our representations do not *deceive* us, but correspond to the will, is their reality [*Über dass unsere Vorstellungen uns nich* täuschen, *sondern dem Willen entsprechen, ist ihre* **Realität**]. This agreement of our representing with our will, with the *thing in itself*, must have a deeper ground, one binding the two. How is it that my representations do not, in fact, show me the thing in itself, but still relate to the thing in itself?[10]

We know that EF, the original dissertation, shows a heavy Kantian influence, particularly Kant's distinctions of appearance and thing in itself and intelligible and empirical character. While the first distinction is not relevant to the purposes of this paper, the second certainly is. The claim in the above citation (i.e., the claim of representations corresponding to will, and crucially, that this correspondence is non-deceiving and constitutive of their reality) clearly does not follow from Kant's critical philosophy. Schopenhauer cannot mean, without going against the most basic common experiences, that all representations, or even representations in general, correspond to the will in the sense that they result from an act of volition. Empirically, it is quite obvious to anyone that not all of what one becomes aware, or is able to become aware, results from an act of volition. One would not know what to make of the claim, say, that my awareness that it is raining is an act of my volition.

The crux of the matters for Schopenhauer, however, lies in the stated fact, that that of which I am aware *is* as it *appears* to me *and like nothing else*. As he puts it: my representations cannot deceive me. The truth of this crucial proposition has been known to empirical psychologists for a long time through simple experiments in which a subject is asked not to think or imagine something, say, a white polar bear. However, we find ourselves unable (a) not to think or imagine it, and (b) to stop thinking or imagining it. What seems clear is that we cannot, in a sense that still remains difficult to describe or explain, unthink what we have once thought, or unsee what we have once seen.

This compelling nature of the presentation of objects in consciousness may be called will. Certainly not just because we cannot will it away, but because we cannot, as cognizers, not attend to it in our field of consciousness, that is, not assert its reality for ourselves. We cannot, to put it simply, not will it. We are now able to interpret Schopenhauer's claim of an identity of cognizing and willing, a claim that holds in both the first and second editions of FR: as representations present themselves as cognitively compelling, necessitated objects, to cognize myself in self-consciousness as subject of cognition is at once to cognize myself as subject of willing, that is, more specifically, as both subject *of* and *to* this necessitation.

Conclusion

Given the complexities and difficulties experienced in the above explorations of Schopenhauer's account of self-consciousness and its subjective identity of cognizing and willing, we may indeed grant him his description of *'miracle par excellence'*. It is surely uncontroversial that a common feature of miracles is their sense of 'mystery' and utter 'inexplicability'. Recall here Schopenhauer's succinct statement in FR, § 42: "whoever truly realises the inexplicability of this identity will with me call it the miracle *par excellence"* (FR 143).

All the same, propositions of miracles that remain unquestioned may eventually either be forgotten or become dogmata. It is not desirable, when reading Schopenhauer, to either forget or submit to propositions that are basic to his whole philosophy, simply because he states their inexplicability. If anything, such statement should make us curious. Perhaps in the same way that the movement of brushstrokes on a painting cannot be explained to a blind person except by putting a paintbrush in their hand and guiding it along a canvas, the claim of a subjective identity of willing and cognizing cannot be explained but only experienced. Perhaps it lies with each and every one of us to disprove the unprovable, and give examples of deeds, acts, bodily movements, for which separable cognitive or behavioural expressions can be found, without, of course, falling back onto a dualism of mind and body, and will and action, which Schopenhauer explicitly questioned and denied.

What may have stopped Schopenhauer from assuming and developing such a perspective himself? Here is a suggestion: had Schopenhauer lived to see the birth of psychology in Germany as an empirical and experimental science, he would, perhaps, have identified with its many findings about the inseparability of cognition and behaviour in animals in general, and in human animals in particular, and seen in them some support for his claims of a subjective identity of willing and cognizing.

As we have seen, these claims are crucial for Schopenhauer's later philosophy, in particular for his thoughts on morality and ethics. He would, no doubt, have been deeply gratified to learn that hundreds of years after his death psychological clinical practices would emerge and become widespread, such as cognitive-behavioural therapy, whose basic claim is that human beings are driven or motivated in their cognition and behaviour by moral and ethical valued directions in life.

Notes

1 The variants between the first and the second editions of FR are important for the present paper. We adopt the second edition as our main reference throughout, referred to simply as FR, with the first edition referred to as EF.
2 This replaces *the subject of will (des Willens)* of the first edition.
3 Added in the second edition with no corresponding § of that topic in the first.
4 White (1992, 127).
5 Koßler (2008, 230).
6 Koßler follows the Aquila & Carus translation (2008) of *Grund* for 'ground'.
7 Koßler (2008, 230).
8 The translation is taken from F.C. White.
9 Koßler (2008, 243).
10 Hübscher, SW 7, 136

Bibliography

Gardner, S. 'Schopenhauer, Will, and the Unconscious', in C. Janaway (ed.), *The Cambridge Companion to Schopenhauer*. Cambridge: Cambridge University Press, 1999, 375–421.
Hamlyn, D.W. *Schopenhauer*. London: Routledge, 1980.
Janaway, C. *Self and World in Schopenhauer's Philosophy*. Oxford: Clarendon Press, 1989.
Koßler, M. 'Life Is but a Mirror: On the Connection between Ethics, Metaphysics and Character in Schopenhauer', *European Journal of Philosophy* 16, 2008: 230–250.
McDermid, D. 'Schopenhauer and Transcendental Idealism', in B. Vandenabeele (ed.), *A Companion to Schopenhauer*. Oxford: Wiley-Blackwell, 2012, 70–85.
Salaquarda, J. 'Charakter und Freiheit', in W. Schirmacher (ed.), *Zeit der Ernte. Festschrift für Arthur Hübscher*. Stuttgart: Fromman-Holzboog, 1982.
Tevenar, G. von. 'Schopenhauer on Sex, Love, and Emotions', in B. Vandenabeele (ed.), *A Companion to Schopenhauer*. Oxford: Wiley-Blackwell, 2012, 120–132.
White, F.C. *On Schopenhauer's "Fourfold Root of the Principle of Sufficient Reason"*. Leiden: Brill, 1992.
White, F.C. 'The Fourfold Root', in C. Janaway (ed.), *The Cambridge Companion to Schopenhauer*. Cambridge: Cambridge University Press, 1999, 63–92.
Zöller, G. 'Schopenhauer on the Self', in C. Janaway (ed.), *The Cambridge Companion to Schopenhauer*. Cambridge: Cambridge University Press, 1999, 18–43.

12 Kant's Theory of Freedom in *Fourfold Root* as the Progenitor of Schopenhauer's Metaphysics of Will

Robert Wicks

Although Schopenhauer regarded himself as Kant's true successor, denouncing Fichte, Schelling, and Hegel for having been philosophically unfaithful to Kant's central insights, he was not uncritical of Kant. In in a lengthy appendix to the first volume of *The World as Will and Representation*, entitled "Critique of the Kantian Philosophy," he set forth his differences with Kant's epistemology, ethics, and aesthetics in a comprehensive survey.

In respect for his great master, Schopenhauer prefaced his criticisms by acknowledging the merits and excellences of Kant's philosophy, mentioning as among the most influential, the arguments in the Transcendental Aesthetic of the *Critique of Pure Reason*. Unquestionably accepting Kant's revolutionary conclusion that space and time are knowable only as features of the human mind which organize our given sensations, and which signify nothing independently of the human standpoint, he celebrated Kant's Transcendental Aesthetic in the following passage:

> The *Transcendental Aesthetic* is a work of such extraordinary merit that it alone could serve to immortalize the name of Kant. Its proofs are so persuasive that I number its doctrines among the irrefutable truths; they are undoubtedly also some of the richest in consequences, and can therefore be considered as that rarest of things in this world, a true and great discovery in metaphysics.
>
> (WWR1 518)

Schopenhauer was undoubtedly correct about Kant's impact upon his own philosophy. The first line of *The World as Will and Representation*—"The world is my representation"—embodies for Schopenhauer, how Kant's subject-centered characterization of space and time carries through to its completion Locke's distinction—originally from Galileo—between ideas of primary qualities and ideas of secondary qualities.

Whereas Locke relativized ideas of secondary qualities—colors, odors, sounds, tastes, etc.—to human subjectivity, asserting their non-resemblance to the physical objects which cause them, Schopenhauer understands Kant as having done the same for Locke's ideas of primary qualities such as extension, figure and motion (i.e., qualities of space and time),[1] asserting their non-resemblance to purely intelligible objects or things-in-themselves: "Thus, *Locke* took the thing in itself and subtracted the part that the sense organs play in appearance; but *Kant* subtracted the role of brain functions too (although not by that name)" (WWR1 495).[2]

"The world is my representation" asserts that the world of our daily experience, in both its sensory content and spatio-temporal form, is a mental product which does not resemble the metaphysical ground of which it is the appearance—namely, how things are in themselves mind-independently. It does not resemble that ground, just as the sweet taste of sugar does not resemble the rectangular sugar crystals whose touch upon the tongue causes that taste. Such is the philosophical basis for Schopenhauer's many comparisons between daily life and dreams—comparisons that were inspired by Schopenhauer's reading of Plato and the Upanishads, and as sustained by modern argumentation, Kant:

> This sort of clear knowledge and calm, level-headed presentation of the dream-like constitution of the whole world is really the basis for the whole of Kant's philosophy, and is its soul and its very greatest merit. Kant accomplished this by taking apart the whole machinery of our cognitive faculty, which brings about the phantasmagoria of the objective world, and displaying it piece by piece, with admirable dexterity and clarity of mind.
>
> (WWR1 497)

The Characteristic Aspects of Timeless Acts

An even more penetrating influence on Schopenhauer's philosophy, though, is Kant's idea of freedom, in reference to which Schopenhauer explicitly mentions the logical inroad from Kant into his own philosophy:

> The solution to the third antinomy, which is concerned with the idea of freedom, deserves special consideration; in particular, we find it quite remarkable that it is precisely here, with the idea of *freedom*, that Kant was forced to speak at greater length about the *thing in itself*, which until now had been seen only in the background. We find this easy to understand, since we have recognized the thing in itself as the *will*. This is really the point where Kant's philosophy leads to my own, or where mine grows from the stem of Kant's.
>
> (WWR1 595)

Central to Kant's idea of freedom and to our interest in Kant's influence on Schopenhauer as it extends from Schopenhauer's 1813 doctoral dissertation, *The Fourfold Root of the Principle of Sufficient Reason*, is the distinction between the intelligible and empirical aspects of a thing's character. Schopenhauer highlights this distinction initially in the first edition of *Fourfold Root* §46:

> Perhaps I could better indicate what is meant, although also figuratively, if I call it a universal act of will lying outside of time, of which all temporal acts are only the emergence, the appearance. Kant has called this the *intelligible character* (perhaps it would more correctly be called unintelligible), and in the *Critique of Pure Reason* . . . he provides a discussion of the difference between it and the *empirical* character, as well as the whole relation of freedom to nature, a discussion which I regard as an incomparable, highly admirable masterpiece of human profundity. In the first volume of his [Philosophical] *Writings* . . . Schelling provides a very valuable, illustrative exposition of this.[3]
>
> (EF 188)

This excerpt confirms that from the start, Schopenhauer accepted Kant's understanding of a person's activity as the appearance in time of an original timeless act, inscrutable, which is presumably what the person truly is. Both Schopenhauer and Kant refer specifically to this timeless nature of individual human beings which in reality is free, but whose appearances in space and time are thoroughly determinable in their mechanical interrelationships.

In *The World as Will and Representation* (1818), Schopenhauer enhances the Kantian distinction between a person's empirical and intelligible character with the introduction of a third aspect of a thing's character, only infrequently realized, namely, its "acquired" character, which proves to be among the most revealing ideas in Schopenhauer's philosophy, as we shall see. To appreciate this significance, let us consider Kant's distinction between empirical and intelligible characters, and proceed to Schopenhauer's tripartite typology of character to reveal the influence of Kant's theory of freedom as it extends from Schopenhauer's early *Fourfold Root* and reverberates throughout Schopenhauer's metaphysics of will, his conception of Platonic Ideas, asceticism, denial-of-the-will, and ultimate liberation.

After establishing that space, time, and causality are organizational features of the human mind, and that we consequently structure our experience as a thoroughgoing causal mechanism, Kant considers the sense in which human beings can nonetheless be praiseworthy or blameworthy for their actions (*CPR*, A546/B574ff).[4] To display this, he observes fundamentally that human beings are aware of themselves in two different ways, namely, as physical bodies and as rational self-consciousnesses, speculating from the latter that there is a nonphysical, intelligible, albeit unknowable, dimension of ourselves in the realm of things as they are in themselves. This intelligible character is who each of us can presume to be in reality, and is that to which points our sense of responsibility. Our respective empirical character—conceived of as a timeless and free act of our intelligible character—expresses holistically, our personal reality as it appears mechanistically in the spatio-temporal world.

When he introduces these ideas about human freedom, Kant explains that "some" physical objects—he has human beings in mind—have underlying their appearance as spatio-temporal objects a dimension that is not appearance, namely, the aspect of the spatio-temporal object as it is in reality. This, as noted, is the object's intelligible character, the rationale behind which Kant presents as follows:

> I call intelligible that in an object of sense which is not itself appearance. Accordingly, if that which must be regarded as appearance in the world of sense has in itself a faculty which is not an object of intuition through which it can be the cause of appearances, then one can consider the causality of this being in two aspects [*zwei Seiten*], as intelligible in its action as a thing in itself, and a sensible in the effects of that action as an appearance in the world of sense. Of the faculty of such a subject we would accordingly form an empirical and at the same time an intellectual concept of its causality, both of which apply to one and the same effect.
>
> (A538/B566)

Kant refers in this excerpt to how the causality associated with the *intelligible* aspect of a sensory object is a timeless act originating from ultimate reality which accounts for the sensory object's action from the standpoint of things in themselves, and how the causality associated with the *sensory* aspect of a sensory object involves spatio-temporal interrelationships which account for the sensory object's action from the standpoint of ordinary experience. Although Schopenhauer was always uneasy about using the term "causality" in reference to timeless acts, and preferred instead the terms "objectification" [*Objektivation*] and "manifestation" [*Manifestation*] to describe the relation more clearly in *The World as Will and Representation*, salient here is the specific context within which the distinction between empirical and intelligible characters appears in Kant and importantly, initially in Schopenhauer's early *Fourfold Root*.[5]

This context is that of human beings and the possibility of their being free, morally praiseworthy or blameworthy, despite how their bodily movements are thoroughly determinable and explainable in mechanistic, scientific terms. In a crucial departure from Kant, Schopenhauer's philosophy expands the scope of the distinction between empirical and intelligible character beyond the moral context to apply not only to human bodies, but to all physical objects.

To understand how Schopenhauer widens the scope of this distinction's application, we should note two general philosophical observations which emerge from Kant's theory of freedom as Schopenhauer understood it—ones which influentially characterize Schopenhauer's style of philosophizing: (1) that human beings can regard themselves from two sides, namely, externally, as physical objects (or as "representations") and internally, as conscious-nesses, and (2) that the internal perspective points to what human beings are in reality. For Kant, the internal perspective points in a metaphysically true direction, but it reaches a limit where the solid experiential terrain ends, and speculative, rational extrapolation must take over with less certainty. For Schopenhauer, more assertively, the internal perspective can lead us all the way to metaphysical knowledge.

In *The World as Will and Representation*, published five years after *Fourfold Root*, Schopenhauer develops his metaphysics from these philo-sophical observations which issue from Kant's theory of freedom. Attending closely to the experience we have of our bodies, Schopenhauer notes the two-sided way in which we are aware of those bodies: (1) from the outside as objects in the spatio-temporal world, or as "representations," and (2) from the inside as subjects of experience. My hand is an object, or representation, like any other in the spatio-temporal world, but I have privileged access to the inner being of that representation insofar as I can feel and move my hand willfully and can use this awareness as the key to understanding the inner being of every other representation before me for which I do not have an inner access.

Underscoring the importance of having a direct experience of his ulti-mate inner being, Schopenhauer turns inward to apprehend his metaphysi-cal essence, searching for a level and quality of awareness, suitably general, that is appropriate to the inner being of all representations. Reason is not a plausible candidate, peculiar as it is to humans, and neither is sentience, since rocks apparently have no consciousness. Arriving at what appears to him as the most rudimentary level of awareness, Schopenhauer identifies a nonconscious, nonrational, senseless, directionless, and relentless impulse at his metaphysical core, which he calls 'will'.

Apprehended independently of spatial and causal relationships, and presenting itself in consciousness only through the thin veil of time, Schopenhauer is confident that we can come close to knowing ultimate real-ity. The situation compares to wearing sunglasses: one can see a tree, and have a reliable idea of what it looks like, but see the tree nonetheless in a col-oration which is not exactly the tree's own. For Schopenhauer, this reality, 'will', is a primal impulse whose manifestation is observable in the behavior of inanimate nature, as in gravitation and magnetism, in plants, in animals, and most perspicuously and subtly, in humans.

At this point in his philosophizing, Schopenhauer is no longer speaking exclusively of the empirical and intelligible character of humans, but of the empirical and intelligible character of each and every spatio-temporal indi-vidual, appreciating that not only humans, but everything, is a manifesta-tion of ultimate reality, or the thing-in-itself, which he has now identified as will: "Now what Kant teaches about the phenomenon of man and his actions is extended by my teaching to *all* the phenomena in nature, since it makes their foundation the *will* as thing-in-itself" (WWRII 174).

Human beings, like every other part of nature, are the objecthood of the will: so everything we have said holds true for them as well. Just as each thing in nature possesses forces and qualities that react to determinate influences in a determinate way and constitute the character of the thing, a human being has his *character* as well, from which motives call forth his actions with necessity. Empirical character is revealed in the way he acts, but intelligible character, the will in itself whose determinate appearance he is, is revealed in turn in the empirical character.

(WWR1 339)

It should be evident that Kant's theory of freedom, which presents the human being fundamentally as a timeless act with a specific character, supplies the template for Schopenhauer's metaphysics of will, through which he understands generally the entire spatio-temporal world as the timeless act of the thing-in-itself, or ultimate reality, which itself has the character of a blind and senseless impulse.[6] Schopenhauer arrives at his position by magnifying the Kantian model of the free human being whose timeless act manifests itself as the person's particular spatio-temporal life, into the model of the free thing-in-itself whose timeless act manifests itself as the entire spatio-temporal world. The magnification has negative implications for Kant's more rationalistic association of the thing-in-itself with reason, for reason now shows itself to be too narrowly anthropomorphic for the purposes of comprehending the nature of ultimate reality.[7]

This magnification of Kant's theory of freedom from the human to the universal context, reflects a general Schopenhauerian style of philosophizing which is also exemplified in Schopenhauer's main argument, mentioned above, that the thing-in-itself is will. In that argument, Schopenhauer observes his own physical body as its stands among other physical bodies, apprehends that the inner reality of his own body is will, and projects that condition to every other spatio-temporal body to conclude that will is the inner reality of all other spatio-temporal bodies, and of the spatio-temporal world itself. Extending infinitely in space and time, the physical world is thereby conceived as a single body—a virtual Leviathan—whose inner being is will. The philosophical context to which all of these implications trace back, is Kant's theory of freedom and the distinction between the empirical and intelligible characters as presented in the first edition of Schopenhauer's *Fourfold Root*.

The otherwise mysterious appearance of the Platonic Ideas in Schopenhauer's philosophy is similarly understandable in reference to this magnification of Kant's theory of freedom. As we have seen, Schopenhauer agrees that each individual human being is the expression of a particular timeless act of will, conceived as the act of will of a timeless thing-in-itself. By extension, he regards each spatio-temporal object as the expression of a particular timeless act of will, and the entire spatio-temporal world as the objectification of a timeless act of will, considered most generally. Each spatio-temporal object as the objectification of will, has its specific character, just as each human body has its character.

Schopenhauer conceives of physical objects in the world primarily in generic terms, maintaining that animals and plants manifest the characters of their species first and foremost, and that the differences between the individuals are relatively negligible. He regards the cat playing in my backyard, for instance, as virtually the same cat that played in someone else's backyard over three hundred years ago.[8] Schopenhauer equates these species characters with the Platonic Ideas as the immediate objectifications of will.

Plato's influence upon Schopenhauer was strong and positive, but it is unfortunate that Schopenhauer's introduction of the terminology of Platonic Ideas obscures the logical source of his insight regarding their metaphysical appearance as immediate objectifications of will. This derives from his reading of Kant, and the assumption that if each human has an intelligible character, then so does every other individual. In the following excerpts, Schopenhauer describes Platonic Ideas as the objective expression of intelligible characters, and hence, as empirical characters:

> Since the character of any particular person is thoroughly individual and not entirely subsumed under that of the species, it can be seen as a specific Idea [*als eine besondere Idee . . . angesehen warden*] corresponding to a distinctive act of the will's objectivation. This act itself would then be the person's intelligible character, and the empirical character would be its appearance.
>
> (WWR 1 188)

The intelligible character coincides [*zusammenfallen*] with the Idea, or more specifically with the original act of will revealed in the Idea: to this extent, not only the empirical character of every person but also of every species of animal, indeed every species of plant, and even every original force of inorganic nature, can be seen as the appearance of an intelligible character (i.e., of an extra-temporal, indivisible act of will) (WWR1 185–186).

In the second volume of *The World as Will and Representation* (1844), Schopenhauer tends to speak generally of 'character', by which he means 'empirical character', and refrains from substantial references to intelligible character, perhaps realizing that the notion of an intelligible character presents the unapproachable mystery of why, as opposed simply to remaining senseless and unconscious for eternity, the thing-in-itself as will manifests itself in the particular kind of diversity we experience. In the second edition of *The Fourfold Root of the Principle of Sufficient Reason*, which was extensively rewritten, the presentation of Kant's distinction is equally softened, with references to empirical and intelligible characters appearing only in passing.[9]

In the course of his numerous references to 'character', however, Schopenhauer refers us to his essay on the freedom of the will, wherein he states that he "wholly supports" (FW 82) the distinction between empirical and intelligible character, adding that the distinction is "among the most beautiful and most profound ideas which this great mind, indeed, which humankind has ever produced" (FW 95). To extract confidently a statement of Schopenhauer's position, we can consult Schopenhauer's essay on the freedom of the will.

In his 1839 essay, Schopenhauer invokes Kant's distinction between the empirical and intelligible characters to explain his own position on the nature of human freedom:

> This freedom, however, is a transcendental one, i.e., not occurring in appearance, but only present insofar as we abstract from appearance and all its forms in order to arrive at that which, outside of all time, is to be thought of as the inner being of the person in himself. Because of this freedom, all of a person's deeds are his own work, however much they necessarily proceed from the empirical character upon its encounter with motives, because this empirical character is merely the appearance of the intelligible character in our *cognitive faculty*, bound to time, space, and causality, i.e., is the way that our own being in itself presents itself. Consequently *will* is, indeed, free, but only in itself and outside of appearance.
>
> (FW 96)

This is Schopenhauer's main position. His conception of the acquired character, which we will now consider, introduces an important and philosophically resonant qualification.

Self-Knowledge and Acquired Character

As Schopenhauer states in the first volume of *The World as Will and Representation* (§55), an acquired character is what a person manifests after attaining a significant degree of self-knowledge: by reflecting upon one's behaviour across time and discerning underlying patterns, it is possible to understand the kind of person one is, and thereby acquire 'character' in the ordinary, laudatory sense. Self-knowledge precipitates as well-expressed character, and Schopenhauer refers to an individual who exhibits this quality as someone who has acquired character.

Schopenhauer maintains that with acquired character, one lives more authentically and artistically, exemplifying who one is in a more consistent and concentrated way. Although it is not possible to change the kind of person one is, there is a measure of control over how one's character plays itself out in the world:

> It is primarily someone's exact knowledge of his own empirical character that gives a person what is called *acquired character*: the one who

possesses it recognizes exactly his own traits, good and bad, thereby surely knows what he may trust and expect of himself, but also what not. He now plays his own role artfully and methodically, with consistency and decorum, which previously was played out quite naturally by virtue of his empirical character, without once, as is said, acting out of character.

(FW 50)

It remains unclear how stylistic control over the expression of one's character is possible, if down to its very atoms, one's body is mechanistically determined within the seamless physical interrelationships of the spatio-temporal world. It would be less puzzling to say that certain individuals as opposed to others are fated to become highly self-aware and to play out their characters with more authenticity and decorum. Along these lines, Schopenhauer's conception of acquired character would not be a prescriptive idea suggesting that everyone ought to be more authentic and give style to their characters, as we find in later existentialist directives; it would merely describe how certain characters happen to manifest themselves.

A sense of freedom nonetheless resides behind Schopenhauer's conception of acquired character. This freedom is located, however, at a higher level of generality than that of the individual person, namely, at the level of the self-determining thing-in-itself as will. Accordingly, and as mentioned, Schopenhauer states that as a rule, freedom is transcendental and does not show itself in the spatio-temporal world, associated as it is intrinsically with the thing-in-itself's timeless activity. He does admit a single exception, though, apparent within the spatio-temporal world, which is the self-awareness of the ascetic:

Thus, in human beings the will can achieve full self-consciousness, clear and exhaustive cognition of its own essence as it is mirrored in the whole world. As we saw in the previous Book, art arises from the actual existence of this degree of cognition. At the very end of our discussion it will also be established that, since the will relates it to itself, the same cognition makes possible an abolition and self-negation of the will in its most perfect appearance; so that freedom, which otherwise applies only to the thing in itself and can never show itself in appearance, can then also emerge into appearance; by abolishing the essence that grounds appearance (while appearance itself continues in time) it can generate a self-contradiction within appearance and in so doing present the phenomena of holiness and self-denial.

(WWR1 339)

Schopenhauer states that the thing-in-itself as will manifests itself as the spatio-temporal world in what appears to be a metaphysical push for self-knowledge, observing how the hierarchy which extends from inanimate matter, to plants, to animals, to humans, culminates in the self-conscious human being. Among humans, it peaks and concludes for Schopenhauer in ascetic awareness. Insofar as will comes to self-knowledge in the ascetic, the ascetic's character is importantly that through which ultimate reality is realizing for itself what it is. Having developed a moral consciousness, it comes to realize that it is a bad energy which manifests itself as a world filled with selfishness and suffering. As embodied in the ascetic, the thing-in-itself as will realizes furthermore in view of the moral consciousness it has developed, that to minimize this suffering, it must minimize itself as the being responsible for the existence of viciousness and pain.

The ascetic's consequent denial-of-the-will becomes thereby the one place in the spatio-temporal world where freedom shows itself. Schopenhauer does not say—but he might well have said, and this is our main point—that the emergence of ascetic awareness as a reflective consequence of compassionate, moral awareness, is none other than the thing-in-itself as will coming to know its own character. *The ascetic is an instance of acquired character on the part of ultimate reality itself.*

Unlike the situation where individual human beings acquire character through a measure of self-knowledge, and exemplify what they are more authentically and clearly, when reality acquires character and comes to know itself in the ascetic, it does not consequently exemplify what it is more authentically and clearly as a world which contains even greater suffering than before. In its traumatic self-recognition, the thing-in-itself as will turns against itself as a result of having developed a moral awareness. Indeed, for Schopenhauer, this world cannot be viewed sanely, except in moral terms: "That the world has a mere physical but no moral significance is the greatest, most ruinous and fundamental error, the real *perversity* of the mind [Perversität *der Gesinnung*] and in a basic sense it is certainly that which faith has personified as the antichrist" (PP2 214).

Overall, the train of thought being presented here, which regards the ascetic consciousness as reality itself having acquired character, is consistent with Schopenhauer's philosophical tendency to magnify the subjects of his arguments to the absolute level and widest generalization. We have seen this in Schopenhauer's core argument that the thing-in-itself is will: he starts with the awareness of his own body, discovers his inner being to be will, and then expands this awareness to conceive of the spatio-temporal world itself as a great body, the inner being of which is will. Presently, we have the concept of acquired character which Schopenhauer describes in reference to individual people who realize the kind of characters they respectively are, expanded and globalized into a conception of reality itself—as manifested in the ascetic consciousness—coming to realize what kind of character it has. It realizes that it is a constantly striving will which feasts on itself, and in that self-recognition, negates itself accordingly in an act of self-denial and purification.[10]

With this, Schopenhauer's concept of acquired character becomes central to his conception of asceticism, denial-of-the-will, and the tranquility-seeking goal of his philosophy. The systematic advantage in this way of understanding the role of asceticism in Schopenhauer's philosophy resides in its derivation from Kant's original and inspirational distinction between the empirical and intelligible characters which we find in *Fourfold Root*, and which is itself the basis for other main aspects of Schopenhauer's outlook. As we have seen, it inspires Schopenhauer's view that the thing-in-itself as will manifests itself through a timeless act as the spatio-temporal world, as well as his view that the thing-in-itself as will manifests itself though a timeless act as a set of Platonic Ideas, or empirical characters.

The moral context in which the distinction between the empirical and intelligible characters is first formulated, extends into how the ascetic embodies the acquired character of the thing-in-itself as will. Subsequent to discerning the bad quality of the substance of which it, and all of reality, is constituted, the ascetic turns away from the world in self-horror. This repulsion does not follow from the apprehension of a logical inconsistency in the manner of Kant's moral philosophizing; it follows rather from the compassionate apprehension of the world's suffering and in the feeling of culpability for that suffering.

Schopenhauer's conception of moral awareness may not be Kantian, but the ascetic's denial-of-the-will does involve the absence of egoism in conjunction with the lack of interest, or sheer absence of interest, in satisfying worldly desires or inclinations, which is a hallmark of Kant's conception of a holy, or divine, will. That Schopenhauer describes the ascetic consciousness as a holy consciousness is probably no coincidence:

> Finally, in the Fourth Book we will see how this sort of cognition, acting back on the will, can bring about the will's self-transcendence [*Selbstaufhebung*],[11] i.e., the resignation that is the final goal, indeed the innermost essence of all virtue and holiness and is redemption from the world
>
> (WWR1 182)

Self-Overcoming and the Promotion of Tranquillity

To appreciate further the general moral context of the ascetic's denial-of-the-will, we can introduce a different sphere of moral reasoning, namely, that related to the Japanese warrior code, since it highly respects certain forms of suicide. When suffering a dishonor, or failing in some socially crucial endeavor, a person who follows the code will preserve a sense of dignity by committing ritual suicide with a knife cut across the abdomen, the cradle of the will. If, within a serious institutional or social context, such as war, one has done something shameful, the respectable and redemptive act is to punish oneself by taking one's own life.[12]

The ascetic's act of denial-of-the-will is comparable to some extent: the ascetic's fundamental, tragic, and harrowing self-recognition is that as a being constituted by will, it is responsible as 'will' for great and immeasurable suffering, in particular of innocent children and animals. It is responsible for its own extensive suffering as it feasts upon itself in its multitude of manifestations, where each living thing is the graveyard of many others. Upon experiencing moral repulsion after coming to know the cannibalistic character of its inner being, the ascetic is motivated to stop the suffering. Since the suffering extends from itself as will, extinguishing the suffering involves extinguishing and over- coming as much as possible, the will which drives everything and which consti- tutes the ascetic's inner being. The self-conscious act of extinguishing the will is interpretable as the thing-in-itself engaging in a kind of ritual suicide.

The ascetic is not motivated to die physically, however, since this would accomplish nothing metaphysically within Schopenhauer's view. The ascetic rather persists in an enlightened condition of near will-less-ness, keeping its will at bay in perpetual self-restraint, and experiencing the peace which fol- lows from having achieved an effectively will-less state of mind. The ascetic is like a burning sun which acts self-consciously to cool itself down as much as possible. It compares also to the archetypical Ouroboros snake which bites its own tail, but which, upon a further act of reflection, is morally repulsed by its self-consuming condition.

The enlightenment involved is consequently not the traditionally under- stood condition and goal of becoming one with ultimate reality, as in Daoism or Christian quietism, since Schopenhauerian ultimate reality—the thing-in- itself as will—is a repulsive, senseless being which produces constant suffer- ing as it feasts upon itself. The thing-in-itself as will is a being rather to turn against morally, than blend into ecstatically. Enlightenment accordingly involves a more subtle and higher-level degree of release from a repellant ultimate reality—a release which, in a kind of cosmic self-cleansing, amounts to becoming free from oneself in the most profound sense imaginable.

We can appreciate in sum, Kant's theory of freedom, and in particular, his distinction between the empirical and intelligible character, as the inspirational and conceptual basis for many of Schopenhauer's central doctrines. With respect to the tranquility-seeking purpose of Schopenhauer's philosophy, Kant's theory of freedom underwrites the idea that as the ascetic comes to know itself, it embodies the acquired character of ultimate reality. Insofar as Schopenhauer embraces and praises Kant's fundamental distinction between the empirical and intelligible character in the first edition of *Fourfold Root of the Principle of Sufficient Reason*, this text shows itself truly to reside at the foundation of Schopenhauer's philosophy and its vision of transcendent stillness.

Notes

1 Schopenhauer is following straightforwardly the remarks in the *Prolegomena to Any Future Metaphysics* where Kant includes also among mere appearances "the remaining qualities of bodies, which are called *primarias*: extension, place, and more generally space along with everything that depends on it (impenetrability or materiality, shape, etc.)," all of which "have no existence of their own outside our representation" (Ak 4:289).

2 Schopenhauer's reference to brain functions—by which he means more precisely "the intellect"—is more perspicuous in the following: "For time, space, and causality, on which all those real and objective events rest, are themselves nothing more than functions of the brain; so that, therefore, this unchangeable *order* of things, affording the criterion and the clue to their empirical *reality*, itself comes first from the brain, and has its credentials from that alone" (WWRII 8).

3 Schopenhauer compliments Schelling in his PhD dissertation, and reiterates the praise twenty-six years later in his essay on the freedom of the will (1839). In the latter, Schopenhauer adds the *ad hominem* criticism that Schelling makes it sound as if Kant's distinction between empirical and intelligible characters were Schelling's very own. In the second edition of *Fourfold Root* (1847), references which highlight the distinction between empirical and intelligible characters, as well as the positive reference to Schelling, no longer appear.

4 In *Fourfold Root* §20 (FR 49n) Schopenhauer also quotes from this section of the *Critique of Pure Reason* (A549–550/B577–578) to highlight Kant's distinction between the intelligible and empirical characters.

5 As early as 1813, Schopenhauer wrote in his notebooks, "I still do not understand how Kant, after emphatically stating that the use of the categories extends solely to objects of experience, speaks nevertheless of the thing-in-itself as the cause of the phenomenon" (MR2, Sheet 6, Entry 157, p. 294).

6 Kant advocates a conception of freedom which is guided by and infused with rationality, differentiating this (*Wille*) from the thought of a purely arbitrary spontaneity (*Willkür*). Schopenhauer's conception of will is closer to the latter, devoid of rationality as it is. It should nonetheless be recognized that Schopenhauer is highly critical of those who apply the notion of a *liberum arbitrium indifferentiae* to individual human beings (*PP, II,* §119), as if each individual were moment-to-moment a free, self-determining master of his or her fate, as a philosopher such as Jean-Paul Sartre, for example, would have it.

7 Schopenhauer intends to apprehend directly in himself, the full and exact quality of how the inner being is in each and every other thing. This apprehension must consequently reveal an inner being which is compatible with what one can imagine to be the rudimentary quality of a rock's inner being. Rationality as a possible quality of this universal, inner being is thereby precluded. In contrast to Schopenhauer, Hegel, who sustains Kant's commitment to reason, aims to discover the world's underlying principle by examining the world's most articulated products to date—human beings, he believes—just as one would examine a fully grown oak tree to comprehend the nature of the oak. Rationality, assumed by Hegel to be the essence of humanity, thereby emerges in his philosophy as the core principle of reality, where in rocks, for instance, it is conceived of as remaining implicit and awaiting development. From the Hegelian standpoint, Schopenhauer misguidedly examines acorns to understand the nature of the oak, when he should be attending to fully mature oak trees. From the Schopenhauerian standpoint, since there is no way ever to reconcile the immeasurable suffering which has taken place in the world, Hegel's developmental model of the universe which forecasts absolute reconciliation and thoroughgoing harmony, along with its attendant conception of absolute spirit, is unrealizable and morally untenable.

8 This example appears in the second volume of *The World as Will and Representation* (WWRII 482), which was published in 1844. As early as 1814, Schopenhauer expressed the same thoughts in his notebooks: "What difference is there between my looking at a tree now and a man looking at a tree a thousand years ago? None; in both cases it is the object tree in the consciousness of the subject; it is the (Platonic) Idea of the tree, which does not know and understand any time" (MR, I, Section 213, p. 130).

 9 See §20 (FR 49n), §43 (FR 145), §49 (FR 154), and §50 (FR 156).
10 Hegel, Schopenhauer's philosophical adversary, similarly presents a philosophy of self-recognition on the part of ultimate reality in its advance through a great chain of being from inorganic nature to humans. At the Hegelian point of complete self-recognition, however, reality comes to fruition by embodying itself most characteristically in a society of self-conscious beings possessed of full rationality, reconciliation, comprehension, harmony, and morality in a heaven on earth and the best of all possible worlds.
11 The CUP edition translates *"Selbstaufhebung"* ["self-uplifting," literally] as "self-abolition." In the present context, however, the idea of *enhancement* is essential to embody and convey. Inspired by the notion of organic development and the dialectical structure of self-consciousness, *Aufhebung* is a particularly Hegelian word, simultaneously signifying preservation, cancellation, and enhancement: a mature stage of development or reflection, considered in view of its immature stage, is yet the same being, a different being, and an enhanced being. In the excerpt, Schopenhauer is signifying how will transcends itself—one could also say overcomes itself—through moral reflection as it remains thing-in-itself throughout the extinguishing of its striving.
12 These are the traditional motivations. Japanese ritual suicide, or *seppuku*, has a lengthy and complicated history which recognizes an assortment of variants on the traditional motivations (Seward, 1968).

Bibliography

Kant, I. *Critique of Pure Reason*, trans. and ed. Paul Guyer and Allen W. Wood. Cambridge: Cambridge University Press, 1998. (CPR).

Seward, J. *Hara-Kiri: Japanese Ritual Suicide*. Rutland, VT; Tokyo, Japan: Charles E. Tuttle Company, 1968.

Index

Ingram Content Group Australia Pty Ltd
Printed in Australia
AUHW011906200423
377267AU00007B/13